D1714902

Old Age in
Late Medieval England

Old Age in
Late Medieval England

Joel T. Rosenthal

PENN

University of Pennsylvania Press

Philadelphia

ACZ-2852

Library of Congress Cataloging-in-Publication data

Rosenthal, Joel Thomas, 1934–
    Old age in late medieval England / Joel T. Rosenthal.
        p.   cm. — (Middle Ages series)
    Includes bibliographical references and index.
    ISBN 0-8122-3355-7 (alk. paper)
        1. Aged — England — History. 2. Old age — England — History. 3. Intergenerational
relations — England — History. 4. Great Britain — History — Medieval period, 1066–1485.
I. Title. II. Series.
    HQ1064.E5R67   1996
    305.26'0942 — dc20   96-14736
                                                                        CIP

To the Second and Third Generations:

To fresh woods and pastures new

Contents

Tables

Abbreviations

CCR	*Calendar of the Close Rolls*
CP	*Complete Peerage*
CPL	*Calendar of the Papal Letters*
CPR	*Calendar of the Patent Rolls*
Chichele	E. F. Jacob, ed., *Chichele's Register*
EETS	Early English Text Society
Henry IV	*Calendar of Inquisitions Post Mortem, 1–6 Henry IV*
Henry VII	*Calendar of Inquisitions Post Mortem, Henry VII*
IJAHD	*International Journal of Aging and Human Development*
Lacy	G. R. Dunstan, ed., *Register of Edmund Lacy*
Lancashire	C. Towneley and R. Didsworth, eds., *Abstracts of Inquisitions Post Mortem*
Langley	R. L. Storey, ed., *Register of Thomas Langley*
Letter Book	R. R. Sharpe, ed., *Letter Books of London*
Nottingham	K. S. S. Train and Mary A. Renshaw, eds., *Inquisitions Post Mortem Relating to Nottinghamshire*
PMLA	*Publications of the Modern Language Association*
Rede	C. Deedes, ed., *Episcopal Register of Robert Rede*
Repingdon	M. Archer, ed., *Register of Philip Repingdon*
Richard II	*Calendar of Inquisitions Post Mortem, 15–23 Richard II*
Rotherham	E. E. Barker, ed., *Register of Thomas Rotherham.*
S&G	N. H. Nicolas, ed., *The Controversy between Scrope and Grosvenor*
Sharpe	R. R. Sharpe, ed., *Wills in the Court of Hustings*
SMW	F. W. Weaver, ed., *Somerset Medieval Wills*
TE	James Raine and James Raine, Jr., eds. *Testamenta Eboracensia*
Yorkshire	W. P. Baildon and J. W. Clay, eds., *Inquisitions Post Mortem Relating to Yorkshire*

Preface

MANY THANKS ARE ALWAYS in order. The National Endowment for the Humanities awarded me a fellowship in the early 1980s, and its generosity, along with that of my university (State University of New York at Stony Brook), made it possible for me to have the time and freedom to begin this study.

Much of the research was conducted at the Institute of Historical Research, University of London; I could not write a book without access to the Institute. As I have spent an inordinate amount of time on this book, debts to friends have grown far beyond a list I can usefully offer here; between footnotes and personal thanks expressed in correspondence and by word of mouth I have tried to express my gratitude, as well as to acknowledge at least some of my borrowing. The continuing and patient interest of many others has also been of value and support, and to be without specific mention here is not to be taken as being forgotten or unappreciated. Constance Berman, Tony Goodman, Constance Bouchard, Rowena Archer, and Caroline Barron are among those who have given me a forum in which I have been able to test ideas and to share findings. Larry Poos shared his unpublished research, and he took an interest in mine when I was not sure of my direction. Linda Clark and Carole Rawcliffe gave me access to unpublished materials on the History of Parliament when I was uncertain about how to close the gap between some vague ideas and hard data. In early days Robin Oggins and Paul Szarmach invited me to speak about my work at SUNY Binghamton. A Toronto conference, organized and supervised by Michael Sheehan, was a valuable way-station; that I can no longer show Michael my work is a sober reminder that we are all working against a deadline. Margaret Labarge, Roger Virgoe, Ralph Griffiths, Edwin and Ann DeWindt, George Beech, Bernie Bachrach, Judith Bennett, Barbara Hanawalt, Barrie Dobson, and Bob Dunning have all put in an encouraging word, sometimes more than once. Other friends, like Jo Ann McNamara, Karl and Sue Bottigheimer and Fred Weinstein, have just helped me remain focused on the good old cause.

Years ago, when I was beginning to publish, a friend and I agreed that if we could not finish a project in a year or two it probably was not worth working on. Looking back, I am not shocked that I was so callow as to make such an observation. What does shock me, rather, is how much free time I must have had for my research. This book represents work at the other extreme of the scholarly calendar: a long period in gestation; in writing; in revising. I like to think it is better for the slow maturation (but I am hardly likely to argue to the contrary). And for advice that was invariably useful, editors at and readers for the University of Pennsylvania Press must be thanked.

As I myself now fall within the chronological boundaries that would qualify for inclusion in my own study — were I unlucky enough to live in the England about which I am writing — I am at least more impressed than I once was by the burdens we accumulate as we go through life. In some ways a scholarly monograph is an explication of a past world, a text created by others and now given to or taken by us, to gloss and interpret, to pull together for its formal if not its final presentation. I offer this comment for what light it sheds on the interpretations and suggestions I present below. At the same time, writing a monograph is a very private enterprise — the author's idiosyncratic and most personal creation, an individual statement now being made public, about some specific aggregation of primary material and of authorial reflections taken from the universe of fate and culture.

Old age has become a "hot topic" by the standards of historical research. I offer a lot of reflections in the pages that follow on how we can study it, and what it may have meant in late medieval England. I do this so old age, along with many other topics in social history, can perhaps become a regular part of our professional agenda, that running dialogue between preservation of records and their interpretation in which we all participate. When we, as historians, work to reconstruct our versions of the politics, the economic system, and the class relations of the long-dead, along with the tale of their institutions and interactions, we readily accept that our subjects are covered and illuminated by the dictum: "Men make their own history, but not of their own free will; not under circumstances they themselves have chosen but under the given and inherited circumstances with which they are directly confronted."

I like to think that perhaps a social historian, relying on soft demography and gerontology, can also offer an analsis of past lives and past society and culture that brings these newer topics into the same fierce light as that we are accustomed to focus on traditional inquiries. Just as the devil should not have all the best tunes, so all the best one-liners should not belong to or only be applied to the work of political historians. And there are not many better one-liners about our task, our discipline, and the purpose of our commitments and our labors than the one set forth so tersely in *The Eighteenth Brumaire*.

Introduction

THIS IS A BOOK that would not have been written a few years ago. It is not about anything and nothing happens. There is no change over time, except that, in the long run, everyone dies.

But from a different perspective, what is more natural than a series of essays and discussions about the life span, the range of sustained activity over time, the *mentalité*, and the behavior of those who did survive, in late medieval England, and who so managed to reach something in the neighborhood of their biblically legitimated span? Survival, old age, longevity, and multi-generational families are facts of life, less common then than now, of course, but memorable as a source of pride and accomplishment as well as a focal point for the inescapable social problems and the joints between the weakest seams in the fabric of "traditional" society.

I offer, in the chapters or essays that follow, a series of analyses of and discourses on various aspects of the social phenomenon that we are wont to sum up as "old age." Though old age seems such a natural part of the human condition, it is important to keep in mind that, to the social historian, it can also be treated as a social and behavioral syndrome, a collection and connection of physical, mental, and interactive responses that are to be expected as a concomitant attribute of life at 60 or 70. Like gender and race and color, it seems a part of the "natural world" around which society has been constructed as a gloss, a reading. And, as we are now apt to say, old age is in some part a social construct, a web of behavioral patterns woven around a biological phenomenon.

While there surely is an iron law of wages, the iron law of aging is better presented by the historian with some relativity; a sliding scale, if we will, on which all who survive are gauged, though at different times and along different scales of evaluation. Because age is both absolute in some biological contexts, and relative in most social ones, we ask different questions, about different aspects of the topic or "problem," in the essays that follow. As we consider and analyze different bodies of sources and data, we pursue different ends and explore different perspectives on a set of more or less common problems.

The topic of old age is a vast one. As will become apparent to even the most casual reader, nothing I offer below can qualify as serious demography. Neither am I going to touch, except for the lightest of brushes, the vast realm of medical and gerontological material now available, focusing mainly on modern Europe (and America) but lending itself to a string of comparisons that seem to lead us from the known to wide realms of late medieval and early modern speculation and uncertainty.[1] The points of similarity (or difference) between the life of the aged in fourteenth- and fifteenth-century England and that of their counterparts in the early modern or modern West, or in colonial North America, or in "the third world" in recent times, or in the realms of anthropological literature, are matters that admit of numerous and intriguing comparisons but that — to the medievalist — should not be forced into more conformity than their nature admits of. Deep comparisons are of limited value, and while the body of literature that tells us of these different societies, let alone of their parallels and analogies, grows at an impressive rate, it only takes us so far and no farther.[2] Sufficient for this effort to test some definitions, dimensions, and boundaries within a single society as confined and informed by the norms of a relatively unified (official) culture and informed by a modest body of quantitative (and qualitative) data. As I have argued elsewhere against the idea of any particular structural-functional form of the late medieval family as *the* norm, I now argue against any single "read" on old age as being correct, or all inclusive, or even preferred. We look at the topic from different angles and we see, as we might expect, different images and different hues.

In recent years an impressive bulk of the scholarly literature on old age in medieval society has been published, largely from scholars who have approached the matter as presented in didactic and creative literature. Much of this work has shown how interwoven the various strands of explanation and analysis — both medieval and modern — actually are. If recent work and a larger concern for the problems of old age as a universal social and historical as well as a literary theme were launched by Simone de Beauvoir, with her magisterial *The Coming of Age*, the current trails along which medievalists wend their ways are being blazed by J. A. Burrow and a host of others.[3] Thanks to their work we have enlightening and accessible treatments of medieval views about the stages of life and the "ages of man" question. The story of the use of art and iconography, to teach and to exemplify, is now familiar and accessible.[4]

Nor do the views and teachings from late medieval society stand as lonely and tide-threatened islands; we know of the ways in which Judaeo-Christian, classical, patristic, and scholastic thought — medical and scientific as well as moral and numerological — contributed to the body of knowledge available to a man such as Chaucer.[5] The medical tradition, from Roger Bacon on postponing the advent of old age through the fifteenth-century Italian treatise of Gabriele Zerbi, *Gerontocomia: On the Care of the Aged*, indicates a concern for a practical and hands-on discussion of the aging process that we might easily overlook, buried as it usually is under the moralities and pieties that constitute the bulk of medieval teaching.[6] There was the realm of the personal and of "social work" beside that of poetic finality and moral symmetry.

Nor should a social historian's "take" on the subject be seen as an exercise merely in the counter-factual or the theoretical. That a fair number of people who survived infancy and their early years actually managed to reach a respectable age should also be familiar material. Josiah Cox Russell set this out some years ago, and little that has been published since has altered the basic picture. According to his tables on late medieval population and life expectancy, that for males born in the quarter centuries after 1300 had, at age 20–24, the expectation of 23.8, 22.14, 23.86, 21.45, 29.38 (for the generation born in 1401–25), and 27.7 (for that born in 1426–50) more years of life. This means that the lives of men who survived infancy and early childhood perhaps ran to somewhere between 45 and 53.[7]

What can be added to this statistical information, and uses data comparable to those of Russell but for somewhat different purposes, is a recognition of the attested contemporary concern with age. We will work with some contemporary sources that are not only rich as a data base but show considerable potential as the starting point of a late medieval "discourse" about such matters. Furthermore, all kinds of material and scholarly writing attest to a level of social and political activity achieved and sustained by many of the elderly; we should be very cautious in using simplistic generalizations about life in the old days being nasty, brutish, and *short*. The latter characterization, at least, is in need of some revision. Indeed, some survived for many years and flourished to the end, if others only made it thanks to the helping hands and open purses we like to think of as part of the nurturing culture of traditional society. Reality was probably bleaker, as it always tends to be.

One purpose I hope to accomplish through these essays is to put old age as a topic or consideration into the agenda of medieval social history, or at least to push it forward with more vigor and assertiveness than has been the case up to now. Studies of family, of patriarchy and prescribed rank, and of social structure will hardly suffer from an occasional but explicit focus on the existence and pull of the three-generation family. The formulation of questions in terms of generations and cohorts and sons' sons can only enrich the detailed work being done on various English counties and localized communities, be they rural or urban. There are still few English counterparts of the papers Georges Duby has offered on young men and their generational identities and roles, and we are no better served when we look at experience and behavior found at the far end of the life line.[8]

But good material is at hand, and is being used, if not specifically to explicate the topic covered here. A good example of how questions regarding age and the aged, the overlap of generations, and links between the elderly and the very young is offered by a recent study of a prominent East Anglian family of the later middle ages on into Tudor and even Stuart times. Roger Virgoe's family history of the Knyvetts pays considerable attention to such issues, and without explicit focus on the subject matter of my study (which we have discussed in general terms) touches many of the same bases; they are natural topics in a family's history, if members of the family happened to live long enough.[9] We learn, in tracing the Knyvetts, that old John Knyvett had stepped aside at the end of the fifteenth century, at least a few years before his death around age 70, in favor of his son; that he and his wife had probably lived apart, with his lady in some sort of honorable retirement and possibly supported by a corrody in Carrow Abbey.[10] In the next generation it was a tale of longevity and patriarchy: Sir William "had lived until he was around eighty years of age and had survived his eldest son and that son's eldest son, so that his heir-at-law was his seven-year-old great grandson, Edmund."

Nor, as we will see, was the mere matter of having survived and having had an opportunity to know one's grandchildren either unusual or a sure path to happiness and family harmony. Though William Knyvett left substantial bequests to the heir of his grandson Thomas, he also had to worry about his daughter Ann, unhappily married to the unreliable

Charles Clifford. In William's will Ann received £20 per annum for 12 years, since Clifford, "by his negligence and misordrely lyving is brought in great daunger and poverte so that my seid daughter lyveth a pore lyff." There is more of such about age and the generations: when death came to Thomas Knyvett in a naval battle in 1512, and then to his pregnant wife in childbirth later that year, a royal decree awarded the upbringing of the orphaned children to their grandmother, Eleanor Knyvett. Furthermore, there was an allowance for maintenance and an annuity of £10 for the old lady herself.[11]

The point of this analysis of Virgoe's work is to show how grist for the mill of old age and its concomitant social issues, as a regular element in all sorts of historical inquiry, is to be found all over the place. Much of the information about age and the aged, three-generation families, and other related topics and questions is constantly being absorbed and embodied into current research, albeit in many cases without much explicit recognition of the direction in which it can lead us. As well as the treatment of Chaucer's view of age and generations in "The Pardoner's Tale," "The Knight's Tale," "The Miller's Tale" — topics we are all likely to cover in the classroom — we have a long list of these questions awaiting us in the sources and publications of historical research. Tales of quarrels that went to court, of last wills and testaments, of careers that reveal decades and even generations devoted to town and local government and elections to Parliament, of local family histories, of prosopographical slices cut from the stories of church and parliament and the universities and the "civil service" all await our scrutiny.[12]

On the other hand, a social historian is inclined to worry about distinctions between the disciplines regarding the use of sources and records. Are the different disciplinary approaches complementary — variations on a common theme? Or are they, in practice, roads diverging from a point of common origin to the extent that their single genesis is but a fading memory? These are not meant as rhetorical questions. As the scholarship unfolds, and as different interpretations of medieval society (as a palimpsest rather than a text) are put forward, I think there is a genuine dissonance between what literature — be it normative, didactic, or creative — said about life and the life span and what men and women actually experienced, both personally and through family and social relations. Men (and women) who looked at their own world with even the most minimal analytic or discursive curiosity *knew* that life was not invariably ebbing away at 40 or 50; the evidence about survival and longevity was all around them.[13] And yet they were content to read and write to this effect, to receive and transmit cultural lore that held messages to which they were attuned regarding the pre-determined and fleeting nature of life; nor did they give much indication of wonder at the discord or dissonance, as best we can read their words and grasp the intention of utterance. Experience as lived, and culture as articulated and transmitted, can run along parallel tracks for a long way without provoking much sense of wonder, let alone of disbelief or distrust in the surveyors who laid out the route.

In the course of preparing these essays I have been struck by the difficulty of picking out the main road of behavior as well as of ideology. In my remarks about identifying a social policy toward the aged and the extent to which they were meant to be the explicit and pre-determined recipients of charity, both the diversity of contemporary expression and of modern scholarly interpretation stand out. Clearly, as we are led by some of the texts, the plight of the aged (poor) was recognized as a serious one, one that it behooved many of privilege and advantage to remedy. But as other texts — and a good deal of studied silence — tell the tale, the fortunate elderly were just part of the deserving poor, the unlucky ones probably beneath serious attention. Modern students have been led by their reading of the sources to look for, and perhaps to see, a more caring society than actually existed. There is no single answer to these questions; ambiguity is one of the elements of the social cosmos.

PART I

SOME DATA
AND DATA
SETS

I

Inquisitions
Post Mortem as a
Window on Old Age

THREE GROUPS OF DOCUMENTS have come down to us, each purporting to contain a treasure chest of data that we can analyze for questions of age, survival, and longevity. The bodies of documents are, in the order in which they will be treated, Inquisitions Post Mortem, Proofs of Age (scattered among the Inquisitions), and the odd aggregation of materials generated by the Scrope and Grosvenor controversy (launched in 1386) before the Court of Chivalry.

None of these materials could be considered reliable, at least not without external support and corroboration, were we attempting to write demography in its up-to-date and empirical sense. Though the information they contain can be turned toward such an end — and will be, to some extent, for want of better sources and data — the documents have a questionable or enigmatic side. But demography as such is not our ultimate goal. Serious historical demography, as treated today, places a heavy emphasis on our ability to ascertain *rates*: rates of birth, rates of marriage, rates of mortality, rates of remarriage.[1] As such, it is largely a quest in pursuit of a normalized statistical grail — a projection from the known to the probable — whereas we are mostly content to snatch at and enlarge on various odds and ends of information pertaining to old age and prolonged survival that have come to hand, regardless why the documents were either generated or preserved.

Our more casual or haphazard approach may bespeak a strange polarization of our sources; a partisanship that places us on the side of the imprecise as against the more precise, an alignment with the haphazard as against the systematic. To some extent there is justice in this charge; we will indeed attempt to make the weaker case not into the better one but rather into one that offers some different insights and conclusions from those found along the road not taken, that is, the road of systematic demographic reconstruction. In addition, the plea we enter is one of "other times, other places"; we forsake twentieth-century empiricism to look at some quantitative materials as they were created and recorded to meet the needs and questions of the moment in the fourteenth and fifteenth centuries. How long people lived, or, to state the question in a more useful fashion, what percentage of people at any given age survived to the next given age, is a difficult question to put to these exiguous records and it is not the question we are primarily concerned with posing.[2]

Rather we are looking for material about the contemporary *perception* of age and longevity: how men and women of the day conceptualized the issue of survival in seemingly precise terms. They took cognizance of years and of chronological age, by count, as well as of the stages of the life cycle and of the physical changes wrought by the changing seasons. They have left us many indications of an interest in how old a particular person was at a given milestone or at a specific point in time. Furthermore, allied to the issue of the perception of age is that of the expression of that age, not just the number of years but how that number is expressed for the purpose at hand. Both the content of the records (the data they preserve and transmit) and the form of their expression (the way they encode or express their substantive content) are worth considering. First we will talk about the problems and limits of the sources and how these problems are inherent in the very creation of the documents on which we build our case, rather than just standing as some peripheral or extraneous factors that happen to be there and that, unfortunately, diminish reliability and accuracy. The three bodies of data we deal with were generated for purposes which make our investigation into age and longevity problematic but which also seem to take us toward the heart of medieval expression and consciousness.

The problem of using the sources we have chosen in order to tease out some precise information about age and longevity is fairly obvious. One difficulty lies in the medieval penchant for expressing quantitative material, especially age, in round and standardized numbers. We all know of the propensity to fall back on a formulaic mode of expression when bringing information back to headquarters: an affectation of a studied disinterest in precision or accuracy, as we see it. To some extent this resort to a rounding off—either upward or downward—is a reflection of an "I don't care" or a "what does it matter" approach. But behind indifference and insouciance are some genuine cultural distinctions between *their* modes of dealing with quantitative information—touching how it was collected and how it was reported—and *our* approach to the same agenda of inquiry.[3] However, lest we become too patronizing, we should remember that governments have been collecting data, presumably at a level of usable precision, since sluice gates on the Nile were a new order of business.

The three bodies of sources of interest certainly contain a treasure chest of seemingly precise information: ages of heirs, individual and biographical details touching on age, the personal and mnemotechnic tools whereby people spoke with utter certainty about a long past event, details of family networks and of begetting and losing, and a long string of self-proclaimed assessments of career length and of the age at which one had cleared one *rite de passage* or another at some far-distant moment. But the sheer bulk of these sources should not hide the problems of using, let alone of relying on them without asking some serious questions.

However—and this is a crucial fork in the road between this journey and that of demographers—our concern is with the contemporary perception of age and the assertions, made time after time and case after case, about its precise nature, about the seeming exactness of the transmitted information. Whether men and women of the day had any common agreement as to how old the old "really" were, or whether the old (from 60 onward, for argument's sake) represented a significant fraction of live births, or of survivals from the age of majority, or from the moment of marriage or first parenthood forward, or any of the other items of the demographer's questionnaire, is hardly relevant. The answer to these questions will be either negative or a string of uncertainties. They certainly did not know of such detail all the time, and probably not very often.

What is of interest to us in the Inquisitions Post Mortem, rather, is how often, and by means of how many different administrative and legal processes and hearings, men of age and some level of social standing were summoned to provide information needed to generate the vast corpus of precise sounding numbers we have. These quantified statements about age, or the years of a career, or the span of years in a certain status or position, or the years that had passed since some event had taken place, were deemed sufficiently accurate and detailed for the legal, social, and economic needs of the matter and the moment. What our local citizenry attested to was what passed muster. Their answers, as given to and/or as recorded by the king's officials, were satisfactory; the bureaucrats returned home with adequate answers and usable data. Sufficient unto the day, or unto the purpose. Men attested; facts were recorded; the wheels of government turned.

This standard of "good enough" was probably a flexible standard. It was met hundreds and hundreds of times, and the material we analyze below is but a small fraction of what is extant. Day in and day out, in a range of hearings and inquisitions and administrative and legal and financial proceedings, in every county of the kingdom, such information was given, recorded, and preserved. Moreover, the standard of need-to-know detail was invariably met by a vast battery of precise and particularized responses, all of them incorporating the substance of genuine or spurious precision, and whether what we have is what men "really" said or rather the result of an editorial process that standardized the diverse substance of actual utterance cannot be determined with any certainty. The sources embody the contributions of hundreds of men, doing some kind of public business, through 140 years of official transcription. It is from this world of presumed exactitude that our three bodies of sources emanate.

If no one individual was likely to testify in such proceedings very often, the inquisitions — as a public data gathering affair or event — were a regular part of public life. A given juror or witness, after his first summons and first testimony, now had a stock of vital information at hand about both himself and his kin and neighbors. Much of it, we know, was numerical and quantitative. If we accept that men knew the coats of arms and family links and genealogies of the local gentry, we certainly accept that they used some signifying quantitative framework within which age, family birth order, and the like were set onto a frame of reference to be used when needed or asked for.[4]

No student argues for the literal accuracy of the ages and life spans given in our sources. Even when the information is accurate by our standards — in those cases where verification is possible by some external check, as for the peers — a modern standard of accuracy seems irrelevant. Rather, the pseudo- or seeming precision regarding dates, intervals, and ages offers an entrée, across some unwritten but critical boundary, into a realm of medieval culture where assertions and attestations were offered with an appearance of precision. The attestations were generated by administrative procedures and were necessary for the closure of such procedures. The recorded responses laid a trail across a seam of psychic and social reality, one along which oral recitation, folk memory, a recourse to numerical expressions, and a community consensus about age and family converged into a continuum that bound together past experience with current relationships and social structure.

Folk memory and village custom were not expressed only in parables, anecdotes, and vague memories about boundary stones and customary works in the good old days. We hear, in the sources, the voice of legal cunning. Maybe it was a case of collusion between interested parties and the neighbors and local folk, alongside the acceptance or the indifference of the king's men. The administrative procedure can be read as an example of "us" versus the outsiders, the official "nosey parkers," but usually there is little reason to think that the outsiders were in any way discommoded by the results. More likely, the collective *mentalité* expressed in the documents reveals a corner of the public arena—the public space, or the moral economy of the locality, if we prefer—in which the various participants contributed a share of information and from which they divided the spoils of a public and collective task, imposed from above but complied with and dutifully completed. In these rituals of memory dredging and record creating, the documents represent closure.

Much of the recent work on memory in the Middle Ages has concentrated on how thinkers and writers made the leap from what is held in the mind's eye—whether as memory of what was already known or as the "creation" of new material—and what is set down, henceforth to be preserved in and transmitted as part of the written culture.[5] The mind both held material and reshuffled it, to great advantage when we turn to such striking and creative examples as the reflections of Thomas Aquinas, and more commonly as basic and pragmatic if pedestrian components in each person's transition (or translation) from recollection to communication. In addition, of course, we know about the powers of retention, as well as of creation, embodied in the oral tradition, the vast scope of the transmitted but unwritten lore of the illiterate. The memory palaces of Renaissance thinkers were as yet unknown on the day the men in a Cambridgeshire village were asked how they knew their neighbor's son was of age when he came forward to claim his inheritance. But we have no trouble accepting the power of collective local lore in a world of rote learning, of sheepherding and manorial accounting, and of market transactions and currency exchanges made on the run.

What is probably more relevant, given the level of society and the nature of the material being called up for the permanent record, is what is what we now refer to as "social memory."[6] The idea Emile Durkheim presented that collectively held ideas assume the power of "social facts," and

the recognition that publicly recited memories encapsulate a "group com-
memoration" of the past — turning it into the reality of accepted memory — are keys to unlocking the psychological and social dynamics behind
an inquisition or the collection of depositions. The intelligentsia had their
architectonic schemes, and lesser folk — literate or not — had their bags of
tricks and devices. We now make much of the idea that not even the literate
were wholly separated from an older and more malleable world of orality
and tradition simply by dint of their acquisition of a "higher" skill and by
their use of writing. Each person's thought process encompassed many
variations, pausing at different rest stops on the road of cognition and
imagination, recollection and communication (whether oral or written).
The medium was, truly, not separable from the message, and often more
than one medium might be employed toward a given end result, a sort of
macaronic internal text in which each person moved back and forth between the facts he or she remembered, the recollection of how and why it
was remembered, and the recorded memory as it became fixed in written
sources. Not that the final form, just because it was fixed by being written
down, was necessarily accurate; it just served to make subsequent changes
in the textual record unlikely.

The growth of governmental bureaucracy went hand in hand with the
use of written records. What government functionaries really wanted from
their efforts was a final written product, the closure to a proceeding as an
administrative "event," as in an Inquisition Post Mortem.[7] The point at
which the administrative procedure crossed the boundary between illiteracy
or orality to that of literacy — from the world of memory and attestation to
that of ink on parchment — was a movable one. Some matters were dealt
with quickly, in one leap from the mouths of one's neighbors to the parchment of the clerks who would record, implement, and preserve the decision. Some questions bubbled and stewed on a slow fire as they mellowed
at the grassroots level; their final form might only take shape after discordant or supplementary material had been collated.

We can think of the seemingly precise records of interest here as the
products of the social process we have briefly described. Their information
on age, identity, relationships, and genealogical links and their elaborate
inquiries into lands and landholding were eventually or ultimately collected
within the boundaries of one document, a memory-synthesizing and sta-
bilizing entity now given permanent existence by the act of written creation
and preservation.[8] As such, the procedures of the inquiry and its end product were steps on the road, moving in a regular and controlled fashion,

from the collective assertion of a "good-enough" memory to the final incarnation in chancery or exchequer — the documentary permanence created at the far end of the deliberations.

None of this discussion is to imply that the Inquisitions Post Mortem are unsullied repositories of "fact." The ground beneath us is pretty shaky if we want to think of them as a precursor of the birth certificate. Nevertheless, they offer the largest body of demographic data we have from their day, and they are, if used with care, a mine of information far beyond any other body of extant material. Like so many other old acquaintances, they have their friends and their foes among historians and archivists — some eager to defend them against slander, and some quite willing to give us a worst case scenario. But regardless where we stand on this spectrum of faith or skepticism, we acknowledge validity in criticisms and danger in use. The faults of the Inquisitions, like their virtues, reflect the perceptions of those who generated and transmitted their findings. The idiom of legal and administrative documents places a premium on information that is formulaic, normalized to meet the convenience of those charged with gathering it and those responsible for "using" it. Popular culture versus vital statistics and modern standards of quantitative accuracy might be the name of the game; for this round, we side with medieval culture and medieval modes of expression.

A reading of the Inquisitions works backward from the data on the age of the *new* heir — the vital fact without which the Inquisition was useless — to a projection regarding the probable or approximate age of the *late* or *former* holder of the property. This is the reverse of a modern obituary notice, which gives the age of the deceased and merely the identity of the nearest survivors. While the ages of the latter can usually be guessed at, from the biographical material and the logic of the life cycle, more precision about the ages of survivors and heirs is unnecessary or inappropriate, given the purpose of an obituary. This can serve as an object lesson in how a level of precision is called forth, shaped, and expressed — as controlled by the purpose of the document or procedure in question.[9] The medieval process was the reverse, and we work accordingly. The Inquisition served as a legal and social notice whereby an announcement went out regarding the succession of the new property holder. That person was coming into his or her own, perhaps at long last, and the attested statements being gathered and recorded — on the basis of local testimony, given to the escheator — about age, status, and relationship were to reassure and to guarantee continuity, as well as to trip the levers that would release or transmit the property.

If the predilection of the Inquisitions for reporting ages in round or conventional numbers is a problem, it is often one that can be contained or controlled for. Against this drift toward imprecision is the fact that the findings of an Inquisition represent a balance — the establishment of a modus vivendi — between the interests of the new heir and those of parties who had an interest in retaining the property in wardship (were there a question about the heir's legal age). Otherwise, the establishment of the critical identity was sufficient. Were he or she a minor, the additional hurdle of a Proof of Age proceeding was in the cards at some future point. In either case, the answers returned and incorporated into the Inquisition were the critical starting point, and not many subsequent inquiries — whatever their problem with details — seem to have quarreled with the information gathered for the original Inquisition. It was taken as the north star by means of which voyages towards inheritance plotted their course.

The weakness of the Inquisitions for expressing ages in round or approximate numbers is compensated for, to some significant extent, by the resort to greater precision on those occasions when knife-edge accuracy may have been at a premium. Ages of infants could be given with (every appearance of) precision; such details lend credibility, even if the detail is rhetorical or folkloric rather than numerical. Though the moment of genuine inheritance might lie far in the future, it sounds credible and responsible to offer returns telling of an heir who is "one and three-quarter years and more, or one year at Michaelmas last," or of another who is "one year and nine months or one year and ten months." Testimony about an heir who had turned three "on the feast of St. Chad the Bishop last," sounds like testimony put together by local heads with serious deliberation and inquiry. Was it correct? It certainly was worded to carry weight and credibility.[10]

When people were clearly of an age not all that near the critical hurdle of majority — as in their early teens — a simple "aged 15 years and more," or something of this sort, generally sufficed. The burden of precise proof, when such a minor heir would come of age in a few years, could still await a future "event," that is the generation of a Proof of Age, with its own procedures. The age given in the Inquisition was good for the moment of this particular proceeding. It had no shelf life; a Proof of Age proceeding, held some time afterward, never referred to the Inquisition nor seems to have acknowledged its (prior) existence. The king's records were in central storage, and were presumably accessible, but locally generated ones seemingly had to be recreated whenever needed.

If the heir to real property were just around the border line of legal majority—perhaps either just below or just safely past—indications of more serious attention to detail are not infrequently recorded. An heir approaching majority but not yet actually there was so identified: "he will be 21 years of age a year from 27 July next." A variation of this theme was, "20 years of age on 24 August next." For someone just safely across, there was great comfort in a report affirming that, "he was born on 20 January 1382 and is therefore aged 21 years and more." Perhaps waiting in line was not too worrisome if one were armed with attested statements that one was already "aged 20 and three-quarters, 2 months, and 12 days." The wait would end just around the next bend.[11]

Once the new heir was beyond the law's most serious demarcation—the age of legal majority—the need for precision obviously became less pressing. If the heir were clearly too old for the question of legal majority to be a serious issue, such formulaic phrases as "aged 30 years and more" or "aged 33 years and more" could suffice for the interested parties; it must also suffice for us. Since the jury returning the information was composed of those with local knowledge, and since the findings usually seem to have been accepted without demur, it behooves us to work from the idea that the ages attested were unexceptionable to and harmonious with local culture and memory, if not accurate by our standards. After all, medieval society was not anumeric. Nor was it a world with a different framework regarding the definition of life, either in terms of ultimate chronology or longevity, or in terms of the stages of the life cycle. To the neighbors, if one were clearly more than 21, one was old enough; if one were well beyond that, a rough-and-ready "30 and more" sufficed. And if one were considerably beyond the latter plateau, a less common "40 and more" or even the occasional "50 and more" did the trick. No vested interests were threatened by such categorization, no larger truths about the law and life were disarranged. A really advanced age was given for the next heir with neither gloss nor explanation. If someone was said to be 55 or 60 when he or she inherited from a parent or sibling, the data just went into the record as offered.

But we should not champion the Inquisitions; analysis, not vindication, is the point here. In many instances the various sets of inquisitions for a given person, returned by juries in different counties in which he or she now held land, display a degree of diversity that causes some uneasiness—to say the least. A widow's son who was variously reported at being 40 or 44 or 50 at the moment of inheritance was clearly a man of mature years; his mother had likely been at least in her 60s, possibly somewhere well beyond. Likewise, a son who was named as being 30, or 32, or "of full age," sets problems we can hardly hope to solve. In the tallying done for the tables in this chapter he would be considered as being in his 30s. At least it seems clear that he was *well beyond* any dispute about his majority, and that they of the jury chose to convey the information in this less precise style does not vitiate its value. The central authorities displayed no inclination to send the jurors back or to seek either greater precision or a synthesis of the diverging assessments from proceedings in different counties.[12]

The formulaic responses — as we elaborate below — were in keeping with the perceived realities and stages of the life cycle. A son now about to inherit from his father and himself already a father of adolescent children was not likely to be listed as simply "21 and more." Common sense dictated that a more advanced age, if not the "real" one, was called for. Nor, conversely, was a son just embarking on marriage and his own life as an adult when inheriting from his father apt to be reported as "40 and more." This would have been out of keeping with the norms of age-regulated behavior, with the customary rate of progress through the stages of life. Local knowledge might be a cover-up or conspiracy, given a sufficient motive, but it also could function as a leveling agent or mediator, pushing the information about innumerable individuals into conventional channels of lived experience as well as into conventional channels of narration about each person's progress through life. If our tables pigeonhole the heirs into neat categories (by age in decades), we seem to be roughly in step with those who compiled the records some five or six centuries ago.

Furthermore, though age is our main interest, identity was every bit as crucial. When the standard answers regarding the identity of the heir were not at hand, we find instances of what we can label as genealogical research, conducted on the run. Whether the information about obscure paths of descent was supplied by the interested parties themselves, whether it was concocted by their supporters to be trotted out at the critical moment for recitation to cut the knot of uncertainty (for closure so all could adjourn for a drink), or whether the jurors were actually sent out to inquire and investigate, is not something we can verify. In any case the routes that led from a deceased heir to his second cousins once removed, or to several first cousins twice removed, or by way of some comparable and circuitous course of relationship and descent, were charted with the contingencies of procreation and survival, as well as of heirs' ages, being taken into account.

In surveying these records we have no indication whether our jurors prided themselves on having done a good job, or, conversely, worried lest truth and justice had not been served. They had been summoned, they had testified, and they had gone home. We rarely have reason, as far as our records go (and it is their story to tell, as they chose, for the purposes of the day) to think the vector of local information was bent too far, either for or against a specific instance of disinheritance.

In one instance a man who had been holding land by courtesy of England from his wife now died. The jury said the heir to the land—the late wife's heir—was John, son of Thomas, son of Richard, son of Amice, sister of John, whose daughter Joan had borne John, and the said John had been the father of Maud, recently deceased.[13] This search only ended when a third cousin had been named. In another case the road of succession and inheritance led to a second cousin, once removed. John, now 30 more and named as the heir, was the son of John who was the son of Edmund who was the son of Gerard. Gerard had been the brother of Robert, father of Henry, and Henry's son was the John whose death had precipitated the inquiry.[14] If those who fed such material to the king's men were inaccurate on such occasions, they were hardly casual. Land was important, and heirs' ages were a not-insignificant factor in the saga.

*   *   *

Having thus offered an elaborate if cautious welcome for the age-related data of the Inquisitions, let us turn to their content. So many of them are extant, and so many have been calendared and published, that a dip into some of the most accessible collections would seem to be more than adequate. We will begin with those published for the last years of Richard II and the early years of Henry IV.[15] Tables 1-1 and 1-2 look at heirs of deceased male landholders, divided by categories of relationship and age (of new heir), taken from these two collections.

A few final qualifications are needed. As is usually the case, we can learn more about men, and about more men, than we can about their female counterparts (mainly their widows). For clarity of analysis and to enhance our comparisons, we have separated the material in the Inquisitions by the sex of the deceased landholder; women who held land will be treated separately. The material about three-generation lines of descent will be analyzed in more detail later when we turn directly on grandparent-grandchild links. Here it is merely reported, though it reinforces the evidence for a longish life span for some significant fraction of those deceased landholders. The "other" category in some of the tables includes a few of the various

TABLE I-I.   Ages of Heirs of Male Landholders, from the IPMs, 15–23 Richard II

	Age at Inheritance					
Heir	<10	11–20	21–29*	30–39	40+	Total
Sons	34	49	42	14	3	142
	24%	35%	30%	10%	2%	
Daughters	8	11	9	4	2	34
	24%	32%	26%	12%	6%	
3rd gen.	5	—	3	—	—	8
	63%		37%			
Other	1	13	10	6	17	47
	2%	28%	21%	13%	36%	
Total	48	73	64	24	22	231
	21%	32%	28%	10%	10%	

*Because of the importance of legal age (21 for men) the categories have been adjusted, or slightly skewed, to reflect *below* 21 and *at or beyond* 21. The sources themselves are tilted toward such demarcation and we follow this distinction, even though it makes for a slight asymmetry in the age brackets. Totals do not add to 100% because of rounding.

TABLE I-2.   Ages of Heirs of Male Landholders, from the IPMs, 1–6 Henry IV

	Age at Inheritance					
Heir	<10	11–20	21–29	30–39	40+	Total
Sons	31	35	34	17	5	122
	25%	29%	28%	14%	4%	
Daughters	3	4	8	4	—	19
	16%	21%	42%	21%		
3rd gen.	—	5	—	4	—	9
		55%		44%		
Other	1	11	10	9	7	38
	3%	29%	26%	24%	18%	
Total	35	55	52	34	12	188
	19%	29%	28%	18%	6%	

heirs from the generations above: aunts and uncles. It also includes many from the same generation; brothers, sisters, a few cousins. Brothers were invariably younger than the deceased, sisters a mixed lot regarding birth order. The "other" heirs of descending generations have been statistically noted: nieces, nephews, and a wide variety of younger cousins and cousins' children.

In addition, the Inquisitions sometimes report groups of co-heirs. When these were sisters or daughters, the tally in the tables reflects the age of the oldest of the group of co-heirs and/or co-heiresses. This practice minimizes the gap between the age of the deceased and that of the (eldest) new heir; we do not want to exaggerate longevity or to inflate ages. The assortment of heirs and heiresses might include one or more sisters, plus the children of other sisters, now dead; all these, both male and female (sons and daughters of the original group of sisters, now figuring as nieces or nephews or grandchildren), came in for a share. When the aggregations included those from more than one generation the whole group has been omitted from the tally; it will be reserved for what qualitative treatment we can bring to this discussion. The number of such groups is not very large, and the age spread of the co-heirs makes them too awkward for statistical treatment, even though they offer some interesting examples of complex lines of descent and relationship.

What do we learn from the data reported in these two large sets of Inquisitions regarding age and longevity at the end of the fourteenth century? The chancery Inquisitions give us over 400 instances of succession for male landholders. The largest single category of heirs is that of straightforward father-son transmission: 142 cases of 231, for late Richard II; 122 of 188, for early Henry IV. In percentage, father-son transmissions are 61 percent and 65 percent of the two universes respectively. What is of special interest to us is that 42 percent of the sons for 15–23 Richard II and 46 percent of those for 1–6 Henry IV are reported as being of legal age and beyond at the moment of inheritance: about half of a group of significant size. When we add the smallish number of daughter-heiresses we find that sons and daughters together — children of the body (who made up, together, some 76 percent of the heirs: 264 sons, 53 daughters, or 317 children as heirs of 419 deceased property holders) — were at and above legal age in 42 percent of the instances for Richard II, 48 percent of those for Henry IV.

If we work backward from the age of the new heirs to the probable final age of the deceased landholder, it is clear that being followed by an

heir of legal age does not argue, per se, for any great longevity on the part
of the deceased. Two consecutive generations surviving to an age of sexual
maturity is not by itself much argument for the *longue durée*. In these assessments we accept the likely presence of the European marriage pattern
as prevailing when we think of age of first marriage.[16] This means a world
of relatively late marriage; "late" is, for most men, in the mid- or late 20s,
for women mostly at the mid-20s mark. If people deviated from this pattern
it was more apt to be for an older rather than a younger mean age. However, the landholding classes, whose lives are reflected in the Inquisitions,
may well have married earlier, given their affluence and a propensity toward
arranged marriage. So for this higher social group we may have a life cycle
that was beginning to produce children when the parents were at or even
below age 20. On the other hand, there is not much evidence, even for the
higher ranks of the peerage, to indicate a world of pregnant Juliets and
teenage mothers.

An heir of 21 or slightly above, therefore, may be taken as the starting
point in a train of argument that gives us a recently deceased father who
had been perhaps in his mid- to late 40s. If some early marriages meant
some younger fathers, we can counter with the certainty that some of the
heirs who inherited were not the first sons but rather the sons who had
survived; many had older sisters of whom our laconic records make no
mention. Nor did all fathers marry at or below the mean of the general
pattern; by definition some had been 30 or more when their first sons had
been born. Nor were all first children born eight or nine or ten months after
their parents' marriage; against the incidence of pregnant brides we must
have couples who needed years of effort to get on track. So, as with many
other arguments based on medieval statistics, the push and pull of compen-
sating factors may well even out: for the universe of heirs of 21 and a little
more, a universe of fathers who had survived to 45, if not closer to 50. This
seems a good point on which to rest.

The next step in our reconstruction in the search for the aging and the
elderly is to look at the sons (and daughters) identified as being 30 and
more, and more. In the first set of Inquisitions (for late Richard II) such
sons comprise 12 percent of the total of sons-as-heirs (17 of 142). In the
second set (for early Henry IV) they are 18 percent (22 of 122): 10 percent
of the first group being in their 30s, and 2 percent in their 40s respectively,
and then 14 percent and 4 percent for the second group. When we bring in
the daughter-heiresses, we have 13 percent of all children-as-heirs named as
being age 30 and more in late Richard II, 18 percent for early Henry IV.

Such children must have meant fathers who had been — to extend our argument from younger to older heirs — in their 50s, or more. This means, to turn from percentages to fractions, that about one landholder in every six pretty surely lived to *at least* the mid-50s.

These findings hardly take us to the cutting edge of gerontocracy. The result is more likely to be a minimal assessment of the age of (deceased) landholders than an extreme one. If some unknown fraction of the deceased had been younger than we suggest, it is likely that quite a few had been older: later marriage and the death of children in their father's lifetime, along with the now-eclipsed aggregation of daughters who had preceded sons, all argue in this direction. When we include the three-generation links — mostly with grandchildren — we have 17 more instances (in the two groups of Inquisitions) from some 419 cases: another 4 percent, one further case in every 25. The mention of a grandchild at all in the Inquisition argues for a deceased grandparent who had to have been about 40 as a biological if not a social minimum: most such progenitors, we can assume, would have been some fair spread of years beyond this, probably well beyond 50. Since we are told that some grandchildren were in their teens and some even in their 20s (or more), clearly some of the grandfathers had been men in their 60s and 70s and, on occasion, perhaps in their 80s.

The "other" heirs to whom we turn, in the occasional Inquisition, add fuel to the fires of uncertainty and variety. Brothers were invariably younger than the recently deceased; the laws of primogeniture suffice to explain this assertion. Sisters could be on either side of the deceased in birth order; neither their ages nor those of their children, were they the heirs, are of much help. The occasional resort to other relatives is interesting, their ages a mixed bag. While an aunt of "60 and more" says little about the last birthday of the deceased, the existence of a (presumably younger) brother of 60 as his heir, or of two nephews of 40 and more, is more helpful.[17] When we come to a first cousin once removed, aged 40, or two such cousins (once removed), aged 50 and more, we have moved down a generation and are probably marking the passing of an elderly man.[18] But cousins could be descended from older aunts and uncles, and the likelihood of impressive age for the late-departed stops short of certainty.

Let us recapitulate before turning to some other sets of Inquisitions. Underage heirs represent about half the pool: 58 percent of the children for Richard II (102 of 170 cases) and 52 percent of all the named heirs; 52 percent of the children for Henry IV (73 of 141) and 48 percent of named heirs. Of those of legal age, more were given as being in their 20s than in their

30s or beyond: 51 children (male and female) in their 20s as against 23 in their 30s or more for Richard II, 42 as against 26 for Henry IV. Thus we can work back and suggest that most of the deceased covered in these Inquisitions had been around 40 or 45 years or a bit more, with a significant minor fraction well beyond this. This accords with other findings on late medieval longevity. And, at the far end, some fathers had clearly reached 60 or more: perhaps it was as few (or as many!) as one father of every eight or ten or twelve. If these are odds that seem moderately long when we turn to individual cases, they are hardly beyond the pale in a world governed by the laws of large numbers. Some of the sons, well into maturity and perhaps already on the down side of their own demographic slope, were just now being called into place to succeed fathers who had come pretty close to their three score years and ten.

At the other end of the "long fifteenth century" are the Inquisitions from Henry VII. These offer even larger aggregations of data, and the material is set out so we can compare their main points with the late fourteenth-century material from Tables 1-1 and 1-2.

Because so many cases are covered in the early Tudor volumes, we

TABLE 1-3.   Ages of Heirs of Male Landholders, from the IPMs, Henry VII, volume I

Heir	Age at Inheritance					
	<10	11–20	21–29	30–39	40+	Total
Sons	81	135	108	82	30	436
	19%	31%	25%	19%	7%	
Daughters	28	24	7	10	1	70
	40%	34%	10%	14%	1%	
3rd gen.	20	14	7	1	—	42
	48%	33%	17%	1%		
Sibling(s)	—	10	12	12	17	51
		20%	24%	24%	33%	
Nieces/nephews	—	11	2	4	8	25
		44%	8%	16%	32%	
Other	2	2	5	9	9	27
	7%	7%	19%	33%	33%	
Total	131	196	141	118	65	651
	20%	30%	22%	18%	10%	

TABLE 1-4. Ages of Heirs of Male Landholders, from the IPMs, Henry VII, volume II

	Age at Inheritance					
Heir	*<10*	*11–20*	*21–29*	*30–39*	*40+*	*Total*
Sons	58	82	98	73	36	347
	17%	24%	28%	21%	10%	
Daughters	21	15	10	6	2	54
	39%	28%	19%	11%	4%	
3rd gen.	7	8	11	1	—	27
	26%	30%	41%	4%		
Sibling(s)	—	—	8	10	10	28
			28%	36%	36%	
Nieces/nephews	6	4	2	1	1	14
	43%	29%	14%	7%	7%	
Other	1	1	2	3	12	19
	5%	5%	11%	16%	63%	
Total	93	110	131	94	61	489
	19%	22%	27%	19%	12%	

Totals do not add to 100% because of rounding.

have divided the new heirs into more categories than for the earlier collections. But sons and daughters still make up the overwhelming bulk of the named heirs: 78 percent of all heirs in Table 1-3 and 82 percent of those in Table 1-4 were children of the man's body. Of these children, 37 percent and then 56 percent were of legal age on coming into their inheritance (in Tables 1-3 and 1-4 respectively), and 19 percent and 29 percent were named as being 30 and more. The male heirs were of age in slightly over half the cases in the first volume: 220 of 436, or 50.5 percent, and 60 percent of the time in the second (207 of 347). Daughters were consistently younger: 26 percent of age in the first volume (18 of 70), 33 percent in the second (18 of 54).

These numbers compare well with those from the late fourteenth century, even though it is impossible to determine whether the swing toward greater age in the later data reflects demographics, that is, improved longevity, or to the vagaries and fluctuations of the investigative process. As we argued for a social integrity in the communal memory revealed by the Inquisitions, we have to acknowledge that there were some matters on which the local community may have been very taciturn. Perhaps the legal and regional culture of early Tudor times placed a premium on age, and neighbors were inclined to attest to greater longevity than they had done a century before.[19]

In the tables for Henry VII, three-generation heirs (grandchildren) represent 6 percent of the total universe of heirs. This category will be analyzed below; a one-in-sixteen resort to this route is worth mentioning. We see a fair number of much older landholders, now outlasting their immediate links (eldest sons) and then giving way at the end to the younger descendants from the third generation. Brothers and sisters were apt to be older heirs, of course, being of the same generation, whereas nieces and nephews probably would have been comparable in age to the children, or a bit younger if they were the children of younger brothers. "Other" heirs are likely to be weighted toward age at the moment of inheritance, since as a group they embrace first cousins and even an odd aunt or uncle. If we look at the age brackets for all categories of heirs, we see that in Table 1-3 50 percent were of legal age and 28 percent were age 30 and more. In Table 1-4 the figures show 60 percent to be of legal age, 31 percent as being at least 30.

We can look at some smaller, regionally focused data bases. They give a few more points for comparison; mostly, they support what we have seen in analyzing the larger printed collections. Tables 1-5–1-7, drawn from Inquisitions for Yorkshire, Nottinghamshire, and Lancashire, put a little more flesh on the bare bones of our statistical material.[20] Without belaboring this intractable material — well hidden by the thick hedges of the "uninformative phraseology of the sources"[21] — we see that a reasonable percentage of heirs only assumed their place in society as land holders when an aged pre-

TABLE 1-5.   Ages of Heirs of Yorkshire Male Landholders

	Age at Inheritance					
Heir	<10	11–20	21–29	30–39	40+	Total
Son	20	23	14	8	3	68
Daughter	3	5	1	1	1	11
Other	1	5	5	6	4	21
Total	24	33	20	15	8	100
	24%	33%	20%	15%	8%	

TABLE 1-6.   Ages of Heirs of Nottinghamshire Male Landholders

	Age at Inheritance					
Heir	<10	11–20	21–29	30–39	40+	Total
Son	22	22	25	11	6	86
Daughter	4	2	3	2	—	11
Other	—	4	5	4	7	20
Total	26	28	33	17	13	117
	23%	24%	28%	15%	11%	

Totals do not add to 100% because of rounding.

TABLE 1-7.   Ages of Heirs of Lancashire Male Landholders

	Age at Inheritance					
Heir	<10	11–20	21–29	30–39	40+	Total
Son	19	29	26	20	14	108
Daughter	4	2	1	1	2	10
Other	6	1	4	4	4	19
Total	29	32	31	25	20	137
	21%	23%	23%	18%	15%	

decessor had finally moved over. Sons and daughters who were now of legal age upon inheritance comprised 28 percent, 40 percent, and 47 percent of the heirs named in the county inquisitions; the figures for children aged 30 and more are, in respective order, 13 percent, 16 percent, and 27 percent.

This method of arguing backward, from an heir's attested age to a predecessor's probable age at death, opened with a discussion of the value of the statements regarding age, and we went from there to argue for at least a reasonable and constant presence of old men — as judged by their direct heirs' attested ages — throughout the century and across the realm. None of this is particularly startling; if it is revisionism, it is revisionism of the mildest sort. No one has argued that old men, as judged by a gentle criterion that placed old age at somewhere beyond 55, were unlikely to be encountered. Instances of greater age — of men probably lasting into their 70s and beyond — were also to be expected. Indeed, the Inquisitions hint at, if they stop short of arguing for, the frequent presence of the elderly. But our statistics give us the confidence — whether spurious or well-grounded — that comes from the use of larger numbers.

*   *   *

We can compare the material on men's heirs with what the Inquisitions tell about women's heirs. As we would imagine, the women — being mostly widows — had outlived husbands and were probably at least as old as, if not older than their husbands had been at death, even if we take into account the disparity between men's and women's ages at marriage. Since the heirs of the women were again mostly heirs of their bodies, they were the fruits of their mothers' earlier life experiences, and the familiar zig-zag of so many women's life courses, with a string of marriages and children by more than one husband, does not concern us.

Because there are fewer cases of women and women's heirs, we have collapsed the data into three tables: one for the data from the two sets of fourteenth-century Inquisitions (Table 1-8), one for those from Henry VII (Table 1-9), and one for the sets of local or county Inquisitions (Table 1-10). In these tables we find that the percentage of heirs already of legal age was higher than it had been for the men: 66 percent, 66 percent, and 61 percent. Women may well have lived longer, in absolute terms, than their menfolk. They also, in most instances, had been younger when the children had been born. When we look at the percentage of women's heirs named as now being over 30, the pattern of higher returns is also apparent: 38 percent,

TABLE 1-8.   Heirs of Female Landholders, from the IPMs, 15–23 Richard II and 1–6 Henry IV

| | Age at Inheritance | | | | | |
Heir	<10	11–20	21–29	30–39	40+	Total
Son	5	21	18	17	7	68
Daughter	1	1	8	8	4	22
Other	1	9	6	2	5	23
Total	7	31	32	27	16	113
	6%	27%	28%	24%	14%	

*Totals do not add to 100% because of rounding.

TABLE 1-9.   Heirs of Female Landholders, from the IPMs, Henry VII, volumes I and II

| | Age at Inheritance | | | | | |
Heir	<10	11–20	21–29	30–39	40+	Total
Son	11	22	29	25	15	102
Daughter	2	2	4	3	9	20
Other	7	12	12	9	4	44
Total	20	36	45	37	28	166
	12%	22%	27%	22%	17%	

TABLE 1-10.   Heirs of Female Landholders, from the IPMs, Yorkshire, Nottinghamshire, and Lancashire

| | Age at Inheritance | | | | | |
Heir	<10	11–20	21–29	30–39	40+	Total
Son	7	6	11	4	6	34
Daughter	3	2	—	1	1	7
Other	4	10	13	5	9	41
Total	14	18	24	10	16	82
	17%	22%	29%	12%	20%	

39 percent, and 32 percent. In addition, the ranks of their heirs contain a higher proportion of "other" heirs than did those of the men, and we find that grandchildren (treated below) and sisters — often of an advanced age themselves — make up much of the differential.

To turn this material upside down we might remark on how few of the women had died at such a young age that the heir was but a child, listed in the Inquisitions as being aged 10 or less. Here, in respective order, the percentages of heirs aged ten and less are a mere 6 percent, 12 percent, and 17 percent. When women were followed by their sons, only 38 percent of the latter group were below legal age; when daughters were the heirs, 55 percent were age 21 or somewhere beyond. Furthermore, many of the 45 percent of the inheriting daughters who were under 21 were cited as being age 14 or more — capable of coming into their own through marriage. So the deceased women had in all likelihood been older women, linked to families and networks of heirs already considerably older; this tells us something about demography and survival, and it hints at social and familial patterns in the widow's life experience that we only can follow in any detail for a few aristocratic women but that must have been a prevailing one at many levels.

As these women of property had been older, so they were also more likely to have been surrounded by older children, to have had older companions, and perhaps to have had some acquaintance with grandchildren. Matriarchy and the culture of old women, whether on their own or in extended family households, is mostly a lost topic, worth investigation but hard to treat other than anecdotally. Such networks clearly constituted a world that embraced many people at different ages and stages of the life cycle: the aging widow herself, her young descendants, and the changing and rotating universe of servants, boarders, and hangers on. The long-lived Margaret Paston and such upper class women as Cecilly, duchess of York, or Alice Brienne, were not anomalies, but rather have been caught for us by the luck of surviving sources.[22]

The statistics we can squeeze from the Inquisitions could be spun out a bit more. However, it is not likely that we would learn much from looking at other collections. As texts and reconstructions of life there is no getting away from the fact that they are dry material, and efforts to trace the weave of family structures and patterns of survival, based on their formulaic findings, are going to be patchy. We can find an occasional vignette that invites a second look. In a few instances the heir is identified as being a clerk or chaplain, an odd twist of fate that bespeaks an unexpected swing in a family's fortune between one generation to the next. When the clerical heir was a brother, the contingencies that pushed him forward are easy to understand. Thomas, V Lord de la Warre was elevated to the peerage in 1398, when his elder brother, lord John, died childless; Thomas was already about 40 and well up the ladder of a successful career in the church (and though he lived until 1427 he was one of the few peers who never married). The Inquisitions reveal a few other landholding families with a similar fortune; a brother in the church and 30 and more, or even one of 40 and more, when fortune's wheel took an unexpected turn. When the clerical heir was a son — a chaplain, now aged 26 years and more — we assume the prior decease of at least one older brother, perhaps of several.[23] Such clerical heirs were rarities, encountered or resorted to less often than aunts and uncles, and their presence in these few instances does not do much to open the window into either age or family structure.

We have referred to odd combinations and clusters of heirs who might be named in an Inquisition when no single male heir was forthcoming. In some instances the trail leading to the group of heirs hints at a long chase; an aged landholder who had just died was only followed by an attenuated group of heirs and survivors, and their competing claims regarding the old man were best set forth at the inquest. A not uncommon collection of such heirs might consist of daughters along with the children of other daughters. One man was followed thus: the son of a daughter, now 17; a grandson (by another daughter), now 10; plus two married daughters (presumably younger sisters or half-sisters of the two boys' mothers), now both married and aged 25 and 24.[24] Groups of heiresses or heirs, related through women, could come in all shapes and ages: cousins of 60, 40, and 23; a brother's daughters, now 30, 28, and 26; a husband's sisters of 60 and 50; plus a third (deceased) sister's son, now 30.[25]

As documents that touch on questions of age, Inquisitions give a few glimpses of impressive longevity on the part of the now-dead. A son of 40 years and more must have meant a father in his early to mid-60s, and if the data are accurate the chances are that the father might have been in his late 60s or beyond. If this is so when a son was named as being 40 (or "40 years and more"), what should we add when the "boy" is identified as 45 or 50 or 58 or 60?[26] One thing we might add to our evaluation of these numbers is skepticism; another is awe.

But these instances of professional distancing can also be overdone. Such advanced ages for heirs now finally about to assume an inheritance are unusual, but they are found, on occasion, in all the Inquisitions. Such things did happen; men and women really lived to be 80 and more. We know that women (as widows) were apt to have older heirs: a son of 60, or one of 67, certainly carried this toward its logical extension.[27] If a late husband's brother, at 60, was now named as his heir, there is also the question of how long after the husband's death the widow survived.

First cousins, named in a few instances, were likely to be of the elderly variety. They were of the same generation as the deceased, and the presence of heiresses and various family dead ends meant they could be older just as readily as of the same age or younger. Thus a cousin-heir of 60, or even 72, is not a certain beacon by which to backtrack: the predecessor might have left the scene when short of such years.[28] Even a first cousin once removed, of a subsequent generation in a genealogical table, could be as old as, or — given the spread of daughters' lives — even older than the dear departed. So such an heir, at 50 years and more, does not irrefutably argue for a predecessor who had been 70 or 75.

But the search for old age and the elderly, not caveats against following leads that point in this direction, is our target. The trail left by the aged across the bare face of the Inquisitions — if rarely a hot trail — is often comfortably warm, and we indeed can close in on a respectable number or proportion of aging heirs, following a number and proportion of aged if now deceased landholders. Clearly, the elderly — like the poor in the gospel — were always with us. How old were those, in years, whom we have considered old? is not a question we have been worrying much about, any more than we have been worrying about how common they were. Approximate numbers, as we have been dealing with here, seem the appropriate raw material for rough assessments of stages of the life cycle, or the generational jump between parents and children and those others who had to wait their turn.

2

Proofs of Age
and the Culture of
Attesting to Age

THE SWORN STATEMENT REGARDING the age of the new heir to real property was an integral part of an Inquisition Post Mortem; the actual age
stated on that occasion subsequently became a basic element in the legal
validation of the life cycle. Regardless whether the age we find in the record
was newly ascertained or merely legitimated, it became codified by the administrative and legal proceeding that embedded it in the records of Chancery or Exchequer. The stated age of a new heir, linked as it was in most
cases to the age of the recently deceased, was the bread-and-butter of the
written record, guiding us through the transition from the old generation
to the new.

When a minor heir reached the point of majority the administrative
procedure that led to a Proof of Age inquiry was now launched.[1] Also under the supervision of the escheator, this inquiry into whether or not the
heir had come to the boundary of legal age came to depend, once again, on
sworn and attested statements offered by the local freeholders, pressed into
service for the occasion to determine the young heir's age. But unlike the
bald statements of the Inquisitions, which rested on some murky and un-
revealed base of research and folk memory, the Proofs of Age also state
the age of the person attesting to the heir's majority, the age of the witness.
In addition to the witness's age, some mnemotechnic device is usually
included — what Maitland refers to as the "talk of coincidences"[2] — whereby
the requisite interval (between event X and today) has been remembered
and the credibility that comes with circumstantial detail is attained.

Those who are skeptical of the reliability of the late medieval inquisitions have not been slow to point to the formulaic and often repetitious and improbable nature of the reasons (and coincidences) produced to explain the sharp edge of memory found in the Proofs of Age.[3] So standardized is the usual assortment of memory-joggers that it seems quite likely that the escheator, or friends and representatives of the heirs suing for majority, or perhaps some local repository of prepared formulae, arrived for the business of the day already armed with a collection of ready-made reasons.[4] If so, the different jurors may just have chosen one reason or another from the grab bag of putative happenings, perhaps choosing them in some random fashion, and then filling in the appropriate names, making their mark, and thereby entering the fixed annals of the written record. Otherwise, from the wide range of possible memories and signposted happenings, we find a suspicious and unconvincing incidence of broken arms, burning barns, and baptisms that coincided with returns from memorable errands and journeys. Who would guess at so much drama beneath the humdrum rhythms and routines of daily life?[5]

The rash of similar events, all reported with total seriousness, hardly enhances the credibility of the Proofs of Age as documents to be taken on implicit trust. Their content, and the honesty if not the wit of those whose statements they incorporate, are easily dismissed as evocative if unreliable. But — as we have argued regarding their peculiar voice — the Proofs are a written fix on a process that reflects oral memory and introduces us, in brief, to the interweaving of events and lives within traditional society. The blending of the internal, the individual, and the external enables us to catch the sense of ritualized public theater, and we need not worry that signs of its pre-rehearsed nature show. As sources, Proofs of Age are the testimony of collective memory, a melding of oral culture *and* its translation into the written form. They link an ostensible knowledge pertaining to years of age and years of interval with the memory of an event so as to produce a series of conclusive statements. And, as we said above, the final written statement sufficed for the law's purpose. Presumably it was also sufficiently consonant with local reality to be attested to on the basis of that consensus.[6]

The data of an Inquisition were less likely to be rounded off when precision was needed, nor was an improbable age for the heir apt to be offered out of thin air. In fact, a real degree of precision, even to the point of "research," was reflected in the witnesses' statements when identity was hard to establish or exact age at some premium. By extension, the discourse embodied in the Proofs of Age, bent as it was to fit a formulaic mold, still had to conform to local acceptance of the probable; whether this was the literally exact seems less relevant. Regardless, it too passed muster at the time and circulated at face value among those whom we have to assume were in the know.

Another aspect of the issue of collecting precise data in this fashion is worth some reflection. The coincidences offered to support the legal findings move from the realm of formal law into that of folk culture; we eavesdrop on the conventions of the community's speech and recollection, set pieces in the mouths of neighbors and acquaintances, expressed to each other and then enshrined within the written transcript. The documents we have, both the Inquisitions and the Proofs of Age, are final products of *process*, of the interaction of local knowledge and memory, either as the result of the pooling of such knowledge, or as a compromise, a modus vivendi between adversarial positions in an inquiry where there had been a real dispute or genuine uncertainty about the responses.

Nor is this process of pushing through to an acceptable conclusion as nebulous as it might sound. Our faith in the modern jury system rests on the idea that some peculiar amalgam of public disinterest, empathy, and receptivity to courtroom logic and the laws of evidence will lead to an acceptable result, more often than not, that for all its faults is hard to improve on. When the presuppositions behind the jury system are stated in this bald fashion the edifice on which our criminal justice system rests seems very fragile. Life and freedom depend on the self-regulating and balancing hocus-pocus of investigations and rhetorical presentations that range from the exactitude of forensic research to the demeanor and digestion, on a given day, of judge, witnesses, lawyers, and jurors. In an uncertain world we balance an important structure on a thin edge and entrust major decisions about people and process to this chancy procedure. Then, once the creaky machine has produced a conclusion, we act in accord with that decision or verdict just as firmly as though the end result were the disinterested product of statistical mechanics, not the bits-and-pieces construct of history, tradition, emotion, and self-interest.

There is in fact little evidence that the findings of the imperfect or imprecise process underlying an Inquisition or a Proof of Age were unacceptable to contemporaries; the heirs named were (almost always) those who did assume control of the property, and heirs claiming to be of age were (almost always) successful in their quest.[7] There are cases where the would-be heir had sought, without benefit of the process, to come into the property, and he or she might then be told to suffer the law's delay. But if we think of a Proof of Age proceeding as an administrative *rite de passage*, not as a "scientific" inquiry into vital statistics, we can grasp the way the local consensus about age was coupled with the seemingly precise definitions of lawyers and royal officials.

The findings of the Proof of Age, along with their formulaic expression, are of interest. Our focus here is on the self-proclaimed ages of the jurors, not that of the petitioner. The witnesses' ages were lore or data that emerged as a logical part of the information offered at a ritualized gathering of men-in-the-know, a kind of market day get-together at which conventional stories were told (or assigned, or fabricated), ages of the witnesses compared for bragging or disparagement, distant events dredged up and cogitated, and links and intersections in lives and families and events chewed over. Memory was a complex structure, socially shaped and focused, and it was now directed to impose closure through the stamp of credibility and authority.

Studies of the legal and administrative machinery and of the interactions of county society and local political culture emphasize the importance of the gatherings of freeholders and gentry when there was common and public business to enact.[8] Occasions on which the sheriff or the judges or lesser officials convened the responsible populace were occasions of ceremony, of pomp and circumstance for the people roundabout. Doing the king's business, whether for a parliamentary election, a session of his courts, or an administrative hearing, was the political equivalent of the ale tasting, the Corpus Christi procession, or the annual pageant of urban theater.[9] On such occasions — or at such events, if we so choose — men of substance moved about with their retinues and retainers, be they lawyers and bailiffs or liveried and subsidized bullies now back from the wars. And in the crowded lanes of villages and towns lesser men either trailed after their betters or did their best to put on their good clothes and show a bit of swagger on their own.

This foray into a world that we visualize as somewhere between the crowd scene of a Breughel painting and the deliberate confusion caused by heavies like John of Gaunt's men showing up in town to dictate the choice of members for Westminster may catch some of the festive and ritualized public behavior that accompanied the process we are looking at, though their purposes were not necessarily those of glee and merrymaking.[10] When the local worthies were summoned to give testimony for their king's use, small freeholders and men of decent but unimpressive substance were presumably on their best behavior. As they were apt to dress for the occasion, and to be seen to have coins available in their purse for the call of the taverns, beggars, and the manly wagers one covered to indicate largesse, so they donned the symbolic robes of dignified participation. At a Proof of Age proceeding one's memory—like one's own age and honorable family antecedents—was a possession to be shared and now displayed as a public commodity; it belonged to the attesting voice. Each juror in turn accepted his responsibility to unveil his age and to link it with his set of memories, perhaps under the escheator's kindly guidance, before his fellows. He showed his slice of the existential event for which memory was now crucial. The personal served the social. His fellows would reciprocate; each was seemingly careful to take his associates and their tales with due seriousness. And the escheator, at the end, put his seal of approval on the collective enterprise when he drew up the final record.

If this explanation of the socializing process behind a Proof of Age gives the proceeding a meaningful social context, then we might say that a descent into and reliance on a formulaic world of questionable accuracy is a small price to pay. Beyond this point, as with the Inquisitions, inaccuracy is easily overestimated. A society's view of the presence of the elderly, and of their longevity and sustained careers, is part of its cultural construction of itself—of the stages of life and the role of experience and deference—rather than a mere matter of demographic or statistical determination. The Proofs of Age allow us to grasp the self-perception and shared reflection on such matters.

An accepted and shared definition of the life cycle is part of the received message—from both culture and biology—that we all carry: the prescribed rules of the game, giving us some idea of how we might hope to pace our time on stage. The Proofs tell us, in bare demographic terms, that the heirs we are concerned with had lived long enough to come to their majority and their property: 21 for male heirs, 14 for females. But of greater interest here are two other kinds of information they offer. One pertains to the stated age of the attesting jurors, often recorded in round numbers, the other to the reasons why the witnesses were so sharp—the "coincidences" that struck Maitland when he looked at these documents.[11]

Like the Inquisitions, the Proofs of Age are formulaic and—absent any specific interest in the history of the individuals or families coming into the property—of greater value when considered in larger numbers rather than as a series of detailed statements about individuals. This means, in effect, that much like the inquisitions, any given group of Proof of Age records is much the same as any other; not an unfair statement, given the law's procrustean interest in standardizing data into pre-arranged questions

and answers. After all, it is the nature of central records to reduce a wide
spectrum of experience and expression into a smallish group of common
forms of behavior. Let us turn to the Proofs printed among the Inquisitions
in the volume for 15–23 Richard II (1392–1399) and take a dozen returns
for a closer analysis.

The dozen we have chosen offer the statements of all the separate jurors: only one juror of the 12 groups of 12 either neglected to state his age
or had it omitted in the course of transcription that eventually took the
document from Dunster, Somerset, its point of origin, to chancery. Of the
143 jurors who stated their ages, 39 declared that they were 60 years and
more, 56 were in their 50s, and 48 were in their 40s: respectively 27 percent,
39 percent, and 34 percent of the totals. None of this group of jurors were
under 40 (though the law did accept men of 30 and more). Nine were listed
as being an "exact" "forty years and more," and a few as 41 and 42. Four
said they were in their 70s: three 70, one 71.

Each jury was assembled on some principle we can hardly hope to
discover: convenience, an interest on a juror's part in participating in local
government, knowledge of or interest in the inheritance at stake, or even
really having a memory of the events or some access to records and testimonies that would enable him to date the would-be claimant. This last is
promising if speculative. Age alone, at least beyond the "forty years and
more" that was the socially respected floor in these proceedings, does
not seem to have been a major factor in the summoning of the twelve
good men.

The component ages for the Proofs under examination are shown in
Table 2-1. All but two of the 12 juries had at least one sexagenarian, and in
five cases of the 12, men acknowledged as being "sixty years and more" constituted at least one third of the jury. Men in their 40s also made up at least
one third of five of the juries; "fifty years and more" was the median age
bracket, perhaps the point in life at which *gravitas* was as yet unimpaired by
the ravages of time and the erosion of memory.

What did these men of full maturity and beyond actually remember as
the event or milestone that still served—from the distance of 20 or 30 or
40 years—to fix the critical point in time so firmly? They remembered the
key date because of the simultaneous occurrence of an event of some significance, often of a personal nature, and so clearly marking the day of the
claimant's birth or baptism that the memory was still fresh enough, so long
after the fact, to answer to the law's demand for verification. Because the
"actual" or "real" events to which they refer could well be drawn from a pre-

TABLE 2-1.   Given Ages of Witnesses in Proof of Age Proceedings, from the
IPMs, 15–23 Richard II

Proceeding (page in volume and date)	Age		
	40s	*50s*	*60s+*
67–68 (16/11/15 R II)	—	12	—
123 (8/12/16 R II)	3	6	3
123–24 (24/9/16 R II)	10	2	—
180–81 (18/7/17 R II)	3	5	4
277 (6/7/19 R II)	4	6	2
350–51 (25/3/20 R II)	8	2	2
351–52 (5/2/20 R II)	—	3	9
352–53 (20/11/20 R II)	3	4	5
510–11 (20/6/22 R II)	1	4	6*
511–12 (1/5/22 R II)	3	8	1
512–13 (17/4/22 R II)	6	2	4
514 (5/2/22 R II)	7	2	3
Total	48	56	39
	34%	39%	27%

* Only 11 participants are reported in this proceeding.

arranged bag of formulaic reminiscences, dressed for the day in clothes of
adequate individuation, it is hard to talk about the better memory of men
of 40 than of men of 60 or 70. If the various formulae for recall really were
just handed out randomly as the business of the day got under way — to
establish the contested question of age, as the ritualized process demanded,
rather than to elevate the import of the incident that made it memorable for
the juror — we are not likely to learn much by comparing the memories of
the elderly with those of their younger colleagues.

Memories were sharp because of a variety of events, and the tales
themselves can be divided into a few categories. There were the men who
remembered the birth or baptism now at issue because it coincided with a
memorable external event, linked only by coincidence or simultaneity with
the birth or baptism of the infant. Mere chance, we are told, jogged the
memory of 50-year-old Gilbert de Babynton, because "on the following
night he was taken by the Scots and led away to Scotland, where he stayed
for the next six weeks."[12] Fire was both common and memorable: "He remembers because at that time a hall of his was burnt down."[13] Odd bits of

drama also set the point in question apart from the usual run of events: "the ferry-boat sank and he hardly escaped with his life."[14] These are Maitland's "coincidences" with a vengeance.

Some men had been personally caught up by their involvement with the family of the moment: servants, godfathers at church, messengers who carried news of the birth, and the like. Six men swore that they had been in the church on the critical Monday and had seen "Henry, bishop of Norwich, and Edward le Despenser, the younger, knight, the godfathers lift him from the sacred font."[15] In this instance the exalted rank of the godfathers would have given a special flavor to the spectator sport, and we have another credible sounding tale. John Walsche was even closer to the great event of the day: "Isabel his wife is the heir's godmother, and he rode with her that day to the church."[16] And for Nicholas Rayjes, now aged 44, the arrow struck the bullseye: "he was the heir's godfather at the time of the baptism."[17]

Some who attested indicated that they had had no personal ties but simply had happened, for some reason or other, to have been there at the critical moment: disinterested witnesses, or so we are told. There were those men for whom a memorable personal event coincided with our central one: a birth, an accident, the departure or return of self or a close relative from a journey, and often a death — a good fixer of memory indeed. A group of men had been in the church at Haule on "Sunday after the said Monday."[18] They had come to witness the marriage of a certain John Jakes to Margery Taillour, and on that occasion "they heard that on the previous Monday Alexander Carent had had this son Edward."

The old men among the jurors may have given slightly fuller accounts of the key circumstances. Maybe they feared that their tales would be discounted, or maybe they were just more garrulous by now. There does not seem any special reason to explain why we would be more convinced of an heir's age by the memory of 70-year-old Thomas de Swynton, who told of "a notable discord between Agnes de Bolton . . . and Alan de Yarwych . . . and on that day [of the baptism] the said Thomas made peace between them."[19] But again we know that this *kind* of memory sufficed to satisfy the demands imposed by an administrative procedure; it bore the weight it was called on to carry.

In several cases the memory of the critical event and its fixed point in time, transmitted as an element in the oral culture, was linked to the writing down of the event at the moment, that is, when the baby was born, not at the "now"-moment (some 21 years later) of the Proof. But it is the memory of something having been written that fixed the date and event, rather than a reliance on any actual proof provided by a written document. This coupling of the two cultures — written and oral — and of the two ways in which events of interest were preserved and contextualized in the lives of those to whom they were of some minor but remembered interest is extremely revealing. To write something down, and then to rely on the memory of witnesses to the process of writing rather than on the content of the document, vividly evokes the scene in the church, as it does of the mystery these men must have felt at viewing the physical "creation" of a text.

There are some other aspects of this phenomenon that bear more discussion than is relevant here. One concerns the number of times memory was set into its context by a recourse to writing. Sometimes it was an actual notation of the birth or baptism, but sometimes it was the process of *something* being written that fixed the moment in memory. Four men attested that they remembered that "Henry de Ferrariis, father of the said heir, asked Benet, vicar of the said church, to write the day and year of the birth in the missal there, and they are so written." [20] The variant is illustrated by the testimony of 64-year-old William Wascelyn: his marriage coincided with the child's birth, and he married "on 6 May after the said John's birth and *the wedding* is noted in the missal in the church of Grimston." [21]

The other aspect of the testimony concerns the verb used (in the recorded testimony) to indicate how the knowledge of the critical event — birth or baptism — was gained. When the events that fix the date are of the sort we have termed coincidental, they are often couched in the phraseology of he "knows this because . . ." [22] Sometimes the attestations are based on what the man "heard" or what someone had "told him." [23] When the jurors had been centrally involved in the business they were prone to talk in terms of "saw." They were now direct and first-hand witnesses: "they saw Robert Hunard and Ralph Smyth . . . lift the said Robert atte Chirch from the font," and "they saw John Northwych, then vicar, baptize the said Robert and wrap him in a linen cloth." [24]

Proofs of Age were documents of empowerment, triggering an administrative procedure that marked an end of something — a minority and a wardship. They authorized the heir to come into his or her own; as such, they were generally "created" around the time of the critical birthday. The age of the heir was usually accepted as offered. Therefore the Proof of Age was an occasion or an event. But it was not the occasion of a de novo investigation, and in keeping with its purpose the assertions of age by the jurors about themselves need not have been accurate, given that the men attesting were of indisputable legal age when the child whose majority was now at issue had been born.

Consonant with this limited "need to know" on which it all rested, the ages of the witnesses that are a basic part of each statement reflect some ordering or stratification of the webs of neighbors and friends, as social hierarchy within a community was played out. The Proofs of Age rarely rely on the testimony of people of great status, the sort of people who would have taken charge of their neighbors by virtue of position and power — or who were inheriting land held in chief. The status of the men who were involved was rather a status gained, on this occasion, by virtue of the right to play a dignified and formal role rather than by dint of having arrived already armed with social standing and unexceptionable credibility. The witness's power to attest was derived from the personal-cum-social lore he would unfold, a casual or even accidental role, played 21 years ago, and now to be repeated, doubtlessly magnified in import and drama as time passed. And for each witness, the mere act of playing the role brought dignity to the role; age and memory became part of a self-creating or self-aggrandizing social persona.

Indeed, the witnesses to the proofs really were a mixed bag of local talent. Many were (or had been) servants, perhaps to religious institutions, sometimes to families of property and power. In their attestations we find that the critical memory may hinge on the tale of an errand run, or a role played in the context of a subordinate position: "he was a servant of John de Cressy, father of Hugh, and he was sent to Somerby . . . to the house of . . . the lady Elizabeth . . . godmother of the said Hugh, and was given 10s. for his message."[25] If tales that do not reflect to the narrator's stature lend credibility, then we have to go along with William Taillour; he was "servant and chamberlain of Sir Ralph de Cromwelle, and because he was not present in the chamber on the arrival of Sir Ralph from the chase aforesaid, Sir Ralph struck him on the neck and felled him to the ground."[26] That certainly fixed the day wonderfully well, even at a distance of 20 or 30 years. The tale also attests, in an oblique fashion, that Taillour belonged; his link to the critical events was, all in all, to his credit.

A close reading of these statements also gives us a view of the nature and functions of community, something that emerges when we think of the Proofs as social discourse rather than just legal data. The documents show that many of the jurors had known each other for a long time. They would now share (or create) a common memory, just as old friends would share a bottle and an evening's conversation or the purchase of a joint wedding gift.

We saw the six men who joined together in attesting to a common memory, that of seeing lord Despenser and the bishop standing as godfathers. The Proof for Constantine Clifton, now a ward under lord Cromwell's care, also drew heavily on a group of men who had been minor members of the Cromwell household: the man sent to fetch Cromwell, the baby's god-father; the servant Cromwell knocked down; Cromwell's gardener, who on that day had been rewarded by lady Cromwell for finding "a nest with white rabbits," for which she gave him "a striped robe"; lastly, the servant of Cromwell's steward. They were hardly an exalted group, well beyond the fringes of liveried retainers, but still joined in a lesser fellowship of service, bound together by minor albeit honorable labor for one of the great men of the realm.

So the bland and unexceptionable Proof of Age — too easily ques-tioned as a credible source because of its formulaic and repetitive na-ture — can be read as a discourse that helps us unlock and decode local social interactions and shared experience — the very world in which age and the perquisites of survival and longevity were weighty matters. Manners, def-erence, cooperation, and common activities were governed and controlled, to some considerable extent, by the bonding of male cohorts and neigh-bors of proximate age, now telling their tales, just as they were by the bond-ing of kin or of social and political equals in a craft or guild. The Proofs of Age offer a testimonial, and a powerful one, to the ubiquity and active pres-ence of the elderly. The documents accept an active and involved role for the aged, with rich details of their formulaic responses, perhaps offered (and recorded) lest they be discounted as too imprecise or too remote to carry much weight.

These men — of 50 and 60 and even 70 years — more than held their own. We might even say that they were the best storytellers, the ones singled out to recite the richest and most circumstantial ritual words in a society accustomed to and even controlled by oralized concepts of proper utterance. The elderly had their place on the stage of public life, and if the Proof of Age offered many of them but a humble role in the drama of trans-mission and inheritance, it was still the best theater in which most of them would ever participate. At least we can say with confidence that the elderly were regularly given parts in the ongoing memory-theater at which the needs of government and the rituals of local social structure and interac-tion — often stretching across the decades or even the generations of the oldest living memories — were merged, recited, and *then* recorded.

3

The Scrope and Grosvenor
Depositions: More
Attestations About Age

OUR THIRD AND LAST OASIS on this data-seeking journey across the sands
brings us to the material generated by the Scrope and Grosvenor controversy of 1386. By the 1380s Sir Richard Scrope (1327?-1403), son of Sir
Henry, chief justice of king's bench, was the senior figure and patriarch of
the Scropes of Bolton and a figure of considerable eminence. He had already been treasurer and chancellor of the realm, joint warden of the west
marches of Scotland, steward of the royal household, and for over two decades a companion in arms of John of Gaunt.[1] He was an important figure
at court and in political and aristocratic circles.

The arms of the Scropes of Bolton—"azure a bend or" (dazure ove
une bende dor)—had been worn with great pride and seem to have been
emblazoned virtually everywhere that members of the family had rested
their heads or left their legacies. And now, horror of horrors, the same arms
were proclaimed and displayed by a mere Cheshire knight, Sir Robert
Grosvenor.[2] Scrope protested Grosvenor's appropriation of his heraldic
identification. In response to the cries of indignation and the pricking of
dishonor, an elaborate set of hearings was conducted, in the mid- and late
1380s, by various teams delegated by the Court of Chivalry to collect evidence so that a decision could be reached regarding the ownership and
proper use of the arms in question.

The depositions collected in these protracted hearings have been preserved. Recorded not for their demographic riches but for what they offered in a quasi-legal proceeding about identity and family as represented
in the use of a specific coat of arms, they nevertheless offer us another body

of contemporary legal and administrative material that fits neatly into the mosaic we have been constructing. Each deponent — and there were several hundred in all, some for Grosvenor, but mostly for Scrope, the more important figure and the plaintiff — was asked to state his name and age when his turn came to testify; for how long he had borne arms (if this were relevant: some witnesses were clerics and religious); when he had first seen the Scrope or Grosvenor arms displayed, and by whom; whether he knew of any break or interruption in the Scropes' use of the arms; whether others had (also) used these arms; and any other questions of this sort that would elicit vital information. The court held hearings up and down the land, in different venues and under different presiding officials, before it had exhausted the information provided by a long line of honorable and deserving men whose testimony was thought worth collecting.

The preponderance of the information clearly seems to have favored Scrope, and it must have come as no surprise when, in May 1390, the verdict was given in his favor. He then forgave the upstart Sir Robert Grosvenor, which meant that Grosvenor was not liable for the burden of L466 13s. 4d. in legal expenses to be assessed against the loser (for a set of proceedings that ran from 9 October, 11 Richard II through 27 May, 13 Richard II, under the ultimate jurisdiction of the constable of England, Thomas duke of Gloucester). All was patched up, between gentlemen, "and they made frynds afor the kinge in the p'lyament howsse."[3] The ceremonial and ritual nature of the reconciliation is also of interest, as part of the public drama surrounding matters chivalric, though it is not our business here.

Each witness was called on to state his present age and, for most of the more prestigious pro-Scrope figures, the years since he had first borne arms (or the age at which he had first borne arms). Thus another contemporary source that teems with demographic and quantitative information is available. Once more, we have the likelihood that the self-asserted ages are inexact, if not mythic in some cases. By the same token, we reassert that a disparity between what was attested and numeric accuracy, as we accept it, makes little difference for our analysis. Men of considerable stature, and very often of considerable age, calmly made a statement about their longevity and career-span that was acceptable to them, as it seems to have been to those presiding over the hearing. Once that was out of the way — their gravity and bona fides having been established — they could tell their story.

What did they say, regarding age? The material presented in Table 3-1 analyzes the stated ages, by decades, of the deponents: those who spoke for Scrope, those who spoke for Grosvenor, and that sizeable group whose

TABLE 3-1.   Age of Deponents in the Scrope and Grosvenor Hearings

Deponents	Age as stated by the deponent					
	20s	30s	40s	50s	60+	Totals
For	10	35	49	53	60	207
Scrope	5%	17%	24%	26%	29%	
For	20	48	44	26	11	149
Grosvenor	13%	32%	30%	17%	7%	
Side	8	15	15	13	7	58
unknown	14%	26%	26%	22%	12%	
Total	38	98	108	92	78	414
	9%	24%	26%	22%	19%	

Source: the ages stated in the depositions in Nicolas, *The Controversy Between Scrope and Grosvenor*

recorded testimony is too tattered to be of much value but who are tallied, with their ages, by Nicolas in his published edition of the records.[4]

The machinery of inquiry and judgment was likely, from the very outset, to give a verdict in favor of Scrope. Apart from the uninteresting matter of the actual facts and historical precedents of the issue, Richard Scrope was a man of great stature when compared to Sir Robert Grosvenor. He marshaled men of such eminence as John of Gaunt, Gaunt's son Henry earl of Derby, Thomas Percy earl of Worcester, and lord Scales, to speak on his behalf. In addition, and of critical importance for our argument, his friends were not only better connected, they were *older* than the men Grosvenor was able to come up with. As the table indicates, a mere 22 percent of Scrope's deponents were in their 20s and 30s (and some of them were already men of considerable status and repute, so the lack of years was more than balanced by their rank): the Scrope case did not rest heavily on relatively young men. Against this 40 percent of Grosvenor's partisans were of comparable youth, being somewhere between 20 and 40. And in this unique proceeding, much more than in the run of Proof of Age determinations, age was likely to be equated with gravity and credibility.

To meet the lack-of-age issue head on, the earl of Devon, a Scrope witness, said that "he is young and had the experience of a short time only." To show what a mere convention this kind of disclaimer was, the earl was almost 30 when he testified.[5] At the other end — and with no need to offer such apologies — are the 53 percent of Scrope's supporters who were aged

50 or more—as they told the tale—against but 37 percent of the smaller universe of Grosvenor partisans who had reached the half-century mark.

Our discussion of Inquisitions and Proofs of Age noted that the ages advanced by deponents and jurors were the numbers that passed the muster of the day. Whatever purpose was being served, whatever weight and credibility propped up by the self-assertions, the answers returned by deponents and witnesses were accepted as not unreasonable; that is, probable enough to be received and recorded, along with the other facts and details they soberly provided. Ultimately, such numerical information made its way into the record as a full fledged and vital part of the proceedings. There are obvious instances of exaggeration, of course, and some men stated an exact age while others were happy to be counted among the "circa" crowd, comparable to the "40 years and more" of the Inquisitions. But, all in all, a lot of quantitative information was being pushed across the counters of the Court of Chivalry, and it was readily being converted by the court into the coin of legal statement with no indication of complaints or doubts about its reliability.

Over one-quarter of the Scrope men claimed to be 60 years and more: 60 of 207 depositions, or 29 percent of the group. This was the case for a mere 7 percent of the Grosvenor men, and only 12 percent of those whose vital statistics are tacked on at the end of Nicolas's volume: 78 of 414 depositions, in all, or 19 percent of the grand total. Even at its least impressive—as among the Grosvenor partisans—the ranks of the elderly were far from depleted, and in the Scrope depositions men of 60-plus stand as the largest single age category, pulling in a bit ahead of the middle aged (the 49 men in their 40s) and the middle aged-plus (the 53 men in their 50s). This is a distinctly gray-bearded collection. Of course, in 1386 Sir Richard Scrope was 49 or 50, and many of his contacts went back to those first initiated by his father.

Since the premium in a deposition was on the length of one's knowledge of and acquaintance with Scrope, as it was on the span of years of familiarity with the coat of arms in question as being Scrope's arms, there was a logic to lining up as many elderly friends as possible, and in having such men come down heavily on their own years of life, on their years of being in arms (covering both weapons and coats of arms), on their years of having known old Scrope, and on the lack of years in which they had seen upstart Grosvenor wave the same banner. So the dynamics of the proceedings favored hyperbole and exaggeration, as they did an emphasis on age. The accounts preserve much of the flavor of court reporting, compa-

rable to what we get in the Year Books and other records of court deliberations and testimony. They are replete with the accounts of ages and the
details of contact and interaction, rambling narratives indeed when compared to the formulaic Proofs of Age as determinants of dates and events.
The depositions are closer to the records of the Mediterranean world, with
their notarial and inquisitorial style. They put us in mind of the cultural
exchanges we know from the work of Emanuel le Roi LaDurie and Carlo
Ginzburg, rather than in the customary annals of English legal and constitutional history.[6]

Some of the old men who deposed were simple and straightforward in
their tales. William de la Halle was 60; he had been armed for 45 years; he
had seen Scrope bear the arms now under dispute.[7] Round numbers, as
always, were attractive; Richard Baker was now 60, armed for 40 years, and
telling much the same tale about which arms belonged to whom.[8] There
were a few deponents from the ranks of the church, some of whom were
also among the elderly: the prior of Guisborough was 66, the prior of New-
burgh 60.[9] Men in their 60s were more common than those at some age
beyond, as we would imagine. However, there were those who claimed to
have reached and passed their biblical quota, often by a considerable margin. As we turn to their statements we encounter some straight claims of
great age: Sir John Loudham was 70, Sir William Marmion 78.[10]

But the tale is much richer than a mere assertion of age, richer than a
claim to long span of years. Some of the testimony takes us back to the
world of the Proofs of Age: the mnemotechnic event that fixes the birth,
or the taking of arms, or the moment of first acquaintance with Scrope
arms. In other instances we get snippets of tales that clearly catch the
essence of verbatim testimony. And some of the younger men, still well
below 60, chime in with testimony that show how a world of folk and social memory—literate but not relying wholly on the written record, nor
making the transfer from orality to literacy until it served some special purpose—preserved a culture that incorporated remembrances of things past,
of multi-generational lore, and of great deeds of our aging heroes and their
even more heroic fathers.

For old age, pure and simple, it is hard to top the depositions of Sir
John Sully, now 105, and of Sir John Chydioke, now 100. Engaging liars.
Sully was "unable to travel because of his age," and his deposition had to be
taken at his home. He had borne arms for 80 years, and had seen Scrope
bear the arms in question in engagements at Halidon Hill (1333), Berwick,
and Crecy (1346). Chydioke said he had been armed in April, 1327—the

year of Edward III's accession, surely an evocative way to open. If these were the champions of (exaggerated) longevity, others offer material along similar lines. Sir Thomas Roos, now 80 and armed for 60 years, said that "though he was an old man, he was not so old as to be able to recollect who was the first ancestor of Sir Richard Scrope."[11]

Memory and age, age and memory: partners that have already engaged a goodly share of our attention. In these depositions we see how younger men bought their way into full citizenship in this world of venerable testimony, sometimes long before their years alone would have pushed them forward. Using the proper mode of speech was not just convention or politeness; it gave stature and veracity. The young and middle-aged men might date themselves, perhaps using the moment of their taking up arms, from an event rather than from a year or a date: William Mauleverer, in his 40s, spoke of being first armed 2 years *before* the battle of Najera (3 April, 1367), "the battle of Spain," as they called it. Stephen de Pulham, about 44, had been armed since Poitiers (1356).[12] James Chudleigh, who did not state his age, said that he saw Scrope carry the contested coat of arms at Poitiers.[13] Sir Guy Bryan, an old and distinguished soldier (born c. 1319) had been armed since soon after Edward III's coronation, and he had seen Sir Richard's uncle Geoffrey carry the arms at the battle of "Burenfus in Vermandois" (Buironfosse, 1339).

These depositions conveyed first-hand knowledge about self as well as about the Scrope family, and they often brought in some of Sir Richard's more distant ancestors alongside kin of living memory. Hearsay evidence was of value; it could push the memory barrier back in time, and some of the young men were among those who transmitted testimony that incorporated such material. But hearsay evidence was at least once removed, and it usually needed some circumstantial framing to give it the same weight as personal, first-hand testimony. Sir Robert Morley, aged about 38, "had heard from his old relatives" about Scrope's arms.[14] So also with Sir Geoffrey St. Quentyn; he had "heard from good lords and old knights and esquires," an often used formula in the depositions.[15] John Bolton, about 60 or 61 on his own, referred to a grandfather who had served with Sir Henry Scrope, Sir Richard's father, in Edward II's Scottish campaigns.[16] For this stretch of 70 years the three generations referred to would more than cover the span.

This is very rich material. We might wonder whether an impartial court would have been less taken than we are with such testimony, or would they have agreed that family tales and old men's reminiscences were indeed high quality grist for the investigative mills? The court of the high constable might not seem the place for casual gossip or unsupported reminiscences. Sir John Trailly, in an airy fashion, backed up his view about the legitimacy of the Scrope arms with a reference to "hearsay from competent knights, now deceased," while Sir John de Wilton was willing to swear, "according to public fame."[17] Sir John Massy had heard "that two of his [Sir Richard's] ancestors had borne the said arms," while old Sir Ralph lord Ferrers (age 72, armed for 54 years) "had heard from his ancestors, who were aged," about the Scrope family and their emblems.[18]

More colors were added to the palette as more men chipped in. Nor was local partisanship neglected: the arms Sir John Bosville had seen displayed at Espagnole-sur-mer were "reputed throughout the counties of York and Richmond" to have been Scrope's, and Sir Nicholas Midylton knew them from the field and from their display in churches at York, Appleby, Carlisle, Richmond, and Bolton.[19] nor was the old "time out of mind" formula the only evocative cliché invoked as memory faded into the mists. Sir Ralph Bulmer "had always heard that the arms had descended by right . . . from beyond the memory of time, and the public voice and common fame [so] testified."[20] No less a figure than the abbot of Coverham — probably an old family friend — went on record as asserting that "it was commonly said that they [the Scropes] came with the Conqueror." Note that he was not saying the arms went back that far, merely that men of such ancient lineage *should* be believed when they made claims about family and honor and because of the length of their genealogical chain.

Lastly, the world of verbal testimony and hearsay was not the *only* basis of authority; the juxtapositioning of orality and literacy that we found in Proofs of Age appears here as well. Some deponents, both lay and clerical, talked about coats of arms that were to be seen in church windows and on the tombs and carvings of churches and regular houses, especially at St. Agatha, Richmond, the Scropes' own ecclesiastical headquarters, and of the ancient nature of various markings. The world of written testimony, like that of iconography and emblem, was combed for support and corroboration. The arms were to be seen in north country churches — on the glass, in paintings, and on family tombs. The abbot of Byland told of a visit Scrope had made to his house when the abbot had been but a young monk. Other knights were present, and one of them pointed to the appropriate decoration, on the ceiling or a window, and proclaimed, "Look! These are the arms of Sir Richard le Scrope." Canons of Bridlington testified to a charter that went back to the fifth year of King Stephen (1140); improbable, but at least specific and well before the formal beginnings of legal memory. Charters with seals carrying the Scrope arms and going back a mere 70 years were enough to convince the abbot of Riveaulx that he was speaking for the right side.[21]

The bulk of the evidence was in Scrope's favor; his eventual triumph was probably predetermined by the weight of his partisans if not by the merits of his case. But the way the brief was presented — resting so heavily on age, on the unbroken and unquestioned chain of memory, and on collective memory and consensus — gives us a look into how the world of the written document grew from and was melded into that of social memory, of family tradition (old and transmitted, or newly created), of fine-spun formulaic detail that gave verisimilitude to the testimony. When a man said he was born not in 1310 but rather four years before the Battle of Stirling (1314), he knew how to win the hearts of the old soldiers at the constable's court as well as how to add the weight of his own testimony. Nor did it harm his case that he was in his mid-70s.

A further point is the age of deponents when they said they has first taken up arms on their own. The most famous of the deponents — with apologies to John of Gaunt, duke of Lancaster — is Geoffrey Chaucer. Though we will look later at his own career and his comments about age, his deposition sheds light on these themes. He opened with the usual preliminaries: "Geffray Chaucere esquier del age de xl ans et plus armeez par xxvii ans." Though he had not been groomed for a professional military career, he had begun in the proper fashion. Beyond the mere interest in having Chaucer appear among the deponents, there is his actual evidence. He learned of Grosvenor's claim — after considerable contact with the Scropes and their arms — when he saw the Grosvenor arms improperly displayed on a sign as he was walking down "Fridaystrete en Loundres." Affronted by this, as any honorable man would have been, he was quite happy to come forward so he could speak on Scrope's behalf.[22]

Testimony from the deponents about the age at which they took up arms conforms to what we would expect; the range, assuming they spoke with some accuracy, was from the mid-teens into the early or mid-20s. Sir Robert Conyers, who had been with the earl of Warwick at Espagnols-sur-Mer, was now 61, armed for 43 years.[23] Nicholas Sabraham, who knew of Scrope arms as they were displayed "in a chapel at Messembre," was 60, armed for 39 years.[24] Old men might resort to round figures: aged 70, armed for 50 years, "before the wars in France were commenced by the late king," or aged 60, armed for 40 years.[25] Were younger men likely to give us more detail? Richard Poynings, now about 28, had been "armed . . . from his youth," while Sir John Massy was 30 and had been armed for 10 years, Sir William de Lye age 30 and armed for 15.[26] The numbers were usually reasonable, but more precise statements like "armed at the siege of Tournai" have a specificity—even if bogus—more consonant with old memory and old soldiers' reminiscences. Vagueness could be a virtue, in that data were such an accepted part of the common lore that their exact source could not (and need not) be remembered: "where the arms of Sir Geoffrey Scrope, or Sir Henry Scrope, or one of the Scropes, were borne, but the places and their names he did not distinctly recollect."[27]

This testimony provides a good instance of quantitative information being incorporated into "soft" memory to make it seem hard. That alone is an indication that numbers lent an air of proof or conviction to data; pseudo-precision seems not to have been questioned, and it was entered into the official records—as we noted with other sources—with great seriousness. To a considerable extent, the swearing to and the recording of the pseudo-precise helped to turn it into the precise. Moreover, quantitative information about age, even if self-asserted and self-proclaimed, was evidently considered to be part of each man's own tale, and the inclination— at least among friends—was to accept it as offered. A man's age, his family background, the tales he had been told, and his personal memory of self and of other were parts of the seamless garment of identity he could cut to his own pleasure and wear as he chose. The details offered in these proceedings are really, in both context and form of expression, the upper class version of the "I remember because it was on the same day as when I broke my arm" in a Proof of Age.

To question the value or veracity of quantitative data was, in part, to call a man a liar. And since honor and shame—the meeting point of the chivalric and customary value systems—were bound up with oaths and depositions and self-defining tales about the olden days—one walked carefully around those who were busy spinning their tales. The story of John Thirlewalle, aged 54 and armed for 32 years, brought in many strands of filial piety and patriarchy as well as his own sense of worth. John's father had remembered Sir Richard Scrope's grandfather, knighted by "good King Edward with the Longshanks." Who would have the nerve to say "nonsense" to a deponent when presented with such testimony; men fought duels over lesser insults.

Just staking a claim to a memory that antedated most men alive was an impressive ploy or rhetorical strategy. We have seen a number of depositions that run us back to Edward II, but almost no one else had pushed, even by way of hearsay and family lore, all the way back to Edward I (who had died in 1307). But even this venerable assertion was not the climax of Thirlewalle's evocative account. When his aged father had finally become disabled, "through old age bedridden, and [he] could not walk for some time before his decease," the old man had still been quick to take up the cudgels on behalf of the Scropes. "Whilst he so lay he heard some one say that people said that the father of Sir Richard was not gentleman because he was the king's Justice"; a true assertion, but when put this way, one that would lead the hearer to the wrong conclusion *unless* it were refuted or qualified. The old man had declared, as his son now testifies, that "if I were young I would hold and maintain my saying to the death." And, we are assured, this was not just the querulous behavior of an old man. It was delivered with the full dignity of aged authority; the son declared in his deposition that the father had been "the oldest esquire of all the North."[28]

Thus one aspect of what we refer to as "the culture of old age" is shown here, reaching out a long and powerful arm across the better part of the fourteenth century to validate honor and to give weight to perceptions of truth and reality. The primitive accumulation of credibility, stored as it was in family and male-bonded memory, in hearsay evidence and its reiteration, and in circumstantial tale-spinning, was inextricably linked to the power of the aged to recreate a believable world. If many aspects of medieval society — limited longevity for most, infant mortality, plague and famine, war and battle, childbed — merged the realities of life with the literary and theological depictions of worldly life as but a brief chapter in God's book, there was also another side to the story. We have seen how omni-present were the aged, just as we have observed the willingness of society to take their claims about age, knowledge, and proper procedure as seriously as they were offered. In some ways, at least, age served itself; in addition, it was well served by many others who did not (yet) have the qualifications to join its venerable ranks.

PART II

THREE-GENERATION FAMILIES:

THE OLD AND

THE YOUNG

4

Three-Generation Family
Links and Inquisitions
Post Mortem

THE THREE-GENERATION FAMILY — the living chain of parents, children, and grandchildren — is an element of considerable power in a consideration of family history and structure and in an assessment of the role of age and the aged as a measure of the quality of life. From grandparents to grandchildren is (another) instance of biology defined and reified to become a social institution; we might say that as gender stood to sex, so the linkage of the generations stood to the bare facts of procreation and survival along a straight line forward in time.

In the simplest or most immediate of biological models, to live long enough to see the birth of one's grandchildren — or, conversely, to come along in time to represent a three-generation overlap and to know one's grandparents — was but loosely linked to the story of impressive longevity.[1] Simply in biological terms one *could* be a grandparent by one's mid- or late thirties, without too great a stretch of imagination or sexual precocity. But given the behavioral pattern we refer to as the European marriage pattern in some form or other, it is unlikely that many men or women, whether toward the top or at lesser social ranks, actually followed a life pattern launched so precipitously.[2] Usually we assume that one was not apt to be a grandparent until at least well into one's 40s, and probably some point shortly after one turned 50 was even more common — for those who survived long enough to get there at all.

In the ideology of patriarchal society, the *man* who survived to see his grandchildren was especially blessed.[3] The tales of the fathers of Israel, culled from the Pentateuch and transmitted through the vast miscellany of rhetorical, educational, and iconographic and artistic illustration that made familiar the biblical basis of medieval culture, gave considerable support to the picture of the old man surrounded at the end by his children's children. Such a father of sons of sons was especially favored, blessed beyond his peers. The Old Testament contained such familiar lessons on the text as the burial of Isaac by Jacob and Jacob's sons, of the detailed listing and enumeration of Jacob's sons and grandsons as they prepared for the journey to Egypt, and of Jacob blessing Joseph's sons.

Nor was the mystique of age and continuity confined to the models from scriptures. In medieval history and medieval lore such a link was also a sign of a particular providence. Though no medieval English king after Edward III had this kind of personal fortune, the heroes of history and literature who could boast of such a clan were clearly to be admired, envied, and emulated. There was the aged Charlemagne of Einhard's *Life*, and the considerably more aged Charlemagne of such tales as the *Song of Roland*. The deathbed scene of William the Marshal, the aged St. Louis going off on his last crusade, and the venerable if self-proclaimed warriors we met in the Scrope and Grosvenor hearings all attest to the power of the model. People recreated it in literature and art, and they sought to appropriate it when possible in biography.

For England, by the late fourteenth century, the sober reality of royal dynastic fortune, if anything, made the image of the king who lived to play the white-haired patriarch an even more exalted role model. While we may agree with G. R. Elton's view of the unhealthy consequences for English history of Edward III's longevity and Philippa of Hainault's fecundity, there is little reason to think that this sensible assessment would have commended itself to Edward's contemporaries.[4] After Edward III — who lived to see both Richard of Bordeaux and Henry Bolingbroke among his children's children — there were no living grandfather-grandchild links between the crowned monarch and male heirs of the third generation as sons' sons until after 1688. It was as though demography mocked the royal dynasties and turned the kings and their sons into an anti-model for their subjects.

In addition to the comforts derived from and contributing towards patriarchal ideology, grandparent-grandchild links bespoke a temporary social and biological truce with, if not victory over, time and mortality. In many societies grandparents are the bonding agents for the family and the transmitters of the lore, leaving the middle generation free to focus on work, war, and sex. The literature of anthropology and ethnology is rich in accounts of institutions and behavior that support this interpretation. We find it reassuring to argue that, despite the paucity of fifteenth-century sources that talk directly to this, many a grandparent was, whether by explicit design or for want of others who would play the role, the cohesive link for the family, both in terms of interpersonal relations and touching the transmission of the culture of the house and its traditions.

Studies that have examined kinship from an historical perspective while setting it against the framework of issues posed by anthropology and sociology have generally offered a positive view of the three-generation bonding force. Where contacts between grandparents and grandchildren are not attenuated because of distance, or feuds and estrangements between the older generations, such links (especially grandmothers and their daughters' children) are apt to be strong, relatively frequent, and in keeping with their presumed importance for the transmission of family lore and bonding. Nor does modern society necessarily stand as colder and more remote than "traditional" society; arrangements for simplified long-distance travel and electronic communication may compensate for the vectors of geographical mobility and demographic scattering.

Late medieval perceptions of old people and young people, though usually revealed obliquely, indicate a world that offers many examples of shoulder and elbow rubbing between the cohorts and age groupings. The Scrope and Grosvenor depositions revealed intriguing glimpses of the way in which old men (and, presumably, old women) expressed themselves — with vigor and exactitude — about events that had touched previous generations. The sons who incorporated paternal lore as part of their deposition, and who thereby were entering into a common cultural memory bank with their forefathers, were but continuing the traditions of family tale-telling. Though Proofs of Age do not talk directly to the point, it seems likely that many an elderly witness spoke with such assurance because the babe in question was the same age as his own grandchildren, and the growth and aging of cohorts enabled the old men to keep things in their proper order.

Physical proximity, often in the form of shared residence, may have exacerbated tensions between the first two generations; if so, how did the third generation, that of the grandchildren, fare in this struggle between grandparents and parents? Day-care and baby-sitting in exchange for bed and board is too simple an equation, and too modern in formulation, to embrace this touchy if extremely common situation. But it does reduce some of the points of contact (and tension?) of this forced reciprocity to the language of a basic exchange from which neither party had an escape.

It may be a familial and residential link more likely to be represented by elderly and widowed grandmothers — whether his or her mother — than by aged men, the grandfathers, though once more hard or statistical evidence is hard to come by.[5]

The instances of grandparent-grandchild overlap that we discuss and analyze here are beyond dispute; they are attested in the records. If the tendency of the aged to exaggerate age seems a universal phenomenon, just being old (in years) is of limited interest. Neither the statistical incidence nor the importance of three-generation family links — in personal terms or in an evaluation of family dynamics — should be exaggerated. It is sufficient for us to identify and analyze the existence and nature of such links. We can begin on some firm ground, though eventually we will drift a bit toward some conjectures about the quality as well as the frequency of the links. Basically, the sources are fairly laconic.[6] A good deal of this search for grandparents (which could also be expressed as "the search for grandchildren") pivots around a search for and a dissection of useful sources: the methodological problems once again.

We can begin by returning to the Inquisitions Post Mortem, already analyzed regarding age and longevity and now reexamined for the light they shed on the existence and identity of third generation heirs. After that we will look at some fourteenth- and fifteenth-century wills, and finally at some genealogical material for the aristocracy. In conclusion, we will offer some general reflections about longevity and three-generation survivals, with a glance at some emotional or personal ties in this world that must have been commonplace but that, to us, are so hard to get a handle on.

*　*　*

We looked at the Inquisitions for what they offered, directly and by inference, on the question of the ages of the new heir and the deceased landholder. We noted some three-generation links; now we will return and look at these in more detail. Of the universe of heirs we considered, in aggregate, from the various sets of Inquisitions, the overwhelming majority were the children (mostly sons) of the previous landholder. Lumping together the heirs named in the seven sets of Inquisitions, we find that children (sons and daughters) made up 80 percent of the heirs of male landholders (1528 of 1913 cases), 73 percent of the heirs of the women (263 of 361 cases). Of the remaining heirs (20 percent for men, 27 percent for women) some were from the landholder's own generation (siblings and first cousins), some from the next generation down (nieces and nephews, first cousins once removed, and a sprinkling of miscellaneous others). In addition, there was a very small presence of heirs from the previous generation: uncles and aunts. But a fair number of heirs, now of interest, were heirs from the third generation: mostly grandchildren, a few great nephews and nieces, and occasionally a great-grandchild.

Also relevant now is the significant proportion of heirs named as being age 30 and more. For the heirs of male landholders, the universe of sons has 25 percent of its members (322 of 1309) already at this early point of middle age; for the daughters of these men, it was still 17 percent at 30 and more (32 of 209). The other heirs, covering those of the various generations, were over 30 in 44 percent of the instances of inheritance (170 cases of 387). For heirs of female landholders the findings are even stronger; of their sons, 36 percent were 30 and more (74 of 204), of their daughters 53 percent (26 of 46), and of the other heirs 31 percent (34 of 108). All males' heirs, in aggregate, give us a group of which 28 percent were over 30 years; for women, the heirs had reached this age in 37 percent of the cases (134 out of 358). In toto, 29 percent of the heirs in the Inquisitions (658 of 2263 cases) were at least 30 years of age.

Thus, as we have said, our paths lead us into middle age, for the new heirs, and into a presumption of old age for many of the departed. But age is elusive, and tracking the link with the heir, as the logic of the life course directs us, is also of value. Grandchildren emerge, and as more than statistical oddities. The Inquisitions, as we know, only trace a family tree as far as their purpose requires; they do not string out their genealogical inquiries any more than they have to, but stop at the first satisfactory response. The presence of the eldest son-and-heir ends an investigation before we learn anything about living siblings or other children. In many instances the stated age of the heir argued for the probability of next-generation children, but such grandchildren were hidden from view unless one of them (or more, when descent through a female made this the appropriate channel because of partible inheritance) turned out to be a needed missing link.

Thus the incidence of third-generation heirs named in the Inquisitions is an occasional guide to the descent of property; that it is also the tip of some unmeasurable iceberg of family structure and survival is unexceptionable but hard to enlarge on. At best, the tally of grandchild-heirs gives us minimum numbers; even when a son's son is the next heir, his own identity hides the presence of siblings (his younger brothers and all his sisters, re-gardless of their ages), let alone that of first cousins by brothers and sisters of the parent.

With these qualifications hanging over us, we turn to the Inquisitions. What light do they shed on third-generation heirs? For convenience, we have combined in Tables 4-1 (for males' heirs) and 4-2 (for females' heirs) the relevant data from seven sets of Inquisitions into three groupings: material from the late fourteenth-century Inquisitions, material from the county or local material (for Yorkshire, Nottinghamshire, and Lancashire), and material from the early and middle years of Henry VII. The incidence of grandchildren as heirs — as an historical and family phenomenon — has been noted. Now we see that a grandchild actually figured as the next heir in 190 cases (of the 2263 that we tallied): 8.4 percent of our total universe, or 1 in about every 12 instances of succession. There was a much greater incidence of such heirs for grandmothers than for grandfathers, that is, for

TABLE 4-1. Grandchild Heirs of Male Landholders, by Age of Grandchild (in decades)

| Set of IPMs | Age of heir | | | |
	0–10	11–20	21+	Total
Richard II and Henry IV	3	5	5	13
3 local sets	3	6	9	18
Henry VII, vols. I, II		24	22	76
Total	36	35	36	107

TABLE 4-2. Grandchild Heirs of Female Landholders, by Age of Grandchild (in decades)

| Set of IPMs | Age of heir | | | |
	0–10	11–20	21+	Total
Richard II and Henry IV	4	7	12	23
3 local sets	3	7	13	23
Henry VII, vols. I, II	8	12	17	37
Total	15	26	42	83

the deceased female holder of property than for the jurors, when they came to assemble the material for the male, which is much as we would expect. The 107 grandchildren who succeeded male property owners were but 5.6 percent of that group's 1905 eventual heirs; the 83 grandchild-heirs who followed a grandmother made up 23.1 percent of that much smaller universe (of 358 instances of deceased women as landholders).

Grandmothers as widows lived longer; certainly longer from the moment of giving birth to the child, if not in absolute terms. Thus a grandmother was more likely to have outlived the intermediate link of her own children (or their children, if we wish), and thus more likely to have been followed at her death by an heir of the third generation. More years of survival for her meant more years of outliving others, more likelihood of the Inquisition having to reaching farther down the chronological line to find the next heir. To be sure, this is an "other things being equal" argument, but it seems logical enough and it is supported by the few data we have.

The next feature to consider is the age of the grandchildren as the heirs. The age breakdown in Table 4-1 shows, of the total of 107 grandchildren named as men's heirs, 36 heirs aged 10 and below, 35 between 11 and 20, and 36 heirs listed at 21 ("full age") and above; the respective percentages are 34 percent, 33 percent, and 34 percent. Against this fairly even age distribution for the men's heirs, the women's three-generation heirs swung heavily toward more advanced ages. The percentage categories for women's heirs, by age of the three-generation heirs, are 18 percent, 31 percent, and 51 percent. Just for comparison, the sons of the male heirs (1309 sons of deceased landholders, as shown in Tables 1-1–1-7) fell into the three age-categories in percentages of 20 percent aged 10 and below, 29 percent between 11 and 20, and 51 percent at 21 or above.

Assuming that the Inquisitions are reasonably reliable, the age of the new heir offers least an indication, within wide boundaries, of the age of the deceased. Though we now have two generations of parenting to worry about, we can ponder whether the behavior of successive generations was likely to move away from the norm in the same direction, or whether they would serve to balance each other when it came to age at marriage and the birth of the heir. Some details, some miniaturized case studies, are embodied in the records, though this kind of information is never presented in more than the most jejune fashion. But presumably the jury's information was no less accurate for a grandchild than for a child, and when we are told the son's son is either aged 10 and more, or 5 and more, or 7 and more, or that he is the "heir as above, age unknown," we at least seem to have a youngish child on our hands. A dead son's daughters of 9, 7, and 4, or a grandson of 1 year and 20 weeks, or a daughter of one year and a half, show the interest in precise wording.[7]

There are more examples of this sort of detail. It can be a matter of specific ages: daughters of his (deceased) son, now aged 11, 8, 5, 3, and 1. But more often it was with an eye on that cutting edge of age, the line of demarcation at which legal majority was recognized and the property could be claimed. A daughter's son of "22 and more on the feast of St. Andrew last," or "a daughter's son who had been 22 on 14 September, 1399," was a way of stating the matter; the grandsons were now legally in the adult world. Sometimes the would-be heir fell just short at the moment we get our fleeting passing glimpse of the march of time: her son's son, by her first marriage, was 20 years and more, or he was 20 and one half. One inquisition left no doubt; the grandson was either 21 and more, or 22, or 24.[8] Whichever alternative we take, it was clear that he made the grade.

Older grandchildren were surprisingly common. Some were well into (if not almost through) their own child-bearing years, if we can accept what we are told, and numerous great grandchildren (born to these proud grandchildren) must have been shielded from mention because of their parents' survival. If the heirs were her son's daughters, now 30 and 28, or "30 and more" (as is the daughter's husband), or two women of 36 and married and 32, then parenthood was likely.[9] A few closer touches appear, as with the son's son who was 31, and whose marriage had been arranged by the grandfather in the old man's lifetime. "The espousals still endure and continue between them."[10]

This last reference hints at a relationship between a grandfather and his grandchildren, if not necessarily anything by way of affection. Presumably the grandfather had intervened, in loco parentis; the patriarchal presence was an active one. With the Inquisitions it is rarely possible to go much farther than an odd vignette. We have a return that tells of a dead son's son, now 9 years old and the old man's heir: the intervening link, the dead son, had been "late his first born son." Though it is a legal truism the poignancy of the tale shows through. In another instance a woman's son's daughter was her heir, now aged 26 and married. The young woman's father had "died long ago in her [the late widow's] lifetime."

Grandchildren for these purposes, as we know, come in four varieties: a son's son, a son's daughter(s), a daughter's son, and a daughter's daughter(s). Except for the first alternative, where patriarchy closed its iron fist, the other possibilities admitted of odd permutations and combinations, since daughters and daughters' heirs would usually partition the property. Too much must not be made of a few numbers. The grandfather-grandchild chain gave us more young heirs than did the grandmother-grandchild one; conversely, grandmothers had older next-of-kin than did grandfathers. When the grandchild was the child of a man's son, the new heir was likely to be younger than when the claimant was descended through a daughter; another instance of the "first-served gets the prize," for a boy, as against the "wait around and if no one else comes forward to claim it, you will eventually be notified that it's yours," for a girl.

Very few grandfathers were succeeded by their daughters' children: only about 17 or 18 such instances of the 107 in Table 4-1 (17 percent). For the grandmothers, daughters produced the next-in-line 13 times, about the same one-in-six ratio as for sons. But this fact has to do with sex ratios, survival, and primogeniture, not mother-daughter bonding. Of course, marriage and virilocal life patterns in the world of propertied folk may have made mother-daughter bonding insignificant in long-term relationships. Being Margaret Paston's son was not always an easy calling, but it probably was a good deal better to be her son than her daughter. Demography is, fortunately, not a sentimental line of inquiry.

The occasional combination of heirs that we find often includes one or more daughters of the second generation and some third-generation children, heirs of a now-deceased daughter (or daughters). By definition, in most of these cases the ages of the second-generation heirs were fairly advanced, and sometimes even the grandchildren were well beyond mere infancy, usually being descended from an older child in a string of siblings (as younger siblings were more likely to still be alive, thus masking the likely existence of their own children). These combinations give a hint of the complications of overlapping and succeeding grandchildren, a phenomenon that may have led canon and common lawyers to lick their chops, anticipating decades of litigation. About the simplest combination among these permutations is a case of a daughter, married and 20 and more, plus a dead daughter's son, now 2; or else a daughter of 40 along with a dead daughter's son, now aged 20.[11] More exotic family patterns are not hard to find: daughters of 30 and more (and married) and of 26 and more and married and of 25 and more and married, plus the 24-year-old son of a deceased fourth daughter.[12] The age spread might be peculiar: daughters of 50 and 22 and a grandson of 25, or a daughter of 30 and a grandson of 19 and more.[13] In an instance of "gavylkendes" succession, a man of Kent was followed into the property by a son's son William, "21 on the Feast of the Exaltation of the Holy Cross last," a brother William, now 16, an uncle Thomas, now 30, and an uncle Edward, somewhere in his 20s.[14]

Grandchildren are the most likely and most common third-generation heir. But grandchildren were hardly an automatic given; sterility and infertility, plus mortality, often over-balanced the social and biological push for procreation, as we know.[15] Sometimes, when most needed, grandchildren failed to put in an appearance; the resort to the dead man's (or woman's) brother or sisters as heirs, let alone to those even farther out in the concentric circles of kinship, testifies to the absence of a three-generation link when it would have been summoned up had it been there. To outlive the children might mean a resort to grandchildren; to have had no children was an early dead end.

At times, in the search for the nearest kin, there was the resort to great-nephews and great-nieces, that is, the grandchildren of a brother or sister. The trail is often a tangled one, but the Inquisitions seem to show about two dozen instances where such a trail was used, and the great-niece or great-nephew told to step forward. The heir was aged 10 or less in five of these, between 11 and 20 in seven, and in the remaining 12 already at the point of legal majority.

All in all, we see a reasonable incidence of three-generation heirs, many of whom had already reached a fairly advanced age when it became their turn to inherit. The use of imprecise or ambiguous kinship terminology is also a problem — disguising grandchildren who are referred to as cousins, or hiding various kinds of cousins (consanguine)[16] — but in many instances the path seems clear. We might be told that the heir is a brother's son's son, aged 8 years and more, or a brother's daughter's son, aged 6 and more. Sometimes the road leads by way of a brother's son's daughter, 30 and more, or a sister's daughter's daughter, 34 and more. Of course, when the claim is by way of the late landholder's sister, she could just as easily have been an older sister; in the last case one would certainly lean toward this. But there is no absolute rule and the small number of such cases makes the inherent uncertainty of little import. When the third-generation link was by way of a brother, the sibling-grandparent was surely a younger brother, the brother's grandchildren younger than a son's son would have been. Accordingly, as a measure of the age of the deceased, the spread of years is even greater, or so logic would seem to indicate.

In a very few cases the heir was identified as being a fourth-generation link. In some instances it looks as though there is some confusion in the record, one impossible for us to sort out. One man was followed by one of those combinations of a daughter, aged 40 and more, and another daughter's grandson, now aged 7. Were the boy descended from a deceased older sister, this is not a stretch of probability, as far as the chronology is concerned.[17] While a daughters's son's son might be aged 6 and more, it is harder to accept a widow's great grandson as 21 years and 3 weeks and more.[18] A combination of a daughter's son, now aged 40 and more (and probably a father, if not more), and of a sister's grandson, aged 22 and beyond, is another that falls within the bounds of probability *if* we accept that the recently-deceased widow had been a woman of sufficient years.[19]

But the search, as we know, is not for demographic data per se, but for expressed instances of age and generational awareness. When grandchildren were named, the jurors — as friends, neighbors, and keepers of the lore that embraced the "who's who" of local families — attested that the third generation heir was the nearest kin. Were they "correct?" Was their information accurate? This is a road we cannot travel with much certainty. However, we learn, from studies of local communities and of the county gentry that these men knew the twists and turns of birth, copulation, and death as it pertained to the landed families of the region. We noted in dealing with Inquisitions and Proofs of Age that what the men of the jury said seems to have been accepted. Attestations about age (offered with a need-to-know accuracy) and identity did become the record, and the king's arm moved accordingly. If government was instructed by these informed voices, the awareness of a larger interest in age and identity may have served to control flights of fancy and to ensure a response in accord with general knowledge and, perhaps, common sense.

While stated ages may be movable feasts, it is likely that the identity of the third-generation heir — when he or she is so named — was a fact around which we can build. If he or she was a firm enough fact on which to base the transmission and inheritance of real property, then he or she was real enough to earn a mark in our statistical tallies. And taking our cue from these tallies, and seeing them as the failsafe net for an otherwise fatal gap in the family's struggle with the tides of mortality, we assert the presence of at least a few sons and daughters of sons and daughters.

If the record must always remain, for the most part, a tabula rasa for anything beyond their mere existence and some of their ages, grandchildren do constitute a base from which to sally forth into worlds of affect and relationship. We are under few illusions about the quality of our material when we juggle medieval quantitative data. But there were old men and old women, and there were grandchildren. The bleak view Peter Laslett offers may be more gloomy than it has to be. If the odds were against being the grandfather's heir, they were considerably better when we turn to the question of whether one might at least know the old man. Better yet, could we fill in more of the blanks, were the odds in favor of getting to know the old woman.

5

Three-Generation Family Links and Last Wills and Testaments

THE LINKS ATTESTED in the Inquisitions between the first and third generation became a matter of official (and subsequently of historical) record only because of the absence of the second generation, with the son's son, or some equivalent heir, now named in lieu of a predeceased father. Had the intervening link been alive and in a position to inherit, the Inquisitions would have made no reference to any of the third generation.[1] Grandparent-grandchild links would have been hidden, blanked out of sight by the intermediaries.

While the frequency with which this next-plus-one route of transmission was resorted to and the fairly advanced age of some of the third-generation heirs may surprise us, there is almost nothing in the Inquisitions to guide us toward any word of affect or any suggestion of relations between the progenitor and his or her next in line.[2] The quality of such familiar and relatively common links was, given the sources we have used, irrelevant and immaterial. The man or woman who had held the land was now dead, and now we have the neighbors' quasi-liturgical responses regarding the identity and age of the heir. We assume that in most instances the deceased had been aware of the absence of the intermediate heir, of the likelihood of the inheritance going directly to a third-generation heir.[3] We are not moving in a culture where people of property were indifferent to such matters.

But as with other demographic materials, what we can pin down on grandparent-grandchild succession offers little entrée into the world of personal or volitional variables. Choices and alternatives about heirs and objects of special affection are not part of the universe scanned by the Inquisitions; they reveal neither the minds nor the lives of the older generation as those about to die might have surveyed the ranks of heirs and perhaps lamented the absent links in the chain of succession. Nor do we have much guidance into the world of the grandchildren — beyond the bare fact of their existence. Demographic pawns might be high born, but they were pawns nevertheless.

Fortunately, we are not quite up against the proverbial wall in our search for some insight into three-generation families, and the Inquisitions are not our only window. By the late fourteenth century we have many wills and testaments, and they hold some promise of a different perspective upon the world of family continuity, including *some* data on three-generation families. Also, whatever the shortcomings of a will as a source, it was not, from its moment of origin, controlled and circumscribed by the legal and administrative constraints that made Inquisitions so myopic and formulaic. The will, to some considerable extent, was a reflection of and a window into a world created and defined by — as well as defining — volition, intention, and social control.

Men and women of property left bequests, on occasion, to those whom they identified as their grandchildren; more precisely, as it was usually expressed, to the child of a child: "Johanni, filio et haeredi Radulphi Barton, filii mei."[4] Beyond merely noting such scattered and not overly frequent bequests, what can we make of them regarding their number and incidence, either in a set collection of wills or as a proportion of the bequests in any given will? As is invariably the case in using these documents, we can extrapolate certain answers and speculations but we can do very little with what is *not* said. And beyond the usual problems of these sources, we also have the questions of kinship terminology, already mentioned when using the Inquisitions, to be kept in mind.[5]

Wills rarely tell us very much about age in a specific or precise sense. A whole group of intriguing questions fall outside their net: the maximum age spread between the parties mentioned in a will, or between the testator and those mentioned; the oldest grandparents of the youngest grandchildren; and other such questions about family structure. Some of these matters can be dealt with by inference, while others remain blank lines. Sometimes we have external biographical information, as for the peers, and the testator's age at the writing of the will — which is almost always within a year or less of death and probate — can be determined. But internal evidence on this matter is rare; a will is the place (or time) in which to talk about one's end, not one's beginning, and final age by itself is of limited interest. The testator's physical and mental condition, not his or her span of years, was the moving force behind the creation of the document, and even those who offered a few prefatory remarks on whether their imminent death seemed timely did not offer numbers to support their pieties about our expected span and the fullness of their years.

However, what is often treated, albeit implicitly, is the stage of the life cycle — as marked by experiential rather than chronological terms — at which he or she now stands. The pattern of bequests to beneficiaries within the family is a reasonable guide here, and the conditional clauses strung around bequests amplify the structure of an otherwise obscure family mosaic. When a man refers to the future welfare or to the uncertain sex or the shaky mortality of the child whom his wife is now carrying, it is pretty likely that he is a father, or a soon-to-be father, *rather* than a grandfather. These comments reflect the burdens and life perspective of men in their 20s and 30s. Hugh Hastings was probably far from the years of a grandfather when he decreed: "Whereby and under the grace of God Almighty my wyffe is insantie and great with childre, which Almighty God of his grace shew to be delyvered and borne in seaftie . . . if it happen to be issue male . . . (or) if it happen to be issue femell."[6] He who worried about the child "en ventre sa mere" was, at best, the likely father of other young children, not of children's children.[7]

If the testator refers — and these clauses, by their nature, invariably are from men — to real and personal property put aside for the surviving spouse or a guardian for the nurture and marrying of young children, we again assume we are dealing with the parent of young children, not one whose children had already moved toward the mysteries of adulthood and parenthood. The same Hugh Hastings we quoted above went on to stipulate that "Anne, my wyffe, have the reule and governaunce of my yonger sonnes and of there lyvelod to they come to their playne age of xx yere, and of my doughters unmarried to they be purveied fore." There is a possibility here, no doubt, of older if unnamed children, perhaps parents on their own by now, but this is not very likely when we consider the general tenor of Hugh's approach to the problems he was about to bestow on poor Anne. The will smacks of youngish parents, of orphaned children with a way yet to make in the world, and, for Anne, of a heavy obligation as a single mother.

When the testator states that any or all of the children are to receive their share of the bequests when they reach age 21 or age 24 (or even 26), the chances are still against the presence of grandchildren, though obviously the odds are growing shorter each year, and for daughters of the upper class they might well have already tipped toward marriage and motherhood. Sometimes the pendulum *seems* to point against the presence of grandchildren, but they were possibly waiting backstage for their summons. One poignant reference to a widowed daughter seems to imply that her husband had died before he had helped her do her maternal duty, and now her father had to come to grips with the fact that he would not survive the next round of negotiations and couplings that might preserve the family.[8] Unusual but rich material is a bequest made by a dying father to a pregnant daughter: "Janet Everingham my doghter, if so be that she be with j doghter I will that it have my felett of perill, and if she be with j son I will that Janet the doghtter of Bertyn my son have the same felett of perell."[9] The will was a working document, designed to instruct and empower those already within an inner circle of familiarity; wording that is ambiguous to us presumably caused no problems then. If we are left wondering about grandchildren, those "in the know" did not have problems with their instructions. Were the grandchildren on the scene or merely anticipated: "lego Eleanae uxori predicti Willelmi Barry, filiae meae, et heredibus de corpore ipsius Elenae legitime procreatis?"[10]

There is also the problem of kinship terminology. It was customary to identify a grandchild as the child of one's child. But terminology is eccentric and inconsistent, and we may be pushing for a precision they did not care about in linguistic terms, or need to worry about in a social and legal context. Within family circles something less clear cut than a genealogical table and a good deal less official than a birth certificate sufficed, and the old referred to the young as they chose — a common privilege of the older generation. The impression we come away with is of many instances of links between the first and third generation *not* being spelled out; many grandchildren singled out and included among the beneficiaries, named but not specified as to relationship. The usage of the Inquisitions showed the ubiquity of "cousin" (*consanguine*), a shorthand convenience that might be glossed on the spot by a modifier indicating that "cousin" is "son of his son," and at times it was deconstructed by a genealogical explanation of the grandparent-grandchild link.[11] But often it is as far as we can go — a monument to casual usage and ambiguity.

Godchildren also bedevil us. Sometimes they (also) were the grandchildren; sometimes they were not. When Jane Stapleton left bequests to her daughter Margarete Norton and to "my son, Sir John Norton," we can be fairly confident that when she turned towards the "John Norton, my godson" who comes in for a "pese of sylver, Parys-warke," she was addressing the child of her daughter and son-in-law.[12] That she had stood as baptismal sponsor was highly probable, though we would not otherwise have any record. There is no ambiguity at all when Isabell Rawson spoke of "Alverey Rawson, myne eldest sonne . . . (and) Isabelle his doughter, my god doughter."[13] In a London will the servant girl, belatedly cut in for a small bequest, was *also* identified as a granddaughter.[14]

But complications and variations are woven into the very fabric of our attempts at family reconstruction. Thomas Meryng at least was clear when he turned to a great-nephew: "my god-child, son unto my broder Fraunces."[15] Lady Scrope's will was a vast catch-all of relationships, acquired in the course of her numerous (childless) marriages over the decades. Was her final mention of "litill John Scrop" meant for a grandchild (of her husband), or one of the youngest children of the next generation, or of another (minor) nephew among the flock?[16] One London will referred to "nepoti meo," then identified as a daughter's son."[17] Since a godson's daughter was the equivalent of a granddaughter in matters of affinity and consanguinity, the links are strong, even if not those of blood by our reckoning.[18] When a great-niece or -nephew is singled out for a bequest, the genealogy is sometimes spelled out. Perhaps less straightforward ties needed to be elucidated, though again we should assume that the executors would know about such matters. Some took no chances: "lego Willielmo Aldegat, nepoti meo . . . Item, Agneti, filiae ejusdem Willielmi."[19]

*   *   *

If we ignore the problems and ambiguities, what do we have to learn from the wills about grandparent-grandchild links? The answer, in quantitative terms, is not very much. Just a few of the many wills are of interest or relevance, not nearly as many links as the Inquisitions led us to expect. Some wills mention grandchildren among the beneficiaries; we have quoted some that are fairly clear about the links. But how frequently do we find these references, and how significant were they when read against the total body of wills and the aggregations of bequests contained in any will of any substance? Do grandchildren come in for any roles above and beyond the occasional inheritance of family baubles and bequests of cash?

Some wills, we know, explicitly mention grandchildren. But there is almost never anything by way of a guide as to why such bequests are made, either as components of that world of volition and sentiment we might hope for at the end, or as pawns in the harsh game of family strategies and social control, of exclusion, competition, and preference. Nor is there often any clue as to whether we are learning the name and identity of *all* the grandchildren on the scene, or whether it is just a favored few, included perhaps to the deliberate exclusion of a bevy of siblings and cousins. Was the preference between grandchildren qua grandchildren, or did it reflect a pecking order the testator had established among his or her own children, perhaps long before grandchildren were a gleam in the patriarchal (or ma-triarchal) eye. The rank ordering of second-generation descendants might just be extended into the third. As the sins of the fathers were visited upon the generations, so might be the favoritism or the hostility.

Some wills of the high and mighty allow a closer focus. That of John of Gaunt is instructive since we know the Lancastrian genealogy, and in this instance we find that two grandsons at least come in for a passing reference: "jeo devise a mon tres cher Henry, fitz ayzn de mon tres chere filtz le Duc de Hereford . . . et a mon tresame filtz John, frere du dit Henry, filtz de mon dit filtz."[20] The same reading can be applied to a few other aristocratic wills; biographical information tells us who was and who was not covered, though few genealogies are so thorough that we can speak with certainty. But for most wills that refer to grandchildren this material merely fills in a few of the blanks in the web of genealogy. There is little indication that grandchildren are mentioned in lieu of parents, though they might be if they were the only link, as in the Inquisitions. Usually when they appear it is in addition to the second generation-beneficiary.

The bulk of the property transferred in a will — in terms of both value and the transfer of obligation and authority — went from parent to child, not to child's child; the main channel of inheritance was usually short and direct. Thus the search for grandchildren in the wills is largely obscured by powerful forces that governed the descent of property, forces with a limited concern for the full tally of living relatives and for patriarchal concerns for multi-generational survival. If grandchildren made a difference in the world we have lost, and if the wills help us pin them down in the landscape of procreation and affection, we should be under few illusions about the cen-trality of the matter — at least by the hard terms of *meum* and *tuum*, which is what wills were mainly about. Though grandchildren undoubtedly had a role in the drama of family life, it was more apt to be within the realms of "to be seen but not heard" than it was of "suffer them to come unto me."

Problems of method aside, what do we find? When we tally the incidence of bequests from a grandparent to a grandchild, we mostly find pretty thin ore. The wills of the Hustings Court of London reveal that of 561 wills written between the accession of Henry IV and the death of Henry VII, only 16, or 3 percent, make an explicit statement about a three-generation link. If we look for such bequests in Archbishop Chichele's *Register*, we strike a richer vein — 13 percent — perhaps as befits the greater largesse of those higher up the socio-economic ladder.[21] While other published collections of wills have not been logged in this fashion, they seem to offer a comparable ratio of wills to this kind of bequest.[22] Clearly, the incidence of grandchildren, as indicated by a tally of bequests steered toward them, is barely at the incidence we reported when we looked for them as revealed by the Inquisitions. Laconic sources are truly the essence of a study of fifteenth-century society and family. Wills at their best may tell us more about ties between grandparents and grandchildren than do Inquisitions, but as a census tally they are more or less exiguous. Without extraneous information they lend themselves to virtually no demographic inquiry about the net of living kin.

When a bequest is made from grandparent to grandchild, it is usually a fairly straightforward one: direct in wording, simple in terms of the transmission at stake, more often than not limited in the number of recipients, and rarely with complicated conditions or controls. A son's daughter who was to receive "duo coclearia mea argentea optima et iijs. iiijd," was probably about average for the world of such benefaction, in terms of the value of the goods and the expression of sentiment.[23] Simple bequests ran from a minimalist, "lego Roberto Aske filio et heredi predicto Johannis Aske filii mei ij cocliaria argenti" to a more expansive, "Willelmo filio Willelmi filii mei unum gladium trenchard et unum baslardum argento ornatum ac unam cincturam rebeam argento stipatam."[24] Really large and impressive bequests are noteworthy for their absence.

Grandchildren who were the principal heirs do not seem distinguishable from their cousins, nor do they stand out in any particular fashion in terms of testamentary disposition. Most bequests to third-generation descendants identified grandchildren in terms of their parents, and most of their bequests were less than imposing; we find only a few that were more impressive in value, and/or more interesting in nature. There is no way of gauging whether such bequests reveal any deeper or more complex ties between the parties, though we might argue that their mere existence has to carry some special meaning. John Bradford was not an especially wealthy man, but his heart was in the right place: "To Alice Watton, my doughter, xl s., to help hir and hir childir." Alice sounds like a young widow.[25] Grandchildren rarely received real property, but in prosperous Bradford a "meisse and oone tenement lyinge besyd the parich church" went to Thomas Tempest, son of Tristram Bolling's daughter.[26] If we were to award a "most interesting bequest" prize, it might well go to Elizabeth Chaworth, "doghter to Elizabeth my doghter," now scheduled to receive "my best Primer, a Franssh boke, a devise of gold, a girdill of purpull silk harnest with golde, a brode clothe, ij draght towels of a suet of Parissh, my best peir shetys, a cofur of euere bounden with selver and over gilt and a fair sprews cofur."[27]

It is hard to determine how many grandchildren even well-documented and prominent people had: in the palimpsest of family records younger sons counted for little, daughters for less, their offspring hardly at all. Wills give glimpses of numbers, as did occasional Inquisitions when it came to a daughter's children and a divided inheritance. In the wills we get some larger aggregations, though almost never on a vast or loquacious scale. Twelve grandchildren, referred to but not named or identified, was the topmost peak, and by a goodly margin: "Item, to my twelve grandchildren, 4d. apiece."[28] Next came half that number: "cuilibet alii sex filiorum et filiarum praedictorum Willelmi Eland et Johannae j peciam albam stantem."[29] A bequest to Nicholas Blakburn, my son, was "for to spend on his three sonnes."[30] John Barton's gifts to 2 boys and a girl, all children of his son Ralph, hardly indicate a vast network, but they are well ahead of most such references.[31] One testator had (or chose to name) 5 grandchildren, by 5 children: 2 of his daughters had had daughters, 2 daughters had borne sons, and one son had a daughter.[32] This specificity has its virtues, and it contrasts nicely with the open-ended but imprecise "every child of my son and doghter" of John Sothill.[33]

Sometimes the pattern was to remember grandchildren by more than one child.[34] In one case we seem to have the children of one child singled out; the impression is that only this one child — amidst an unspecified stock of others — had kept the line alive, and now his offspring were being suitably rewarded.[35] But these are glimpses into a unmapped territory, a land of mysteries destined to remain unsolved. The pattern that emerges is that there really was no prevailing pattern. No cultural paradigm asserts itself to steer the wheel of favoritism and behavior.

The Inquisitions revealed that grandchildren as legal heirs were not uncommon. Wills, by themselves, say virtually nothing of this; were we just to follow their lead we would never suspect the one-in-twelve or one-in-fifteen resort to the transmission of estates via such a route. The wills offer few leads regarding the transmission of property. It is possible that a few of them single out grandchildren as recipients in the absence of the parent.[36] But even here there is little certainty that an unmentioned parent had to mean a dead parent. The shortcomings of a will, as a document that can provide a full picture, are only too well known.

Since most of the bequests of interest are relatively simple matters, both in terms of material objects and regarding any conditions surrounding the transfer, the impression is that they constitute a bond or link between an aging adult and a relatively young child. The Inquisitions indicate that, though grandchildren might be well beyond the infant and toddler stage, only a fraction of such heirs were apt to be at legal majority. The wills shed little comparable light on age and age spread. The pregnant daughter we saw was going to start at the beginning, in terms of her child's status. A bequest toward a granddaughter's marriage conjures up a picture of someone still young but perhaps now moving toward the stage of life where such matters were thinkable.[37] There is a will in which a father refers to a son living in a different village. This evokes a picture of a grown-up son, off on his own and perhaps "starting a family." But this is mere speculation. A few wills refer explicitly to underage grandchildren, still within the embrace of parental care: "To Thomas Thurland, the sone of Richard Thurland my son, cc marc, to be delyverd when he commys to xxj yeres of age."[38] Whether he was 2 or 20 at the critical moment is left unsaid. Some wills hint at an even more tangled web: "my doghter Alianor with ye mariage of hir son Darcy over yat yt I have bequethed hir in my Codicell so yat she be rowled by hir moder my wife."[39] One grandfather did couch his bequests in the protective caveat of "if any survive."[40] A son being instructed to serve as guardian of his own son is hardly unusual, in terms of responsibility, and it probably makes clear the tender age of the third-generation party.[41] On the other hand, the older grandchildren of the Inquisitions put in an occasional appearance.[42]

We have concentrated on a dynamic that runs from grandparent downward to grandchildren. Actually, of course, the three-generation family could run in both directions: a child being below the testator and someone from the parental generation above. A number of wills reveal that there was a flow of bequests upward or backward, as well as downward or forward, as there was survival from an older generation, outliving the younger. Bequests to members of the generation prior to the testator fall into two categories. The simpler is when members of the generation above are simply named as beneficiaries. Mothers were the most common category to be mentioned in this way: "I yeve to my lady my moder my pleyn cuppe wt armys, for a remembraunce, to pray for me, or "matri meae, xx libros."[43] John Grene, as befitted a canon of Wells, worried about the tolling of his bell: "to my mother, if she be alive, 20s."[44] There are also fathers, and fathers and mothers, and sometimes the two lumped together as parents: "to my father and my mother, 20s., and to my father a green gown furred," along with, "to Thomas Steur and Agnes his wife, my parents, 10 marks."[45] Parents-in-law also appear: "lego patri uxoris meae meam zonam argenteam et unum tabelam ov le menyhe."[46] Others of this generation are sprinkled about: a mother and an aunt; a mother, two sisters, a brother, and an uncle; "Roger, my uncle."[47]

The other category of generation-before provisions imposes some specified responsibility on the older relative. The future care of a sibling of the testator might be enjoined: "to my fadir c li. of lawful money of Englond, to the maryage ward of my sister . . . or els to do what hym pleases with itt."[48] Or it might be for the testator's children: "Indenture betwene me and my fader that John my son shall have it for terme of his life."[49] The testator's mother might be asked to help dispose of worldly goods: "Agnetem Parker matrem meam . . . ad vendendum omnia terras et tenemente."[50] So little of this rich and complicated story can be deciphered; wills are documents of instruction, not explication. We would like to know more of the family ties of Thomas Dalton, merchant of Hull, who asked his mother to assume care of his wife.[51] Aging parents can be a problem for their children; no wonder a dying testator was explicit about shucking the burden as he prepared to leave: "I will that my em [uncle] Sir Robert Clayden haf it to do ther with al as him thynk best, and that he se to my moder that sche be wel loked to."[52]

* * *

There is not much need for an elaborate summary of our findings. Wills offer direct and explicit evidence of the existence (and acknowldgement) of some grandchildren, but hardly in such volume as to add a great deal to what we have already learned. Qualitative information from the wills takes us a bit farther, perhaps, but hardly into any newly illuminated arenas of family feeling or generosity. Grandchildren, when mentioned at all, came in for reasonable tokens, for some passing regard for their futures, and probably for some treatment wherein partiality was mingled with distinct indications of disinterest or indifference; actual hostility was dealt with by a policy of silence. Grandparents, like other categories of testators, both offered and withheld, promised and revoked.

Should we conclude that grandparent-grandchild links were of little import? that no one really cared? It is hard to refute this, if we are prone, a priori, to lean in this direction. I would offer, as an alternative reading of these thin texts, that the grandchildren were a hidden albeit a rarely discussed resource, left unmentioned because wealth rarely flowed directly to them and because fulsome feelings towards family and descendants were not often revealed in written sources.

If reading the wills does not make us sentimental about the existence and importance of three-generation links, it does show sides of family and interpersonal behavior not otherwise visible. We know of the way Margaret Paston cut her daughter Margery out of the family after the latter married John Calle, the family bailiff. When her turn came Margaret wrote a will replete with bequests to different grandchildren, including "Custaunce, bastard doughter of John Paston, Knyght." And among these bequests we see the gift of £20 to "John Calle, sone of Margery my doughter . . . when he cometh to the age of xxiiij yer." If John failed to make the age level needed, his brothers William and Richard would stand in.[53] Were these bequests part of a reconciliation that otherwise escapes our notice? Or, alternatively, was it the bowing before forces of public decency and shame—even for Margaret Paston—but in no way an indication of any softening of personal feelings? Since the family continued to employ their bailiff, qua bailiff, we can go in either direction as we play with this unyielding text.

Ambiguity is the essence of much life within the family: between the married couple, between siblings, between those of each cohort, between the generations. Accordingly, it is hard to know when the text of a will leads and when it merely follows. Was it used to forge family strategy, as against when it simply reiterated established patterns of interaction. If Margaret Paston remains a puzzle, we can turn to a warmer side in the will of a grandfather who spoke, with touching memory, of £40, "to be yeve unto Anne Vavsour, doughter unto my son John Vavasour, which I cristened, toward hir mariage." Nor was he just partisan toward the girl; if any of her brothers went to Oxford or Cambridge for a bachelor's degree they were to receive 20s. And if they went on, to receive a master's degree, another 40s. was to come their way.[54]

These odd and rare touches are a tribute to the occasional expression of a warmth of feeling, of positive bonds and ties across the generations.

There is the testator who remembers his "grawndame" — an argument for her longevity and for some sustained interaction. We should also note that the bequest only amounted to 3s. 4d.[55] Others worried lest their children not be sufficiently devoted and responsible, as parents, much as we worry today — in both directions — as the generations replace each other. The testator's daughter would hold the property (a flock of "shepe") for a while, but it eventually was for her son, the grandson: "I will she remember John, her sonne and myne . . . as he shall be abyll to set up husbondry, if she leve so long."[56] Sometimes it is the terminology itself which is evocative: the grandchildren were to get the goods, from the man's brother, since his own son had predeceased him: "unto yei be on age: Unto ilkon of my barne's childere xxs."[57]

In these odd moments, at least, we can turn to the three-generation family, as revealed in these glimpses and vignettes. They are memorials of the lost world of the long-dead and of their unrevealing records. We have to stop here. It is nowhere written that we, as historians, are in any way privileged to learn those matters which they sought to keep to themselves.

6

Three-Generation Family Links and Some Aristocratic Genealogies

THE INQUISITIONS TOLD US something about the existence of the three-generation links of living relatives, though not nearly as much as we might have wished. The wills, even less revealing in some respects, shed light on other aspects of a relationship that we believe to have been more common, in life, than its trail across the records might suggest. A third area to search for grandparent-grandchild links is in the genealogical material that we can recover for the peerage families of the realm.[1] Here we expect little that would indicate the quality or strength of the bonds between or across the generations, but an examination or comparison of the years of grandparents' death and grandchildren's births — a chronological cross section in the great book of "begetting" — will give us some bedrock information about this aspect of age and survival.

Aristocratic families have been chosen for this exercise on the basis of accessible information. We have looked at approximately a hundred or so peerage-family patrilineal chains that run at least part of the way from late Edward III or Richard II to the end of the fifteenth century. The goal here is to pin down the incidence and duration (in years) of overlap between a man and his son's son, such years being the reach of the three-generation link. This period or interval of overlap only covers those men (with the occasional granddaughter to represent the women) directly on the chain of patriarchy: peers, their eldest sons, and those sons' (eldest) sons. Younger sons and brothers rarely appear, hardly more in evidence here than in the Inquisitions. Needless to say, women claim but a fraction of the attention devoted to their various menfolk; as heiresses they can enter, but only in the absence of their betters (which means their brothers, and which also means not very often).

The inquiries of peerage historians and genealogists, like those of the jurors assembled to offer material for an Inquisition, focus on ascertaining that there was a son in the offing. Were he absent, then perhaps his own son might be pushed forward, the next best thing. We saw how little the "need to know" focus turns us toward the full family structure and the larger net of relatives, ignoring even close kin who are not needed at the critical moment. The ignored and neglected relatives constitute a vast if forever lost population, generally beyond historical reconstruction, another story destined to remain untold. Women, however, do figure from time to time in genealogical inquiries, insofar as such information was recorded to determine the succession of titles and the death dates for peeresses, especially for widowed peeresses. Since her death would unlock her dower land for a male heir of a subsequent generation, her demise was an event worth noting and even, we suspect, worth celebrating.[2]

Counting families is never a very precise affair; it is the human equivalent, perhaps, of counting manors, and we know from the "gentry controversy" how tricky that exercise proved to be.[3] Peerages had both a narrow logic — defined by primogeniture and male descent — and a broader logic, in that they could be kept alive through an heiress (in the absence of male kin) as she moved toward marriage. Furthermore, new peerages were bestowed on younger sons of peers as well as on their older brothers; when fortune smiled such patriarchal broods as the Nevilles or the Beauchamps or the Bourgchiers collected titles both new and old, and it is pedantic to wonder about an exact count of how many "families" are covered in our tally.[4] Thus the exact number of families we have followed through *The Complete Peerage* does not necessarily correspond to the number of peers recognized by law or summoned to any single session of parliament.[5]

The largish group of upper class families dealt with here can be divided into three categories: those with at least one instance of an overlap between a grandfather and a grandchild (male or female) in our period; those with an overlap between a grandmother (but not a grandfather) and a grandchild; and those with no three-generation overlap that we can spot. Though different families are tracked for varying lengths of time, the results are quite interesting. In the first category there are 61 cases, in the second and third 19. Thus in 80 percent of the cases — 80 of 99 families we have followed for three or more generations — there was at least one instance of the overlap of a first and third generation.[6]

This is a strongly positive finding. Given how little we found about overlap in the wills, this healthy rate of return is gratifying. But our success is qualified by a few further considerations. In many of the 80 positive cases there is but a single instance of an overlap, in the course of anywhere from three to five or six generations. Given the goodly age reached by so many peers, this is pretty close to a minimalist finding. Survival to age 50 meant a life that was more than long enough to give one a good chance of seeing one's grandchildren, and the average longevity for the peers between 1350 and 1500 was in the early or mid-50s. Thus the overlaps between generations are to be expected, mere experiential results that follow directly from what we know about longevity and fertility.

There is no line of historical exposition so powerful that it must carry all before it because of its internal logic. The world of demographic speculation and reconstruction, like that of affection and family ties, is very much one of pluses and minuses, brought together for a final balance on the ledger sheet but with no predetermined sum (be it positive or negative) on which we must agree. Peers' sons and most of their daughters probably married at an early age, a factor that would certainly facilitate the arrival of grandchildren; if a man lived to reach 50 and produced a son not long after his own marriage, he was "even-money" to see grandchildren. But families that lasted over time sometimes seemed to alternate long and short lives, and longevity and family continuity were but loosely correlated.[7]

The difficulty London merchant families encountered in raising sons and sons' sons to bridge the chasm of three or more generations — gauged in terms of stability and replacement rates — was hardly a problem unique to the aspiring bourgeoisie.[8] Comparable problems crop up everywhere. In the Inquisitions we saw instances of clergymen named as heirs. In some cases these men may have remained in the church, content to inherit for life and then to see the estates move collaterally into the next generation. We looked at the odd case of Thomas, lord De la Warre (c. 1345–1427). Here we have a younger brother, well established in an ecclesiastical career, now called on to serve as a peer.[9] Thomas never married: any grandchildren (and future lords De la Warre) in this family had to come as a result of his sister's marriage with Thomas West.

But given the ages and proclivities of the two generations whose co-operation we need, at least one instance of a grandfather-grandchild link, somewhere along the line between 1370 or 1380 and 1500, was the prevailing story. In many cases, of course, there was more than one link, more than one yoking of grandfather and grandson. We can begin with some simple examples. There was John, lord Berners, and his line. John lived a long life (1407–74). Though his son and heir, Humphrey, died in 1471, Humphrey's eldest son, John, had been born in 1467. So the generations are intertwined; the overlap between the grandson's birth and the grandfather's death is a comfortable seven years. However, we can see that this kind of instant success was easier said than done. Humphrey himself died young, a casualty of the wars, and his son John—he who had known his grandfather and who survived into his mid-60s—eventually died without surviving legitimate male progeny. The thread had held for the family to be positive on the tally sheet, but no more than that.

Other families add variations to the theme. William, V lord Harrington (1390–1458, only a peer himself because his older brother had died without children) named an heiress-daughter, Elizabeth, who died in her father's lifetime.[10] But she had married William Bonville, and their son William was about 16 when her father died. Again, both the first William Bonville (1393–1460) and the son (William, died, sine prole, 1460) produced by the Bonville-Harrington marriage managed to get themselves killed; the latter accomplished this while in his teens (being about 18). Knowing one's grandfather for a few years was perhaps of limited interest in a world where so many barely knew their parents.[11]

While the correlation between longevity and three-generation overlap has to carry some weight, there are limits to the argument that those who lived longer had more opportunity for almost everything. The Cliffords offer a good take on this proposition. In the fifteenth century the lords Clifford shot through life at an accelerated pace; four successive peers died by violence, all at youngish ages. Yet three of them contrived to be born while their grandfathers were still around. John Clifford (1388–killed [x]1422) overlapped for about a year with Roger (1333–1389); Henry, "the Shepherd Lord" (1454–1523) for a year with Thomas (1414–x1455: killed as a Lancastrian at St. Albans); Henry, XII lord Clifford (c. 1515–1570) with Henry, X lord, by about a decade. In the two earlier cases the overlap was but a curiosity, too brief to mean much in terms of relationships; the bond could have had little meaning for its younger partner. The grandfathers may have been more sanguine. We do have accounts of the rejoicing that greeted news of an heir's birth, as in Proof of Age testimonies, and we should not be too cynical about family feeling just because the record is usually a blank.

The Percys of Northumberland had a family pattern similar to that of the Cliffords. They could boast of five successive male heirs dying by violence *and* of three instances of grandparent-grandchild in the five generations; an extreme instance of the co-existence of mutually exclusive models. The Percy men lived longer, on the average, than the Cliffords, which would seem to improve the odds in their favor. Henry Percy, Hotspur (1364–x1403) was aged 4 when his grandfather, Henry, lord Percy (1322–1368) died. Hotspur's son — already an orphan for 5 years — was aged about 15 when his own grandfather, the first Percy earl of Northumberland, was killed at Bramham Moor (1341–x1408). And that son of Hotspur lived until 1455, when he died at the first battle of St. Albans, by which time his eldest son's eldest son was already 6 years old. These are odd tales; we might argue whether families like the Cliffords and the Percys focused on their bad luck or their good luck.[12]

With fewer dramatic circumstances and less splash in national affairs, the survival and coincidence of the generations for other families follow a similar course. The lords Ogle never were very prominent, but when Ralph, III lord Ogle (1468–1513) was born his father was alive (by 1440–1486), his grandfather but recently dead (Robert Ogle, c. 1425–1465), and his great-grandfather still hanging on (Robert Ogle, c. 1406–1469). Though this solution was obviously unusual, not even the patriarch Robert was really of such great age, and many of the aristocratic families had men and women who long outlived Ogle, whether their descendants stretched to the fourth generation or not. The Greys of Wilton give us a family with two successive peers who carried memories of their grandfathers. When Edmund, IX lord Grey (c. 1470–1519) was born, his grandfather (Reginald Grey, 1421–1494) had over 20 years yet to live. Edmund's elder sons would have had at least 5 years with his old father (John Grey, d. 1499). The eldest son, George Grey (1494–1514) died childless at 20, leaving his brother (Thomas, 1497–1517) next in line. Thomas likewise died without a son-and-heir, and he was followed by two more brothers, who had (finally) been born after their grandfather's demise: Richard c. 1505, William in 1509.[13]

What is always lacking in this material is the magic word that takes us from the world of formal structure to that of the flesh and blood of interaction. The evidence seems to be that grandchildren, though perhaps a source of considerable pleasure and pride (as well as of utility, when needed), did not figure largely in the records of their grandfathers' lives. Did such men have leisure and taste for domestic life, or were they — at the top of their world with their patriarchal responsibilities — indefatigable political creatures? Even the records of the royal household in the thirteenth and fourteenth centuries, when it was fecund and produced grandchildren in abundance, say but little about them as individuals. The administrative records are mostly a tale of expenses for nurses and nannies, of extra revenues for clothing, and of the need for larger traveling expenses when the household went on the road. The veils are thick and our analytical scissors not up to the task of cutting through them.

Some odd twists of family life are hinted at, though certainty about internal family dynamics is unlikely. When George Neville, V lord Abergavenny (1469–1535) was born, his grandfather (Edward Neville, 1404–1476) had 7 more years to live. George was the oldest of 8 children; most would have been born too late to have any recollections of the old man. Lord Bonville, we know, was eventually succeeded by his great-granddaughter, Cecilly, who married Thomas Grey, marquis of Dorset. The old man died in February, 1461, a Yorkist casualty after the second battle of St. Albans, while Cecilly, born early that year, succeeded him directly as his heiress. But this impressive overlap of four generations had little personal meaning. Hugh, III lord Burnell (c. 1347–1420) lived a long life. His son and heir, Edward, predeceased him, one of the few English nobles to fall at Agincourt. But Edward's three daughters, born between 1391 and 1414, lived to make good marriages and to carry a goodly score of tales and memories of the three-generation family, to be transmitted to their own children, if and when they so chose. William, V lord Ferrers of Groby, was another peer with a long life span (from 1372 to 1445).[14] His son's daughter Elizabeth, who married Edward, lord Grey of Ruthen, was about 26 when he died, and she eventually became grandmother to Thomas (1453–1501: created earl of Huntington and then marquis of Dorset in 1475), and 30 when the old lady died.

The sources concentrate on eldest sons, the main characters of the ongoing political and genealogical drama, and we have to grope toward the identity of most of their younger brothers, let alone of cousins. In peerage cases where the resort would be to a younger brother, his age can often be determined. Some of the families whom we have counted did fall back on collateral inheritance — from a childless older brother to a younger one and his descendants — and still saw a three-generation overlap; the younger brother too was born while the grandfather yet lived. The Hastings family offers an example, as both John (1466–1504) and George (1474–1511) had some overlap with their father's father, James (1412–1477).[15]

In some of the 61 families with a grandfather-grandchild overlap there was actually more than one instance. We have mentioned the Ogles, with their string of three-generation links. The Scropes of Bolton, with a run of father-son links from the late fourteenth century to the turn of the six-teenth, could boast of only one grandfather-grandson tie, though some of the wives, the (widowed) peeresses, lived to establish such links along fe-male lines. Richard, I Lord Scrope (plaintiff in the Scrope and Grosvenor controversy) lived until 1403; by this time his son Roger's son Richard was 9 or 10. After Richard most of the men failed to stay a long course. The peeresses, by contrast, lived longer and often knew their grandsons. Mar-garet Tiptoft (widow of Roger, 1373–1403) was around until her grandson (Henry, 1418–1459) was 13: Margaret Neville (widow of Richard, 1394–1420) had a 26-year-old grandson (John, 1438–1498); Elizabeth Scrope of Masham (widow of Henry, 1418–1459) had a 30-year-old grandson (Henry, 1468–1506). And these ties cover the years between grandmother and eldest grandson; younger siblings presumably had a turn, if a shorter one.

We have been talking about links between a grandfather and a third-generation descendent. In some families there were links between at least one grandchild and his or her grandmother, somewhere along the line, *in addition* to a grandfather, as with the Scropes. In such cases the old lady was often the survivor of the marriage and her years of survival as a widow, after the peer's death, could run anywhere from a mere one or two to a full generation. In the latter case, if there had been grandchildren at all—per-haps coming long after the old man's death—she would have had ample opportunities to build ties and to play the social role consistent with being a grandmother *and* being an upper class dowager.

The story that the Scropes offered can be found in numerous other instances: the lords Abergavenny, the families of Bardolf and the lords Latimer (Neville), and the Zouche family, another line that ran along father-son descent across the generations, furnish good examples. To work backward, John Zouche (1459–1526) overlapped with his grandfather Wil-liam (1402–1462); William (1373–1415) with his father's father (William, 1321–1382); the latter William with his father's father, William (1276–1352). In addition, Maud Lovel, grandmother of William (1321–1382) lived until 1346, for another instance of the step-grandmother ties we noted above (Elizabeth Despenser, second wife of William, lived until 1408, when her husband's grandson, William Zouche, was at least 6 years old).

There were some 19 families with a three-generation link *only* between grandchildren and grandmother. Since we now have numerous studies of

middle and upper class families and know about the high incidence of elderly and long-lived widows, the sustained presence of the grandmother is
much what we would expect. As with other permutations, some of these
families had one instance of the overlap, others two or more. The years of
three-generation overlap could be too few to make a strong and lasting impression on the grandchildren, or they might run to decades and carry the
grandchildren well into young adulthood. Families like the Beaumonts and
the Botelers were familiar with such overlapping, though we have little idea
of what they made of it.

The widowed grandmother as a bridge between the generations sounds
probable. Maurice Berkeley's grandson and successor, Thomas, was but 3
when the old man died in 1508. But he was 9 or 10 when Maurice's widow
Isabel, died; were the years of this interval critical years in the boy's development? Isabel's father, Philip Mead, had been thrice mayor of Bristol,
and who knows with what tales of the Cannings and Cabot families, and of
the Merchant Adventurers, she had regaled the youngster? In at least one
case the step-grandmother was a link with something more exalted than
what the male line could offer. After lord Botreaux died his second wife,
Margaret Roos, outlived him by 22 years. Perhaps the Botreaux grand-
daughters (the eventual heirs) were happy to keep the tie with Margaret,
for she not only remarried a peer (Thomas, lord Burgh, d. 1496), but she
had started life as a granddaughter of the earl of Warwick.

*   *   *

None of this is startling or diverging from what the demographic
sources indicated was a reasonable norm of family continuity. Studies of
families of any prominence, including studies of the gentry or county elite,
find plenty of instances of old men and old women of the third generation,
still on the scene and continuing to play a role in affairs. In some cases the
role was a public one; sustained involvement, sustained service. In others it
was directed toward the private arena: wills, philanthropic activity, family
matters to be tied up while there was time. But whatever the sphere of
action, the presence of both the first and the third generation in the same
circle of enterprise and interaction is a common tale. The material offered
here merely reminds us that we can find all sorts of layers of life and interaction, once we decide to seek them.

What we do not find is much idea of how people across the bridge of
an intervening generation felt about each other; how important such ties

were, in life and in ideology. They did devote attention to such family matters and issues of visiting, nurturing, and socializing: the evidence of the Paston Letters alone gives us confidence for these assertions. But how much did the personal links that jumped a generation figure into the whole tale? Literature abounded with examples — uplifting ones, to tell people what to emulate, and horrifying (if exciting) ones, to indicate what was to be avoided. The woman who slew her own grandchildren was not the role model for the many, we assume, and her unnatural behavior carried its obvious moral for those who heard the tale.[16] If we want a softer touch, can we turn to tales from historical records and find at least a hint of demonstrated affection? If we are willing to be eclectic, we can find some comfort, as in the case of the man who requested, in his will, burial beside the grave of his grandmother.[17]

Though we did not discuss the Proof of Age material in terms of what it contained about three-generation ties and the family histories of the older witnesses, we can return for a final anecdote. In a Proof from the reign of Henry IV we have one of those memorable coincidences — the recollection of a man, who "gave a hare to William the grandfather who told him that his family had been increased because Beatrice his daughter had given birth to Isabel."[18] So there had been rejoicing, and of such sort as presumably to stick in men's minds, years later, because the second generation had done its duty by producing the third, and because the first had lived long enough to be involved, at least vicariously, in the rolling over of the life cycle and the experiences that go, appropriately, with its changes.

PART III

FULL LIVES
AND CAREERS:

SOME CASE STUDIES

7

Retirement, for Some,
at the End of the Road

STARTING FROM THE IDEA that we are looking for facets of life experience that were not beyond the reach of those who did survive to reach old age, we now explore some paths toward problems and experiences that might have been encountered as one neared the end of the journey. We have had a try at combining an analysis of soft demographic material with the reconstruction of three-generation family chains: old age as perceived and reported, and old age as represented (if not created), de facto, by the overlapping of grandparents and grandchildren.

We turn here to two other lines of investigation. Though there is no whole story of age in historical society any more than there is in contemporary England, there are still some lines of approach we have yet to explore for late medieval England. Beyond the soft demography and world of interaction as defined and shaped by attestation and self-perception, and beyond the wealth of material that we will look at from the once-removed realms of literature and cultural history, there are some aspects of the topic that emerge from an exploration of social history.

Retirement, toward the end of life *and* as part of old age, at least for a few, is a topic of considerable interest. We can view retirement as both a practice and an institution. Another approach — to be tested below — entails looking at some careers, from various levels of secular and ecclesiastical service, and trying to gauge the role played by those beyond the chronological milestones that mark old age. As well as age in life, and stages of the life cycle, there is duration of active life to be considered. In the Scrope and Grosvenor hearings we encountered the practice of indicating when one's active life, as a mature individual, had begun: the age one had first borne arms. Many of those tales had proclaimed decades of service and activity.

We will see that it was also an accepted convention to talk about a point in life when one *might* lay down one's arms, as well as pick them up.

Retirement from active life is a perennial issue, and if the full history and documentation of retirement lies within the boundaries of modern history, there is still a good deal of medieval ground to claim before we strike our colors.[1] It might come in the form (or guise) of voluntary retirement; as such, it was usually an option exercised or invoked by the affluent. In this upper class incarnation it entailed a deliberate, often explicit decision to withdraw from the full rigors and obligations of life and service and from one's role in the labor force, wherever that happened to be. Alternatively, retirement could be involuntary; the notice that a man (as it invariably was) had become redundant or superannuated, because — we are told — of age and its attendant woes. In this instance retirement was the final step on the vocational ladder; the subject was an old man, not about to recover from this ultimate demotion or to rejoin the chase.[2]

The vast amount of literary and didactic material available to a well-read and attentive lay person in the later Middle Ages and relating to some aspect or other of old age, is truly impressive. We assume it was "no coincidence" that Caxton published a version of Cicero's *De Senectute* in 1481; with his keen antennae for shaping consumer demand, he usually guessed correctly about what would be of general interest. The bulk of the relevant literature — to which we will turn later — concentrated on the number of the stages of the life cycle, on the inevitable loss of powers at some (early) age, and on the moral meaning of our autumn and winter. Most of this body of writing, whether popular or learned, was theoretical or abstract. It was normative and, as such, little of it — including a fair amount of medical material — was written with an eye on extracting empirical data regarding health and behavior, or on enlarging on the at-hand lessons of lived experience.[3]

Accordingly, there was a lot of easy-to-come-by contemporary wisdom, distilled from a vast body of lore and available as a guide to such questions as when one became too old for a given activity (war, sex and love, counsels of state, or the chase). However, there was not much by way of advice regarding alternate pasttimes and activities for those now grown too old for their former pursuits and their previous levels of engagement. Most of what practical wisdom there was tended to stick at unexceptionable pieties about the aged having more time, finally, for spiritual contemplation.[4]

On the other hand, we should not think of the conventional wisdom of medieval society as being unduly callous or particularly short-sighted. There was no prevailing ethic, no body of teaching that said one *should* work until one literally dropped over, just as there was no ethic that said the elderly should be left in the woods or on a convenient ice floe. Perhaps it was more a matter of advice *not given*. The wisdom literature was simply not translated into personal options or family alternatives designed to make age easier to bear, let alone into social policies applicable on a broader basis. Or, if it were done — and this is arguable, at best — it was either at the level of implicit social policy, or as piecemeal and unsystematic articulation. Such wisdom and compassion as were available to ameliorate the woes of the aged were mainly the balms of the smaller communities, smaller economies. And lastly, the implementation of any advice, regardless of source or values, depended on the ability of the individual or the family or some benevolent social institution to subsidize the course now being counselled.

But that there was such a practice and institution as retirement, easy to identify and to dissect, is not in dispute. Evidence for this is easy to find; it will only surprise those eager to assume that modern institutions must have modern roots and no others. The medieval practice or institution obviously did not embrace all the old, and the comfort it offered, in both tangible and psychological terms, probably varied from the almost-nonexistent to the extremely lavish. But that it existed at all, and in some fashion across much of the social and economic grid of society, is of no little interest.

*   *   *

The most critical transitions along the life line are those encountered on entering full maturity and then on passing into old age. Both of these transitions — from youth into maturity, and from maturity into old age — were movable feasts. Though the accompanying rituals and demarcations might be complex, they were easily read within the society. But while "coming of age" was noted by law and carried an official set of new freedoms and powers — compensation for the need to assume the burden of adulthood — no single social step or ceremony marked the movement from the prime years into those of old age. Furthermore, the burdens of age were cut to an individualized cloth — depending on strength, status, and degree of socialization or alienation regarding family and support networks. Social and personal demarcations varied with chronology and with individual will or vigor. Neither, in most cases, was there a fixed age at which all who had lasted were now deemed, in a uniform fashion, to be ready for their last transition.

However, these elaborate discussions about the stages of life, or the entry point for old age, or of the nuanced gradations of age, offered wisdom about what one *could* do, or what one *should* do. The advice focused on what was generically do-able; it was imprecise, universalistic, and detached. In reality variation—often articulated with a striking indifference to the realities of life—was the essence of the matter. Some men aged rapidly and said they were more than ready to step down. Caxton, when about 50, had remarked that "age crepeth on me dayly and febleth all the bodye"[5] (though despite these lugubrious sentiments he remained active up to the end of a life that ran to about 70). Osbern Bokenham, monk and poet, made much of his age and of the dangers of incipient senility; there is no reason to believe a word of what he says.[6] Hoccleve's comment about the "ripeness of death," now coming over him at age 53, had little to do with his own biographical thread, which stretched to somewhere between 65 and 80 years. Literary conceits often had no relation to demographic facts, not even to the life experience and circumstances of those now giving them utterance.

If some men made much of the onset of old age, others were determined to hold it at bay as long as possible. In early Tudor times Lord Dacre petitioned for a release from his duties, all because of "myne age, debilitee, disease of the goute, and my leg which troubleth me very sore." The gout had become so bad that "I may not stir, if fire should bren my bed, without help."[7] He was about 57 when driven to such a piteous complaint: a long career, and one that had embraced a good deal of military service, was winding down.

In the literary and medical speculations about the stages of life, writers recognized old age as a distinctive final period. When the whole scheme of life was a fairly simple one, as in Horace's presentation—with but four stages of life—old age was simply that which came after mature manhood; details about years are left vague. When we move to authors whose arguments were more elaborate and whose stages of the life line more numerous— running to six or seven or ten or twelve—there might be a number of intermediate steps between the first entry into the house of age and the last episodes of the long trail. A life drama of seven acts, and surely one of ten, would have to accommodate sub-categories within the larger rubrics. Each sub-set of age, moving in chronological order, would have its appropriately increasing plateau of decrepitude and feebleness. In the speech in *As You Like It*, the final stages indicate steady and inevitable deterioration, until we arrive at the nadir of "sans eyes, sans teeth, sans everything."

As we turn to the plight, the circumstances, and the life-coping strategies of some elderly men, we are struck once again by the disparity or dissonance between what was so casually asserted and what people knew from life experience. Literary figures had little difficulty presenting sharp gradations when they discoursed on the stages of life. Some accentuated gradualism and continuity; others posited distinct chasms and leaps between the stages of life. But when, in "real life," people actually began to feel the advent of old age, and how they recognized and reacted to their new condition, are harder questions to fathom. The church was a likely player when boundaries and definitions are at stake; here it assumed an active role. Sometimes ecclesiastical institutions took a lead in displaying sympathy and compassion for the problems of age. For examples of special treatment, often calling for a dispensation or license, the church proves to be a storehouse of kindly examples. We can look at the reception accorded the request of Peter Percii of York. He received a dispensation in 1451 for promotion "to all, even holy and priest's orders," because he and his sexagenarian wife wished to separate, she to "live in chastity and devote herself to holy meditations," and he to "serve God in all holy orders." Old Elizabeth had borne Peter no children, and "for the last twelve years [had] not cohabited."[8]

In another such case the injunction decreed that there should be no public gossip or scandal when 70-year-old John Langley of Worcester gave his "handmaiden and servant," Joan White, now "a woman of fifty and more," various presents. "No suspicion of the sin of incontinence can in future arise in regard to them, by reason of their age, all power of committing such things being on the contrary taken from them." Though tongues might wag, the simple truth was — or so it was entered into the record — simply that "he cannot do without the service of the said woman without great danger of his person."[9] Sometimes the license was to allow marriage for those beyond the age of child-bearing, while at others it was simply to eat meat during fasts, "on account of their weak constitution and old age."[10]

These records indicate some public sensitivity to the problems and needs of the elderly. However, they barely hint at the level of concern or analysis toward the gradations of old age advanced by authors who had wisdom to proffer. Bartholomaeus Anglicus had followed Aristotle's lead and asserted that age, "senecta," began somewhere around 45 or 50, with old age being followed in time by the dotage. In one's 50s one was still under the sanguine influence of Jupiter; by the 60s this had yielded to the melancholy that showed the sway of Saturn.[11] François Ranchin, an early author on geriatrics, followed Galen's division of the later stages of life with elaborate sub-categories: vigorous and robust old age, then mature old age, and finally decrepit, deadly, fatal (and final) old age.[12] Paré (1517–1590), a respected physician, also followed Galen; his explication involved an old age that began just past 35. In the first 15 years after this milestone or mid-way point, one was still capable of happiness and of dealing with business. But then, in "mature old age," those capacities faded and one needed help with food and clothing. Finally came the decrepit stage; the body died away, there were lapses into childhood, and there was only the grave to look forward to.

All this was fascinating, if a bit melancholy. It was also, for the most part, removed from a good deal of common experience. Chaucer's friend Deschamps looked upon the years after 40 as a "surrender" to enemy forces; his *Lay de la Fragilité Humaine* painted the aging process and its inescapable condition in the most gruesome colors.[13] Individual theories abounded and writers could take their pick from a wealth of interpretations and theories. Erasmus, usually a voice of common sense, saw death as coming at 50 or before. How such positions assumed their canonical status is a problem for the realm of the history of ideas; it is enough that common lore rested heavily on Cicero (with 46 as his dividing line) and Isidore of Seville (who held out for 50 as the point of irreversible decline) or Augustine, who argued for 60 as the boundary line.[14]

When John Smyth wrote his history of the Berkeley family, in the late seventeenth century, he mused on the coincidence that he was writing while in his grand climacteric year, that is, at age 63 (the product of the propitious numbers, 7 and 9) while at the very same age the fifteenth-century Lord Berkeley was zealously moving to prosecute the family's feud with the Countess of Shrewsbury. Berkeley's passion for litigation and Smyth's for the family's history, taken together, would put the lie to those who saw decrepitude as inescapable at such an age. Smyth was greatly impressed by other numerological features of the family history; Lord Maurice had been survived by a wife who "just soe long survived her husband as to make the period of both their ages alike." And then she died: "to lay her bones by his in that 70th year that bringeth completeness to the daise of man."[15]

But while few were able to arrange their longevity to conform so neatly to a prescribed numerical paradigm, let alone to please a subsequent historiographer, many of the good folk of fifteenth-century England did survive. And many of them, as we would expect, were hardly averse to picking up an occasional privilege or dispensation because of their years. Even business debts, voracious as death and taxes, might be written off because of the "age and infirmity . . . and other causes," pleaded by one aging debtor."[16] Xenophobia, likewise, saw gray hairs as a reason for an exception; when aliens were ordered to abjure the realm or to obtain a license to remain, the three groups exempted from this stark decree were denizens, German knights of the Hanseatic League, and "those who are impotent through old age."[17] More of this special pleading is to be found, once we look for it, and these cases typify the way authorities dealt with the peaks and valleys of the human condition. An 80-year-old woman was allowed to give up her vow of a pilgrimage to Rome, provided she find a substitute.[18]

But the aged turned to look at themselves in the glass, as well as telling others of their plight. John Manyngham says, in the preamble of his will, that he was "felyng myself enfebled and duly visited by sundry infirmites in my body and right unweldy in this my decrepite age." But he spoke with no apparent sense of having been short-changed in life: "Remembering also . . . God hath give me long tyme and space of life."[19] Stephen Scrope was more like Caxton; he acknowledged life's ravages when still on the younger side of the ledger. He was only about 50 when he spoke of a "sicknesse that kept me a 13 or 14 years ensuing; whereby I am disfigured in my person and shall be whilst I live."[20] Lord Scrope, a cousin, had made no bones about his enfeebled condition; in his will he referred to himself as "senex aetate, debilis corpore, sanus tamen mente."[21] Some of this language was rhetorical boilerplate, a conventional way of noting the passing of time, the fleeting nature of all things worldly. But it was also an assertion of seniority, whether this carried many privileges or not.

If the large question is what kind of life did old people live, the answer must begin with an acknowledgment that we will almost certainly wind up with the usual mix of uncertainty and diversity. Many varieties of data speak to the issue; none can be seen as providing a definitive answer. The stages of the life line — whether dictated by literary treatises or by the actual biography — are inescapable realties. As men (and women) grow old they and those around them recognize that something distinct, something different, is occurring, within and without. In demographic terms the old obviously were distinct; even the pre-statistical world saw that those over a certain age, or those with certain life experiences now behind them, could be contrasted to the waves of the young always pressing forward.[22]

In addition, even the dimmest of observers noted how few, in any given universe of live births or young adults, survived to anything approaching old age. Cohorts who had banded together as apprentices or comrades in arms were steadily and cruelly thinned as the years ticked away. But to note the obvious is different from being able to say how heavily such an awareness shaped consciousness about age, quantitative evaluations, and the natural wearing down with the years. After all, the aged were hardly rarities in their world. When we examine some elite careers we shall see the tremendous volume of material arguing for continuity and sustained involvement, above and beyond mere survival from maturity into the halls of age.

*   *   *

Let us return to retirement and withdrawal. One of the keys to a recognized distinction between maturity and old age (or "post-maturity") is the idea or institution of retirement. Though we may think of retirement as a modern phenomenon, in so far as it has become a major social institution, we have no trouble identifying it — both as concept and practice, albeit on a limited basis — in the fifteenth century.[23] We can look back and say that retirement was an idea in search of a structure on which to rest: personal wealth, community charity, or some idea of institutional commitment and subsidization, as with some fortunate clerics and some select groups of civil and royal servants, might make it possible. But at best it was applied on a limited and sporadic basis.[24] Though it was there, it was only for the few, and even for them only on a haphazard or hit-or-miss basis.

The phenomenon, if not evenly distributed across the socio-economic grid, was at least sprinkled across the land; in towns and cities; in the mansions of the great; in abbots' lodgings, priests' houses, and bishops' palaces; and sometimes in peasants' cottages and hovels — where physical needs were urgent, succor hard to find. Just as everyone was likely to know someone with living grandparents (or living grandchildren), so one might well know an elderly cleric or local burgess or royal servant or feeble grandparent or widow or widower who had been pensioned off, retired with some kind of stipend and some indication of special regard for debility and waning powers. There were always the mute if numerous armies of superannuated agricultural workers and cottagers, cared for (or not) within the bosom of the traditional family, looking to casual charity and marginal forms of self-help. There were also, no doubt, many if short-lived homeless and friendless, destined for an early end because of the lack of resources and the good fortune to move others to lend a needed hand.

We can identify a number of types or versions of withdrawal from the work force: the many faces of medieval retirement. In some cases age was indeed a major factor, explicitly linked to the special status that interests us. When old age was coupled with infirmity and disability in discussions of retirement and of pensions, as it often was, it was age that was most often cited as the main reason for the need to withdraw, to retire. In light of what we have said about the power of literary models in shaping consciousness and perception over behavior and experience, and in deference to the power of ideas about the stages of life and the gradations within those stages, the idea that people could withdraw because of their years is but a logical conclusion to the discourse. Indeed, we may choose to see retirement as the predictable extension of these discussions, though the logical next step, in so many cases, was also the step-not-taken.

What we do not find in fifteenth-century discourse or administrative records is any priority accorded to a social synthesis or a generalized policy about the variations and idiosyncracies of the aged and of their common condition. In public life the man of waning powers who perhaps *should* have retired was a familiar figure. Edward III had offered his people a pitiable spectacle in his last decade, although a king — especially one with a dying crown prince and an under-age grandson — had no place to go, nothing to do but to stay the course. A century and a half later Henry VIII was likewise broken by premature old age and decrepitude. Though he was but 56 at his death, the realm had obviously suffered from and through his long decline, and there must have been a widespread (if unvoiced) sentiment that he had lasted too long.[25] Conversely, in a society where men were called on to labor in hereditary and prescribed stations, and where they were expected to toil in some vineyard or other — an injunction with both moral and economic messages — casual withdrawal might be judged rather harshly. Dante, we remember, took a dim view of retirement from the see of Peter.[26]

As those born to great positions were expected to risk great swings of the wheel, so those in exalted office were expected to continue to serve.[27] Lesser folk had to accept their lot, the position to which they had been called; in an analogous fashion the high and mighty were to be stoical about their special burdens. But while some accepted and honored this lofty standard of service and commitment, others of high rank were willing to look, at times, for a way out. Perhaps it had to be a way out with honor, but an early exit from the public arena was not always unwelcome. We find references to retirement or withdrawal because of old age at the highest levels of society and service, and some combination of age and ill health, plus long years of honorable service, might lead to a request for a discharge from public life. It might come in the form of "medical excuse," perhaps masking favoritism, perhaps really indicating a recognition of diminishing ability and strength.

The excused absences from the House of Lords offer some suggestive data.[28] Between the accession of Richard II and the death of Edward IV some 30 secular and ecclesiastical peers were given explicit permission to absent themselves. The list covered 11 peers, 16 bishops (including one bishop of St. Davids), and three mitered abbots. These absences, in effect, were permissions to withdraw from public service; some may have been temporary, but others clearly were either permanent or at least open-ended. Since the service of a peer to his monarch was a serious obligation, the excuses are read in the context of departure from the life-long duties that attended high position and status.

The 30 recipients of these excuses (including Lord de la Warre, the former priest) provide a glimpse into personal problems and they way in which they were expressed in a public formulation. Of the bishops, some were excused because of specific maladies, curable or incurable. There was sympathy for bishop Lacy (d. September, 1455) in February, 1435, now "prevented from riding on horseback by long standing disease of the shin bones."[29] In some instances it was the general characteristics of old age rather than a more precise affliction that lay at the root of the problem. Bishop Heyworth (d. March, 1447) was excused in 1439, "by reason of his age and infirmities,"[30] as was John Arundel of Chichester (d. October, 1477), in 1474, "on account of his debility and old age" (and so with Beckington in 1452).[31] Illness plus age sufficed to get Adam Moleyns his excuse, in response to a petition "shewing that he is weak in body and sight and constrained in conscience to oversee his cure and in consideration of his long labours and usefulness"; he had been a bishop for 5 years.[32] In 1461 Lyhert of Norwich (1446–72) was allowed to send proctors to parliament. His personal service was not demanded, "in consideration of his age and long service in France and elsewhere and of his desire to follow things divine."[33] This point was perhaps so unusual that it justified a mid-career rededication; better late than never.

It looks as though some combination of good service, debts for favors done, and probably some real measure of ill health might go hand in hand. Of the 30 excuses about two thirds were triggered by age or age-health problems. The total of 30 is not very large, for the course of a century, in a peerage that averaged some 30–50 secular peers and 15–20 bishops along with the mitred abbots, at each parliament. Some of those excused did return; their withdrawal had been but temporary, their illnesses curable or at least endurable. Lacy lived for 20 years after his absence because of his painful shins, Beckington 13 years, and Lyhert 12, though the latter two had alleged old age among their difficulties. Though this condition was hardly going to improve, its cruelest manifestations may have abated.

Some of the men clearly were dying when they were officially released, including some whose excuses make no mention of cause. John Arundel was gone within two or three years of the Parliament from which he was excused. Moleyns, already "weak in body and sight," was murdered within a year; an angry mob intervened to make further medical bulletins academic. In August 1464 William Booth received a life exemption from future attendance; he was dead by the end of September. In his case at least, the putative "debility and old age" was more than a ritualized formula.[34]

The winds of court gossip and rumor, if not of genuine inquiry, could well have determined the facts behind each request. Bishop Clifford clearly was announcing his troubles to the world: "While riding to Parliament he was suddenly struck with illness which in the course of one night disfigured his face and made the whites of his eyes and his whole body from head to foot as if they had been smeared with saffron. It took away all his appetite and he could ride no further. He looked at his face in the glass and was ashamed that any one should see him. He begs therefore that the members of the council will excuse him to the king."[35] This sounds like jaundice, and his lack of reticence, along with his willingness to provide such detail, is striking in this circumstantial narrative.

When we turn to the lay peers the tale is much the same. Lord Vesci was exempted from parliamentary service, in 1455, because of "age and infirmity." By then he was probably well into his 60s, though he had 13 years yet to live, and his second exemption in 1462 was for life. The Earl of Oxford was allowed to absent himself, "for good service in France, Normandy, and England, and in consideration of his infirmities . . . [and] if he should come of his free will he shall enjoy all privileges as other earls or barons."[36] He was about 52 years old in 1460. As with Bishop Moleyns, his death (at Edward IV's orders in 1462) makes questions about health and expectations superfluous. Exemptions to William Botiller, Lord Sudeley, and to John, Lord Beauchamp of Powick, referred to "debility and age," and allowed that "he shall not be compelled to leave his dwelling for war."[37] Sudeley was around for another 12 years, Beauchamp 13. Though the royal heart might harden against one who had fallen from favor, it may have been difficult for the king to ignore pleas of debility from capable servants and familiar companions. In 1426 Bishop Langley had offered to send proctors to represent him. He was just too ill, he said, to attend in person.[38] In this case the illness was not mortal and he returned, eventually, to give his king and church another 11 years of service.

This treatment accorded the those at the top was in the context of favors sought and granted with excused absence as a half-way house between active service and retirement. Full retirement should be marked by explicit articulation: lunch, gold watch, speeches, and drinks. In the absence of the ritual occasion the level of activity simply slides downward and a new, if lesser, stage of life is entered, if not specifically delineated. Sometimes the exemptions and excuses were the genuine prelude to retirement, to full and final withdrawal. At other times they accommodated a passing need or a temporary disability, expressed in the idiom of service and honor. The excuses — sought and granted — show that at least there were respectable alternatives to the endless string of summonses and calls to duty. Life could wind down as well as end with a bang.

*   *   *

Beyond the special considerations shown to the rich and famous, we can see the king's government toying, in other ways, with the idea of retirement from service, at least when this coincided with the king's own purposes. In addition to the dispensations given to peers and bishops, we get a whiff of a "retirement policy" as applied at a more pedestrian and localized level. We have an instance of an old soldier asking for that which he thought his labors and honors had gained for him, and he must be but one voice of the hundreds, or even thousands, cast up by the French Wars.[39] Nor was the issue always individualized. Groups of coroners were retired, or dismissed from office, for reasons that allegedly stemmed from their age and diminishing powers. The reasons may have been genuine, or they may have served to hide political or personal motives behind the phasing out of these minor functionaries. But regardless what political agenda was served by these en bloc changes in personnel, it seems likely that the men involved were also aged and of declining years when given the push.

Forced retirement for coroners was not exactly the turning point in the road between a medieval service ethic and the rise of the civil servant. Nevertheless it is worth some comment. The move to replace the coroners was, in administrative terms, translated into action by letters close from chancery to the sheriff, and in a typical case the county official was instructed to supervise the election of a new coroner, since "William Hales of Kirketon . . . [was] too sick and aged to travail in the exercise of that office."[40] The king was now moved to act in this peremptory fashion because he had learned from "credible witnesses" that so many of his once-trusty servants were no longer fit for duty.[41]

For reasons probably related to the coup of 1399, not the welfare of his minor officials, Henry IV launched a considerable turnover among the local functionaires. The striking feature of this action is that the coroners were ostensibly being replaced because they were held to be too old. We see the same thing, again on a fairly large scale, a generation later; this way of doing business went on through Henry VI's minority. Between 1422 and 1429 there were about two dozen instances of such "forced" retirements of coroners. Between 1429 and 1435, 25 coroners from counties or their subsections, for instance, the ridings of Yorkshire, were adjudged to be too old or too sick. Between 1435 and 1441 the *Close Rolls* show that new coroners were to be "elected" in at least 20 counties; the incumbents were "too sick and aged," or "too weak and too hampered with divers infirmities."[42]

So far we have looked at two contrasting patterns of withdrawal that point towards retirement; privileged permissions for men of status, and polite encodings of enforced departure, imposed from above on more prosaic royal servants — but ostensibly imposed because of *old age* and *failing strength and skills*. The concept of allowing men to go to pasture, or of turning them out to pasture, was present. Beyond that — into the realms of an articulated view of the life cycle and social responsibility for those who were winding down — we cannot proceed.

Municipal records open other dimensions of the issue. The boroughs depended on a goodly supply of labor to oil the machinery of local government. Such labor was largely honorific, and men of substance sought service and local office to display status as they ascended the municipal cursus honorum. In good times there presumably was pressure for the ranks to open, to allow more men and new men into the charmed circles. Con-

versely, when population trends and economic forces pointed downward —
as they did, fairly regularly, in the fifteenth century — the pressure was on
the town fathers to recruit and to retain the necessary personnel. At such a
time the individual impulse was to escape, certainly if the escape could be
covered with some modicum of honor. A look at municipal service in York
indicates that "most often aldermen were allowed to resign without pay-
ment or fuss but others had to pay and one or two had quite a nasty time
with their colleagues. John Tong, mayor in 1477, had to ask several times,
'for God's sake,' to be dismissed because he was 'broken by great sickness'
before his demand was granted."[43] A few years later another such official, a
"man of great sickness and diseased with gout," had to pay £10 to acquire
a life exemption from municipal burdens. The city council took his money
and accepted his plea, but the mayor was instructed to see if more money
could be squeezed in return for his exemption.[44] So much for being taken
care of by neighbors and brothers in the world we have lost.

For the City of London we have an abundance of relevant information; the *Calendars of the Letter Books* are a gold mine concerning age-related
aspects of public service. Men of 70 and more were allowed to escape
from duty on municipal juries simply by virtue of their age; many more
were excused when they argued some compelling combination of ailments
and disabilities in lieu of or in addition to age. Nor was this but an odd
or occasional channel of escape. There are hundreds of such exemptions
through the course of the century. In Richard II's time there are about half
a dozen petitions a year, and handfuls of petitioners can be named in a
single exemption. As with the replacement of the coroners, whatever other
motives were at work, the wording of the business concentrated on age and
its attendant disabilities.

Whatever the economic and demographic trends, it was but business
as usual when a citizen of London was "discharged by William Walderne,
the mayor, and the aldermen from serving on juries, etc, except on urgent
occasions, owing to increasing old age."[45] When one citizen requested a
discharge from his duties an investigation was launched to determine "if he
be found to be seventy years of age." In this case the old man was more
than vindicated, "he having been found on inquiry to be over seventy years
of age and afflicted with deafness."[46] The normal deterioration from health
to decline to decrepitude is not hard to chart; exemptions were granted
because of "deafness and other infirmities," or "failing sight and deafness,"
or "deafness and increasing old age," or "as he was afflicted with colic (*colic
passione*) and old age," or "owing to his suffering from sciatica and other

infirmities," or "owing to ill health," or "owing to his being afflicted with stone," or "on account of deafness."[47]

The mayor and sheriffs were told to exempt Ralph Hogman, grocer, from the assize or juries if he indeed were 70, "that age having been prescribed by the Common Council as the limit for such service." In addition they were "to restore any distress" they may have caused by their zeal or incredulity. Old Ralph "should be discharged," presumably to be called no more.[48] William Bys also got away, but with a few strings; he was free from "serving on juries, watches, etc, owing to increasing old age," but he had to find a substitute for "the watches of the City and his ward."[49] Usually, however, "the ancient custom of the City," allowed a discharge without conditions, it being a sort of thank-you for service rendered.[50]

The collective weight of so many entries like these — some with illuminating details and some merely noted in the terse language of routine business — is to reinforce the idea that there was an articulated recognition of the need to slow down, if not to bow out. If this form of public consciousness is a policy regarding the aged, in some embryonic form, it was perhaps one that could only be nurtured in a place such as London, with its huge labor pool and its variety of public and private resources. London presumably had a supply of men and sufficient prestige to ensure that a long line of younger sons and aspiring outsiders would clamor for a place in the queue. Few other secular settings were as conducive to official tolerance of individual need. Furthermore, there is no indication that Londoners were forced to buy their way out, unlike their less fortunate counterparts in York. But at age 70 enough was clearly accepted, under some circumstances, as being enough.

*　　*　　*

For the best analogue with the modern retirement and a retirement policy we can turn to the church. Here, as with the City of London, we have a special combination; the recognition of a common and pervasive social problem, a large pool of labor, and some ability to marshal resources to implement a policy and ameliorate a problem. Moreover, the church had one peculiar headache — the lifelong duration of clerical status. Church personnel did not have a private or family life to which they could turn when their public role was worn out. Thus superannuation for ecclesiastics had to be incorporated within and supported by the church's own embrace. The old could not be turned out to someone else's pasture. If anything, it was

into the Church's pastures that others steered their elderly; corrodies, benefices now claimed for and used by aged clerics after careers in royal service,
and other routes along the roads of pluralism and absenteeism that now led
to home. If London's use of its own might end when they reached 70, not
so with clerics. The church commanded such a vast labor force that its clerical ranks represented a normal population and age curve — given that it began with men and women in their mid-teens or early twenties — and the
problems peculiar to either end of the life line had to be taken into special
account.

Various arrangements and kinds of arrangements were available
whereby individuals found shelter within the church's bosom. Some were
variations on retirement at the end, but others were closer to annuities,
arranged for a long term or even for life. Corrodies allowed or enabled the
laity to live within ecclesiastical precincts, and they might be subsidized by
an inter vivos transfer of goods, perhaps long before old age had set in. Or
a corrody might be claimed by an ecclesiastical or secular patron to support
a servant or associate, and in such cases the payments may have been closer
to an annual salary than to a retirement buy-out or a pension. Ecclesiastical
houses themselves paid pensions, and here it could either be for succor in
old age or for services, perhaps yet to be rendered.[51]

This is not to argue against corrodies and pensions as a net whereby a
tumble from an active career into the deep well of age and debility was
made as gentle and as comfortable as possible. At Thornton Abbey, in the
good old days, there had been "certain alms called little corrodies, which
were formerly wont to be given to serving folk and to friends of the canons
who had fallen upon old age or loss of strength." Now, alas, "such alms and
your abbot's alms dish have for many years past been sold for certain sums
of money, not without the guilt of simony and avarice." But reform was
coming: "henceforth such alms be in no wise sold, or given, as is aforesaid,
and assigned under such form, but in the form of old accustomed."[52]

When a corrody was arranged to cover retirement within a regular
house, the terms of daily life might be spelled out in detail. One presumably
bought in at whatever level one could; the records of Launceston Priory tell
of a corrodian who came in on a par — for food, drink, clothes, fuel, and
favors — with the prior's esquire, while his servant was pegged against the
standard of the prior's servants. Nor was the corrodian's horse neglected,
just as we have instances of dogs as well as servants being remembered.[53]
The aged prior of Blyth, now retired "on account of old age and infirmity,"
was to get four white loaves a day, along with three gallons of beer, two

dishes of meat (and three of fish, on fish days), 100s. per annum for wines and spices.[54]

Later we will look at the bishops and see how active this particular elite remained through the course of life. If and when a bishop began to fail there were the options of honorable withdrawal and retirement, of pensions and comfortable leisure. The same options and alternatives, in scale, were available for an elderly and ailing abbot or prior, usually within the walls of his own house in company with lesser brethren who might be residents of the infirmary in their last years. When the dean of Irthlingborough College was adjudged "broken in health by reason of old age," and could no longer bear the burdens of his office, others were to visit the sick and preach on Sunday in his stead.[55] And at the pitiful end of the road, we have the abbot of Peterborough, asking to be relieved of his duties, "by reason of his want of strength and old age and the sore infirmities which he daily suffers and that daily grow upon him."[56]

But it was really among the lesser clergy—the uncommissioned ranks in the army of ecclesiastical labor—that the problems of age, illness, and declining mental and physical powers were most in evidence. Such men, often working in considerable isolation, posed the knottiest problems in terms of the care they needed and the pastoral care they were to deliver to others. If the secular clergy had to cover some 9,500 parishes (plus the vast number of unbeneficed positions in chantries and schools), it seems likely that a good 25 percent or so of the men were at or beyond age 50, and that at least some 10–15 percent were probably 60 or more. Of these, we can only guess at how many were in real need of replacement and retirement; how many could cope, albeit at a slower pace; how many could go to the end without help.

Certainly the records show that for some in need there was some aspect of retirement as an option—if not always an affluent or comfortable one. Priests who could no longer perform their duties could, on occasion, be turned out to pasture. If there is no evidence of a systematic analysis of the problem, let alone of a systematic solution, episcopal registers show that worries about such men were a regular item in the administrative agenda. Aging priests *might* be accorded relief from labor and, on occasion, receive a comfortable or even a handsome pension. Of course, when there was a pension for a secular cleric it was usually met by siphoning revenues from the benefice, to the partial impoverishment of his successor.

These generalizations can be fleshed out anecdotally if not systematically. An unfortunate priest who had to step down in 1414 was consoled by his bishop, a superior who recognized that retirement was a necessity here, not a mere indulgence. The priest was "broken down by age and weakened in sight by palsy of the eyes, and for years has been incurably troubled with many sicknesses, as notoriously [he is] now troubled."[57] How much intercession and special pleading had preceded this catching of the bishop's attention, merely to salvage one old soldier in the ranks? When "age and infirmity" forced the rector of Chilbolton to resign, Waynflete replaced him and stipulated that his pension was to be 10 marks.[58] Archbishop Chichele's bureaucrats turned a sympathetic ear to Walter Causton, prior of Dover, whose removal was not because of any "demerits," but rather because of age. He got a chamber in his old house, plus 10 marks a year, for life.[59] Under the burden of age and physical or mental distress monks could leave the cloister and canons their residential duties, though usually they would be taken care of by their own.[60] Some needed lesser dispensations, as the priest who "on account of his old age and bodily weakness," was allowed to eat meat during ecclesiastical fasts.[61]

But there was no hiding from the fact that even the most dedicated could break down. The archdeacon of Salisbury was so afflicted with gout that he was permitted to carry out his duties through a deputy.[62] A chantry priest, "old and ailing," was also allowed to use a deputy; that the latter was "removable at will" may argue for some hope of recovery, or it may indicate just one more way unbeneficed clerics were kept dangling in insecurity and near poverty.[63] Certainly, few parishioners in Abbot's Ripton expected their rector to resume his duties. He was broken with age, infirm and blind, and unfit to exercise his office; the parish was without a cure of souls.[64] A combination of mental and physical infirmities *and* old age *and* blindness more than sufficed to end of the working career of the rector of Lanreach,[65] as were the burdens of 90 years *and* paralysis for the rector of St. Martin's by Loo, Cornwall.[66]

These cases sound all too typical, and there is no reason to think they are anything but the tip of the iceberg. The percentage of the priesthood so afflicted and comparably long-lived and able to retire on an adequate pension must have been but a fraction of those whose need for such treatment was both genuine and visible. For the many who inhabited that world of failing powers and diminishing resources—recorded and preserved in the occasional bleak complaint from abandoned parishioners or in the records of an episcopal visitation—we can imagine a tale of innumerable parishes served by the senile and the feeble, of the masses left unsung, of marriages and baptisms unperformed. Bishop Rede learned that the priest of Finden "had been afflicted through many years continually and incurably with severe and diverse infirmities and particularly with the complaint of deafness as he is now notoriously afflicted, so that he is now rendered altogether useless for the cure of souls entrusted to him."[67] And how, we ask, did the good bishop become aware of this situation? Alas, not by anything approaching a regular personnel review. Rather, it was "by public rumor, and the notoriety of the fact which by no subterfuge can be concealed reporting it in many ways."

For clerks fortunate enough to catch the sympathetic eye of a superior, retirement could be a not uncomfortable chapter at the end. Men on the higher rungs of the ladder might draw lavish pensions. The prebend of Oxton and Crophill in Southwell Minster was put to grass with a life annuity of £16, and the prior of Bolton in Craven — from the "commissioned" ranks of the church — was to get £12 per annum.[68] The latter's money was expressly drawn from the priory's regular revenues; his successor bore some of the burden of this generosity, just as heirs to a secular estate had to endure the dower shares payable to long-lived widows for years and years. The canon of Osbaldwick's 40 marks in York Cathedral was a good deal more than handsome. The rector of Great Torrington's pension of £20 was at least some compensation for the old age, weakness, and blindness that led to his resignation and retirement in 1453,[69] and his successor was threatened with excommunication and the sequestration of revenues if he defaulted on the payments. The archdeacon of Stafford, "stricken with sudden illness," was to receive 50 marks a year, drawn from the revenues of Tutbury priory.[70] We have details about the rector of Norwold, now "almost a sexagenarian . . . constantly unwell . . . on account of the unwholesomeness of the climate." He was allowed to receive his revenues while residing "in an honest or religious place, or studying letters in a university, or serving some ecclesiastical prelate."[71] Were he so conscientious, we might ask, what had he been doing throughout his career? But if an experienced bishop asked for leave to devote himself to matters spiritual it is small-minded to cavil at a mere rector now turning to otherworldly interests.

Lesser citizens of mother church understandably got by on lesser sums, like it or not. Most of the pensions authorized by bishop Rotherham were below those smallish amounts on which many a parish priest already had to make do while on active service. In a vast hierarchy where chantry chaplains often received but £5 a year and where beneficed clergy might to lucky to get 10 marks, a pension of £5–8 was passable. John Appleby's £5 6s. 8d. from a rural vicarage was probably more than fair.[72] But others, pensioned off on £4 or 5 marks or even 4 marks, were clearly at, if not well below, the poverty line. Some form of supplementary income or a cut of agricultural yields, or local charity, was badly needed. The vicar of Wath received but £2; presumably the lack of resources in a poor living tells why did he so much worse than the vicar of Dewsebury, with a comfortable £10 per annum.[73]

Priests appointed to parish churches could be saddled with the obligation of covering their predecessor's pension.[74] Such payments were usually rendered on a quarterly basis, and badly needed by the former incumbent, "by occasion of his bodily infirmity and senile age," and to be paid promptly and fully lest he be reduced to begging, "to the disgrace of the clergy."[75] Shame and honor evidently were motivating forces in England as well as in southern Europe. Fortunately for the old priest, there was some sense of the seemly and the church too recognized that it lived in the public gaze.[76] It were best if the pension were paid properly and promptly, "lest he be seen begging."[77] It was embarrassing to learn that an aged prior, relieved from office and duties "because of bodily weakness and blindness," had his pension "maladministered" by the lay supervisors appointed to take care of him.[78]

Retired priests probably lived in cottages in their old parish, cared for by local housekeeping resources and dependent on some combination of an ability to pay, to inspire affection, and to be a focal point for shame and scandal. The former prior of Dover, surely an aristocrat of the church, had his own chamber in his old house, along with a servant, and 10 marks when he moved off on his own.[79] But what of a mere rector, pensioned off because he suffered from some combination of gout, colic, and other ailments, and told to reside for life in some honest place? One priest was given a perpetual vicarage, in his old age, so he need not reside in any of his incompatible benefices.[80] This kind of tangle indicates how the juggling of personnel and their divers duties and sources of income could create a bureaucratic nightmare of such complexity that no one could be sure of who was responsible, whom to charge with the old man's upkeep.

*   *   *

This survey of retirement is a tapestry of rags and patches, of brightly illuminated if short swatches of gaudy color set against dark stretches with few lessons of hope or joy. For every datum we can uncover innumerable others, probably alike in substance, are hidden from us — but visible then, part of the pattern of on going social interaction and biography. If we can focus on medical and age-driven dispensations for peers and bishops, for aging citizens of London, and for some of the vast army of clerics, we are likely to be tapping no more than a small, albeit a representative fraction, of the social response. We know that at the manorial level arrangements were made — usually but not always between parents and children — regarding how the old were pensioned off, as the land of the older generation was turned over to the labor and control of the younger, in return for an agreement regarding living space, income, and personal relations through the duration of old age.[81] We also know that such arrangements might turn sour; backbiting, if not back-stabbing, with the cruel spur of inflation and taxation and of changing family structure and ambience, might have raised the tension level to and beyond the bearable. But if we state the negative case as the probable lot of countless men and women, we should not allow it to dominate our story. Arrangements for rural retirement, if imposed by necessity rather than choice, must have been adequate and acceptable in some instances, and in many cases pretty much the only option.

Furthermore, if few towns were as indulgent as London, not all were as mean-spirited as York. Guilds, fraternities, and other voluntary and membership organizations helped take up the slack of those whose needs were increasing and whose contributions were going in the opposite direction.[82] The charity of the church, as well as that directed towards the church, was rarely steered towards the old in an explicit fashion, though it did touch many of concern to us.

The retirements we have considered constitute the respectable facade upon the social structure. The data leave open many questions about values, personal options, and sentiments. Many of the retirements were those to which men were driven. Even putting the best face on this material, it is hard to see a great surge of what we might term voluntary, let alone "early" retirement. We have moralizing about the final stages of the life line, but no one spoke about the potential pleasures and opportunities of golden years, now upon them, except for homilies about spiritual freedom from sensuality. Could we but hear old Agnes Paston, now perhaps turning her thoughts to the deferred pleasures of travel (that oft-postponed pilgrimage to Santiago or Jerusalem), to develop hobbies, to work in the garden, to volunteer for the parish guild. The use of corrodies indicates that people anticipated years in which care-giving would be necessary, and they made plans for the transition. But in terms of what old people did with their time we know almost nothing. Maybe, by the time people stepped aside, they had reached a point in life where their level of activity just diminished; the quality and quantity of life would run down in tandem. But if we are willing to be harsh about medieval society's lack of articulated compassion for the aged, we should also remember that there was little perceived need for men to step aside just so the young could have their day in the sun. Most of the retirements we have looked at were necessary in terms of age, health, and vigor. However, the reasons were either that the old man *could* not go on or that he no longer wished to go on. We did not see pressure on him to step aside so his juniors could come forward. If he was able to stay in line, and if he chose to stay in line, tough luck for those behind him.

In some contexts the idea of the generation or age cohort provides an insight into the ways younger men take over from their elders.[83] Society, as a system within which the old and the young stand as both rivals and partners in a long distance race, comes into focus when we look at the transition of personnel on the basis of age. But hierarchy also meant staying in place. Kings did not abdicate; few bishops stepped down; old peers smiled as sons and grandsons stood beside and behind them and had to bide their time. For the few among the elderly who sought to step aside and who either were allowed to or were free to choose to, the world clearly had some compensations. This is not much, on the scale of what may have been possible, or as judged against modern standards of health care and human dignity and of personal options. But, on the other hand, "not very much" can be a good deal better than nothing at all, and some people in the fifteenth century were seemingly happy to take whatever was available and whatever they could get — in terms of leisure or cash and comforts — when they, or those around them, decided it was time to step down.

8

Careers and Case Studies of
the Peers

SO THERE WAS RETIREMENT, as both an institution and a practice. Much depended, of course, on whether one retired or was retired; power, affluence, and life alternatives, before and after retirement, were the critical variables. But by focusing on these cases and examples we can present another gloss on the theme of the ubiquity of the aged, on the social recognition of if not sympathy for their plight, and on their ability — in select areas and studies — to claim some share of resources to carry them through the final stages of the life line. As their fates and fortunes varied and diverged, so did their options and life patterns.

No useful purpose is served by trampling through the records in search of every old man (and woman) we can find. That they were present, more or less everywhere, and in reasonable numbers, is by now one of our givens.[1] If the various sources are too inchoate for demography in its more rigorous guise, they do allow us to give some clarity to a general view about longevity and survival. How can we apply this to supplement our view of late medieval social structure and social relationships? We certainly want to move from a random list of those who survived to a more contextualized application of the information. What we are seeking are boundaries or social confines within which such variables as longevity, career length, and life choices assume a more precise meaning, in both individual and behavioral terms.

In this and the next two chapters we will look at three discrete groups: the secular peerage, the English bishops (between the accession of Henry IV and 1500), and a fair-sized sprinkling of professional and creative writers whose lives and production patterns can be traced. All these groups are large enough to be of statistical significance, and they all offer anecdotal and qualitative as well as numerical evidence.[2] These groups can be pinned down and defined; the first two with considerable precision. What proportion of each can we follow toward the milestone of old age — as it was seen and accepted by contemporaries — and how active were the survivors, in the later stages of their careers? Insofar as we can make estimates based on activity, expression, or contemporary evaluations, were there aspects of the lives or careers that look to be specific attributes of old age, of a successful struggle for survival? Sometimes questions about the kinds and levels of service rendered at different ages can be posed, and when we look at creative writers we have suggestions about the way in which the productive career years might be set against the length of life.[3]

Having said that a random search for the elderly is of much less help than an analysis of some closed groups in determining how society "worked," we will nevertheless begin with some random dips of data. As so often with our sources, a fair amount of information is at hand, although it must be readdressed because our questions are rarely those for which the records were designed. To run through late medieval literature looking for jokes about May-December weddings is an amusing pastime; it tells little about *real* ages at marriage or how behavior was recorded and judged in a social context. On the other hand, if the picture formed by satirical and estates literature is not be the "reality" an historian searches for, it certainly was part of the contemporary consciousness. It was written and circulated against the backdrop of socio-economic norms within which the elderly enjoyed a good deal of prescribed power, a considerable share of the wealth, and a grip on decision-making offices and high status. If we find too much ambivalence simply to accord age, per se, a privileged position, the chances are that age was cobbled together with experience and authority to command a considerable dominance for those within its ranks. Creative literature may emphasize jocularity at the expense of the aged; hierarchical society probably did not.

In fact the real tilt was more likely to be toward deference and privilege. A sermon of the day enlarged on the fourth commandment and called for the respect due to "every virtuous old man."[4] Clearly an unexceptionable message, but as sermons were drummed into the lay consciousness with regularity, this kind of idea was part of life's platitudes. An even more positive view was expressed in the intriguing (and self-serving) conceit that one did not age on those days on which one heard mass. What a boon for church attendance, if not for public credulity: "That day schalt thou elde nought, Yif thou bee studefast in thi thought on God, that is verray."[5]

These are interesting ideas, though there is little point in worrying about how literally they were offered, let alone received. They certainly are more pointed, in their validation of age and the aged, than the customary saws of wisdom literature: "Old people are envious of the young, and they know much because of their age."[6] Old men in positions of authority were perhaps as much the norm in daily life as were the endless stream of silly, covetous, and lecherous old figures conjured up by the poets. As an eighteenth-century anthropologist noted, "So inseparably connected are age and authority in early periods, that in the language of rude nations the same word which signifies an old man is generally employed to denote a ruler or magistrate."[7]

In secular society some men came to the fore early and remained there through the full course of their lives. The peers are among the most obvious of the groups with such an age spread or composition. Called early and generally maintaining high status and visibility through life, the peers who survived into old age were probably more likely to gain prestige by virtue of longevity than to see it slip through their fingers. Some, as we will see, lasted and remained impressively active until the end. Aside from the peers, there are other groups we can track, composed of those who began early and who stayed the long course. Knights of the shire and burgesses of the towns come to mind when we look for illustrative material on durability and public visibility.

A cursory look at a group of parliamentary knights — those elected for Somerset in the parliaments between 1386 and 1421, and, by way of comparison, men elected for Bristol in those years — gives an idea of the extent to which prosopography and longevity and careers can be linked.[8] These two groups have been chosen more or less at random from among many such aggregations: there is no reason to think their tales unusual, their lives and careers in any way other than average for men of their position and experience. We see that the knights of the shire were usually more prominent than those chosen from the boroughs; a reflection of this is that their biographies tend to be better known than those of their urban colleagues.[9] For Somerset 23 men can be identified as knights of the shire for the 32 parliaments between 1386 and 1421. We can turn to the *History of Parliament* for approximate birth and death dates for 13 of the 24: one died in his 30s, one in his 40s, and eleven lived until past 60 (with four actually reaching their 70s: two to 70, two to 76). For the other 11, the best we can do is to pick them up at the first point at which they are recorded in the sources. Considering this as the start of the working career (and as such it may pick the man up while he is still in his teens), we find that between the first mention and the date of death, two men (of the 11) had careers of 20 to 30 years, six between 30 and 40 years, two between 40 and 50 years, and one more than 50 years.

This is impressive material, and it speaks for itself. Three of these county knights eventually rose to the peerage: William, lord Bonville (1392-x1461), Walter, lord Hungerford (1378–1449), and John, lord Tiptoft (c. 1380–1443). Their careers illustrate how the opportunity for upward mobility was correlated with longevity. Bonville only became a peer in 1449, when in his mid- or late 50s, Hungerford in 1422 when aged 44, and Tiptoft in 1428 when in his mid-40s. Furthermore, the summons to Lords came respectively 28, 25, and 22 years after their first election. Thus we see that long careers are not unusual, albeit the ultimate level of success for these men was exceptional; some who could ford the tricky waters of local and national politics were (also) those who lived long lives. If swift turns of fortune's wheel are the image in popular fancy, genuine success stories are more apt to have a gradualist and/or accretionary theme. The longer the life span the greater the opportunity of going to the head of the queue.

Other Somerset biographies show that, except for the final step up into the peerage, these three were not so different from many of their contemporaries in either service or longevity. Robert Hill of Spaxton (1361–1423) offers a comparable record, though he never rose above the distinguished heights of the House of Commons. Son of Sir John Hill — a member of parliament and then a justice of the king's bench — Robert sat in four parliaments: November 1414, 1415, March 1416, and 1419. His first appointment to public office, on a royal commission, had been back in 1397, and he served long stretches as a justice of the peace (1399–1410 and from 1410 to his death). He was four times sheriff of Somerset and Dorset between 1408 and 1423. Neither his legal career nor his sister's marriage to lord Harrington hurt his efforts to make a mark, and he left a sizeable estate to go along with an impressive record of power and involvement. Another case study that shows how survival, influential friends and relatives, and long life all reinforced each over as part of the secret to mobility and success.

Hugh Luttrell (c. 1363–1428) was another of these long-lived knights. He sat four times for Somerset, plus twice for Devon, between October 1404 and 1415. Through his mother he was a grandson of the earl of Devon. He entered royal service as a commissioner of oyer and terminer in 1393 (and he continued in that position until 1427). Though he also had served John of Gaunt in the 1390s, it was his Courtenay ties that guarded him against possible reprisals from angry Lancastrians. He was in his 50s when he served as lieutenant of Harfleur (1417–21), as seneschal of Normandy (1419–21), and on a commission against West Country Lollards (1417). He returned from the French wars in 1421, and he remained active in public affairs while turning his personal attention to rebuilding Dunster Castle, on which he spent over £250 in the 1420s. Neither Hill nor Luttrell are more than good case studies of common patterns; a long life meant more time in which to keep climbing the stairway to fame and fortune.

The 28 men who represented Bristol in these years offer another variation on the theme, though because we know less about them it may be in a minor key.[10] Though we only have life dates for Richard Cheddar (who lived to about 58), we can use the working career dates for the rest. Three had careers that ran 10–20 years, seven of 20–30 years, eight of 30–40 years, and eight of 40 and more (peaking with Thomas Norton's 51-year span between his first mark in business and his death, after a career that included seven parliaments).[11] Furthermore, these are minimal career-spans; there may have been years of activity before the first recorded entrance. Town records offer a somewhat different career pattern for the urban bourgeoisie, as municipal office seemed more apt to go to men in middle age than to those at either extreme. An important figure like John Burton represented Bristol in five parliaments between 1417 and 1432. His office holding in town was even more spread out; it began with a term on the common council in 1413 and it ended, 40 years later, with a term as mayor (for the fourth time) in 1450–51 and as a commissioner to raise a loan in 1453. John Leycestre had been active in trade during Richard II's reign, and he had sat in parliament (May, 1413) well before he served as sheriff (1417–18) or mayor (1424–25, 1430–31). If such men were not at their full three-score-and-ten, at which point their London counterparts were seeking relief from office, they were certainly not far behind in counting the years. Furthermore, this kind of analysis could be extended to cover virtually every parliamentary constituency, touching both the individuals and the collective representation. Findings much like those for Somerset and Bristol would undoubtedly be the norm.[12]

Let us look at some secular clergy. Though the sources are patchy, at best, and though they are not a social group or statistically bounded universe in the proper sense, we can assess some career and survival patterns, since the *Fasti Parochiales* for Yorkshire provide some material of interest.[13] As we might imagine, we cannot assume that every incumbent is named or all dates known. Nevertheless, enough instances can be found where we have the date of appointment and of death or resignation to indicate the duration of some long careers; that is, of incumbents who held a single living for 30 or more years. This span is about what we might consider a generation, or a professional man's years of active contribution, and if we add to it the years of legal majority—when an ecclesiastical career would begin—we are probably picking up an incumbent pretty near the start. A 30-year span might make a full career in the church, as in any other track we can follow, but it is hardly of striking duration. It is enough, however, to at least take our man to the brink of what medieval commentators would consider the near side of old age, of *middle elde*. Those who put in much over 30 years in the church were pretty sure to be men whose lives ran to 50 or 55 years or more, and we can safely include them in a tally of the elderly, if hardly of the ancient.

From the *Fasti* we can see how long and short tenures in a particular living were apt to alternate; a cyclical rhythm seems almost a rule. But it was only a tendency; sometimes a specific living saw a string of incumbents pass through at rapid intervals, whereas another had a few men cover a century. But if the dance of short and long tenures is close to a pattern, it is a checkered one regarding careers. We find an example of this of syncopation with the vicars of Folkton, the rectors of Lowthorpe, or the vicars of Rudston.[14] At Folkton 8 men held the living between 1401 and 1500; they served 3, 3, 6, 12, and 17 years (with other periods of service left unstated). At Lowthorpe 12 men, between 1407 and 1504, served the church for terms of 2, 21, 7, 2, 1, 4, 6, 23, 14, 3, and 15 (with one undetermined). At Rudston, the 12 men named between 1413 and 1516 served for terms of 7, 2, 3, 26, 13, 4, 1, 13, 13, 1, and 21 years (one here too as undertermined). In toto we have 27 men who served an average of only 9 years; only 11 were in place for somewhere between 10 and 20 years; only 4 for 20 years and more. Ecclesiastical careerism, not mortality, is probably the reason for the rapid turnover and the short periods of service to the separate churches.

Some of the vicars and rectors died in office, but mostly men left because of resignation. Usually this meant a move to another position, not the end of the working career. Mostly by surmise, if the records do not indicate to the contrary, we assume short service as an indication of a move, while 20 or 30 years is likely to mean a priest who either died in office or resigned because he was old and ready to end his career. We can look at the data in a slightly different fashion. In volume III of the *Fasti* we find about 313 men who, between the late fourteenth to the turn of the sixteenth century, held the various benefices and livings covered in the volume.[15] Of these, 44 served a single church for something between 20 and 29 years; 27 served for 30 years and more, 4 for over 40 years, 1 for 50.

These dates mean that one cleric, of every four or five whose service can be dated at each end, put in 20 years or more in a single benefice. While this fact alone hardly argues for a clergy of staggering longevity or age, it reveals a good sprinkling of the middle aged, if not of the elderly. Sometimes we learn that the longer periods of service were indeed ended by death or a (final) resignation. When William Blase was presented to Addingham, in April 1414, he followed an elderly predecessor now going off to collect his life pension of 100 shillings per annum.[16] Richard Phalthorp did a bit better; when he left Giggleswick in 1485, after 38 years service, he drew a fairly healthy 10 marks.[17] A vicar of Kettlewell resigned in 1412, in the presence of his successor; his flock had enjoyed his labors for 45 years.[18]

Other branches of the church would doubtlessly present a similar tale, had record keepers (and modern editors) been as cooperative as they have been for Yorkshire. The regular clergy are helpful here. The great abbeys were run by men who were chosen for life, with the prospect of dying in office a regular part of their outlook (though we know that some were pensioned off). A tally of the mitered abbots reveals that most houses bridged the century with between 5 and 10 men in command. Granted, this is a fair variation for both life span and years in office; it again shows the alternation of long and short terms, as men came and went. In most houses there seem to have been one or two abbots who lasted well beyond the paltry average of 10–20 years we get from simple arithmetic. At Abingdon, where 10 abbots presided between 1396 and 1504, William Ashenden was in charge for 33 years (1435–1468), John Sante for 26 (1469–1495).[19] Thus a lot of men — either elected at advanced ages or dying young — only enjoyed brief careers in their leading roles. Ashenden had been a noted builder for his house, and his opportunities to leave a mark — like those of the Somerset and Bristol men who climbed and climbed over the years — were enhanced because he "lived to great age."[20]

Some major abbeys managed to put together a run of men comparable to those who had ruled Cluny in its early days.[21] At Bardney in Lincolnshire a mere five abbots sufficed to span the years between 1404 and 1507. Richard Horncastle covered the last 34 of these, up to 1507, "when he resigned by reason of his great age." But even here the good run of five men does not reflect any truly amazing tenures; rather, it is the absence of any short terms — the absence of the pattern of alternation — that makes the difference.[22] At Coventry Richard Crossley "governed near 40 years," from about 1399 to 1436, and John Litlington answered for Croyland for 38 years (1429–67).[23] Litlington, like Ashenden at Abingdon, was known as a great builder. Resignations by old and failing men, looking toward some period of well earned rest, enter into a discussion of long service; John Deeping after 30 years at Peterborough, John Stowe after 31 at Ramsey, and Thomas Spofford — abbot of St. Mary, York, and then bishop of Hereford — returning from episcopal burdens to end his days in retirement in the cloister.

The champion in the game of longevity seems to have been John Chennock "abbot [of Glastonbury] nearly 50 years."[24] He too had been a builder of his house, as were many of the long-lived and elderly abbots. Given the problems of fund raising and the pace of construction, the odds were much greater that a man who presided for 30 or 40 years would complete a project than even the most vigorous and affluent abbot with a mere 15 or 20 years in which to cultivate his pet projects. The amount of construction Benedictine abbots carried out in the century, as best we can separate fact from a tendency to lionize the heroes and their labors, is surprising. It does not conform to views about declining houses and declining enthusiasm. Longevity (of the abbots) may have been an important factor in gauging the success of these enterprises.

*   *   *

We can follow up on some of these ideas about the correlation between age and career-success when we turn to several closed elites. The secular peers and the bishops offer two fixed groups about whom we know — by the standards of 15th century sources — a considerable amount. The secular peers are the best documented lay elite of the realm.[25] With the exception of a royal prince or two, men did not become peers until they were 21, if their fathers had pre-deceased them, or until their fathers died and they received their own summons. Thus we are working with a universe whose members had already reached legal age. And if the individual writ of summons was the de facto creation of a new peerage, or when the title came by way of marriage to the heiress of an established peerage, the summons to Lords might elevate a man who was already of some considerable years (as with our friends from Somerset: Bonville, Hungerford, and Tiptoft). And because we begin with a group of men who, for the most part, had already survived to at least age 21, data on survival and longevity are going to be skewed towards survival, towards success in the race of life.

In some part because of their peculiar demographic composition they offer good material for a case study. Compared to most others in their world their demography can be established within a reasonable margin of error, and their ranks reveal a whole string of elderly men, having and retaining visible positions of power and status throughout the course of long lives. While the peers seem typical of the groups who dominated secular and ecclesiastical society, their tales are readily known and easily told. If one view of medieval society is of a world full of men already active in their late teens and early 20s, another shows us legions — perhaps the same men, viewed through the lenses of 40 years down the road — still active while having long passed their 50s and even early or mid-60s.

Table 8-1 presents some demographic data on the peers' longevity; the material extracted from *The Complete Peerage* seems accurate enough for a rounded-off guide. If we begin with peers born between 1351 and 1375 and then proceed to divide them by birth groups (by quarter centuries), we see that survival beyond age 60 was relatively common. For the entire universe of five birth cohorts, 72 of 267 peers (or 27 percent of the total) lived to at least age 60. Of these, 45 men (or 16.8 percent) died in their 60s, and 27 (10.1 percent of the total) reached 70. For each cohort, moving forward, the

TABLE 8-1.   Survival of Peers, by 25-Year Birth Cohorts

Age at death	Born					
	1351– 75	1376– 1400	1401– 25	1426– 50	1451+	Total
20–29	11	7	4	7	6	35
	31%	20%	11%	20%	17%	
30–39	17	14	4	12	9	56
	30%	25%	7%	21%	16%	
40–49	18	8	16	17	7	66
	27%	12%	24%	26%	11%	
50–59	3	12	13	6	4	38
	8%	32%	34%	16%	11%	
60–69	7	12	5	10	11	45
	16%	27%	11%	22%	24%	
70+	4	7	10	5	1	27
	15%	26%	37%	19%	4%	
Total	60	60	52	57	38	267
	22%	22%	19%	21%	14%	

Data extracted from *Comple Peerage*. Totals do not always add to 100% because of rounding.

proportion surviving to 60 was 18 percent, 32 percent, 29 percent, 26 percent, and 32 percent. Every cohort had at least one man who lived into his 70s, and there was actually an average of five such men, per group, plus an average of nine who survived to be sexagenarians. There were some champions of heroic longevity; we know from Josiah Russell's work, and from some of the peers, that a truly long life was encountered from time to time. And coming from the other direction, there is nothing in a study of longevity that offers evidence of "a demographic collapse of the late Middle Ages." If such a collapse was a real phenomenon it must be identified through demographic rates, rather than in information about the maxima of survival.[26]

We estimate that the average life span for men in late medieval Europe who reached at least age 20 or 21 ran into the early or mid-50s. Our peers, as a group, fall fairly neatly within these boundaries. We can think of the 27 men who reached 70 as balancing the 35 who died in their 20s, and in statistical terms they also compensate for the 56 men who died in their 30s and the 66 who reached age 40 but not 50. The presence of aged men was a constant across through the century.[27]

The peerage, as a group, is tilted toward longevity, of course; we have a larger component or proportion of old men than we would find among some other groups we could look at, since we start with men who had already reached legal age. However, the Somerset knights put up some pretty good numbers when it came to survival, and it may be that the peers were on a par with other upper-class groups. Syvia Thrupp pointed out that among 97 London merchants, 24 lasted to an age somewhere between 59 and 70, 10 reached 70 or more (a post-59 survival rate of 35 percent).[28] For colonial North America — perhaps not a bad comparison with late medieval England — there are findings of the same sort. In seventeenth-century Andover the data lead to the view that "those who did survive to adulthood could anticipate long and healthy lives"; of 92 men, 29 died before reaching 60, 16 died in their 60s, and 74 lived to at least 70, 31 percent, 17 percent, and 51 percent respectively.[29]

Nor are the Andover figures all that eccentric for the northeastern colonies in their early, heroic days. In Plymouth Colony 23 percent of the adult males died before 50, 18 percent while in their 60s, and 59 percent after age 70. This was a hardy stock, no doubt, and those who reached adulthood could look forward to 40 or even 50 more years of activity.[30] Nor should we forget the political and constitutional factors at work. An aristocracy that relied on de novo recruitment and for succession *when* the father died would contain fewer men in their 20s and 30s and more men in middle age than would a random slice of population. If the men who sat for Bristol rarely went to Parliament until they were in their 40s, as was the case, they comprised a universe that we only pick up at a point in age when 34 percent of our five cohorts of peers (91 of the 267 peers) had already died.

The quality of life, as well as its quantitative assessment, is of interest; so is an inquiry into the level of sustained activity as men aged. How long did men in high positions last as active figures? The material on retirement, mostly relating to clerics and citizens of London, leads to a picture of survival often coupled with decline. The hale and hearty among the aged are not likely to figure as petitioners for relief, so their presence in their world might be unnoticed when we concentrate on pensions and people being turned out to pasture. In addition, the excuses sought by peers and bishops regarding age, illness, and disability were specific in focus. Such tales of age and failing powers did not place the petitioners in a social context, and they highlighted the inability to serve and the ravages caused by aging.

We can turn, by way of contrast, to some who still could serve, and who often did so. The public role sought by and accorded the elderly is a universal problem, regardless how, when, and why a given society draws the line between middle and old age, between full and diminished responsibility. When we looked at various facets of retirement we were not greatly concerned with individuals; we knew little of their personal situations, let alone their psychic and social adjustment. We just saw that they and/or their colleagues thought they were ready to bow out. In modern society we can look on the "golden years" as a time, perhaps, when fathers make way for grown-up sons. But this may be fantasy, a utopian view of the life cycle, and it may cover over real hostility between generations. Perhaps to step down — let alone to be pushed aside — was mostly to allow a rival, a replacement, to take over, and to have one's own position irreversibly diminished. That the successor was a son may have made the transition easier for some, but we can also think of reasons to argue that it made it harder, more contentious.

From the royal family in the twelfth century we can draw the lesson that Henry II was too dilatory and begrudging when it came to delegating power to his sons. However, we can also read the records to confirm the view that even at his most choleric the aging Henry was probably a better judge of men, a wiser and more capable controlling hand on his many subjects and projects, than any of his boys. The medieval polity had no loyal opposition, let alone anything as cozy as a senatorial use of the House of

Lords. In the fifteenth century there was little scope for a partial-but-continuing status if it became disconnected (because of age) from full service. If many an aging peer reached a harmonious modus vivendi with his sons as a personal and working relationship, this was fortuitous. Control of the visible and ceremonial parts of power was in general as vital as control of the estates. He who was seen to slow down was likely to be acknowledging his own relegation to the outer circles. To accept the inevitable was to begin the irreversible descent.

When we considered the church's action on retirement and pensions, we saw signs of contemporary sensitivity to the way in which men broke down. If this constant need to renew the personnel was dealt with at the parish or town level, what were the problems when high office is under consideration? Lesser men laid down lesser burdens; the high and mighty had fewer options. Kings, in fact, had no place to go. A biographer says of Henry II that, "although, not at fifty-six, particularly old, even by medieval standards, he seems to have been worn out by as lifetime of arduous travel and the incessant endeavor to impose his will upon the world,"[31] and the sober tale of Henry VIII's final days is a familiar one. If the more fortunate could hope to live on, hale and hearty, for decades, many others near the top presumably had little choice but to admit that "age crepeth on me dayly and febleth all the bodye," as Caxton had lamented, even though they were still short of their three score and ten.

As the peers aged they might seek excuses from parliament, but otherwise they rarely lodged complaints about age and its accompanying woes. Nor, as we suggested, can we confidently accept all the complaints they did register about age and decrepitude at face value. On the other hand, who would deny some element of truth behind the excuse granted to lord Sudeley: "corporis sui debilitate, ac senio variisque: infirmitatibus adeo contractus existit." After all, there really were lots of old men among the peers, and their active lives had begun early and often had been strenuous, not to say dangerous.

Table 8-2 gives a list of peers who were granted excused absences from Lords, along with some career-length data. Obviously, some of the men got their dispensation when they were well on in years. However, only the earl of Oxford was singled out when actually within a few years of death, and in his case it was an execution, not failing health, that ended his career. For most of the men there was a reasonable interval between the excuse to withdraw and death, though peers such as lord Sudeley or Beauchamp of Powis or lord Vesci were getting on when excused; 67, 47, and 68 respectively.

TABLE 8-2.   Peers Who Received Excuses to be Absent from Parliament

John de la Warre (c.1345–1398): Excused for life 11/1382 and 10/1397: bad
    sight
Richard FitzAlan, Earl of Arundel (1346-x1397): Exempted for life, 4/1394
    (because of political disfavor)
Aubrey de Vere, Earl of Oxford (1340–1400): Excused 11/1397 because of
    incurable infirmity
Thomas de la Warre (c. 1355–1427): Granted 3-year absence, 1/1402
William Lovell (1397–1455): Excused 2/1446 because of long royal service;
    Excused for life, 5/1453, because of infirmity
John Tuchet, Lord Audley (1398-x1459): Excused for life, 10/1447
Henry Bromflete, Lord Vesci (c. 1390–1469): Excused for life, 5/1456;
    Exemption renewed, 2/1462
John de Vere, Earl of Oxford (1408-x1462): Excused, 11/1460, because of in-
    firmity and good service
Ralph Butler, Lord Sudeley (c. 1395–1474): Excused 2/1462 for life because of
    age and weakness
John, Lord Beauchamp of Powick (c. 1417–1475): Excused 10/1462 because of
    old age and debility
Fulk Bourgchier, Lord FitzWarin (1445–1479): Excused from attendance,
    5/1474

Based on Roskell, "The Problem of the Attendance of the Lords in Medieval Parliaments,"
Bulletin of the Institute of Historical Research 29 (1956): 201–4.

The table supports the picture of long service as a regular part, or concomitant attribute, of a long life. Lords de la Warre, Bromflete (lord Vesci), and Boteler (lord Sudeley) had already been into years of middle age when first summoned, and between their first summonses and the excused absence they had put in terms of 3, 7, and 21 years. Obviously, most of their years of service — especially for the first two — were already behind them when they reached the peerage. One further consideration, beyond our immediate concern here but worth mention; except for the earl of Oxford, the men tallied in the table were minor peers, holding minor peerages. Lord Fitz-warin, who died at 34 in any event, was a member of the extensive Bourgchier family, and his inclusion on the list of the excuse-seekers probably testifies to ill health or the onset of a fatal ailment. Otherwise no one here was a name to conjure with; perhaps the old age and disabilities were easier to accept when the petition was from a minor peer. The major peers either enjoyed better health or were less inclined to seek escape from their wonted duties, no matter what their disabilities. They were needed, regardless of their condition; *noblesse oblige* once had a literal meaning.

TABLE 8-3.   Age of Peers in Some Fifteenth-Century Parliaments

	Ages					
Parliament	20–29	30–39	40–49	50–59	60+	Total
1406	13	12	6	9	1	41
1429	11	12	7	2	1	33
1453	6	17	11	16	6	56
1482	7	9	12	4	10	42
Totals	37	50	36	31	18	172
	22%	29%	21%	18%	10%	

Since peers were often summoned before they were of legal age, for simplicity in compiling these tables ages are just by decades; there is no distinction, for younger men, between "not yet 21" and "21 and more." The data are extracted from *CP* and *Lords Report on the Dignity of a Peer* (London: House of Lords, 1829), vol. 4.

Against these glimpses and claims of infirmity and disability we can also set a very different picture, one of vigor and sustained participation. If we look at some fifteenth century parliaments we can see how the old men in the aristocratic ranks regularly comprised a fair percentage of those summoned (though their presence in these parliaments actually comes to a lower percentage than their overall survival rate in the peerage). The data are presented in Table 8-3. The peers summoned to the Parliaments of 1406, 1429, 1453, and 1482 give us an aggregate of 172 men. Of these, 37 (22 percent of the group) were in their 20s when summoned to the relevant session, 50 (29 percent) in their 30s, 36 (21 percent) in their 40s, 31 (18 percent) in their 50s, and 18 (10 percent) in or beyond their 60s. In each parliament elderly presence could vary from a single peer (of the 41 summoned in 1406 and the 33 in 1429) to 10 (of 42; 24 percent of the Lords) in 1482. So in simplistic terms the old men were an obvious and regular part of public and political life. In a world of hereditary and life-long honors we would expect this. Nor is there any reason to think that contemporaries found it strange, in so far as they noted and remarked on such matters.[32]

Beyond their presence and role in parliaments, most of the peers were heavily involved, through life, in public life and service, far beyond the mere question of attendance. At least half of those who lived to 60 or beyond played some specific role in the king's service when in their mid-50s and later; the average life span — which they obviously exceeded — was not their quitting point. Sustained and prolonged service, as a theme, is a good foil to set against that of retirement and withdrawal. Tasks undertaken by, or imposed upon, aging peers ranged from the ceremonial to the dangerous. At various times their duties brought men of 55 or 60 or more to the judicial bench, the county circuit, or the battlefields of France and the northern borders.

Sometimes the burdens seem appropriate for an old man; honor and few heavy labors. There were presumably no strenuous demands placed on the earl of Arundel when he served as steward at the coronations of Richard III and shortly afterward of Henry VII. Lord Berkeley was an old man when he carried the sword of state on ceremonial occasions for Henry VII, and he was earl marshal for Henry's queen. Lord Grey of Ruthin, almost 70, bore the second sword at Richard III's coronation, while the aged duke of Norfolk acted as the royal steward. Norfolk came to this affair fresh from having borne the great banner at Edward IV's funeral: "the lord Howard, the kinges bannerer, rode next before the fore horse, bering the kinges baner upon a courser traped with blacke velvet with dyvers scochons of the kinges armes, with his morning bode upon his hede."[33]

Ceremonial tasks were easy to perform, and elderly peers rallied to such calls. Indeed, peers were jealous of their prerogatives; to be passed over on such occasions was a slight, not easily forgotten even were a man covered with years. But many of these same aging peers, alongside innumerable rivals and lesser and younger aristocrats, were also needed for difficult and dangerous work; elderly lords of the realm and the field of battle were hardly strangers. When Henry Fitzhugh prepared to go to France in 1417 he was charged to lead a company of four knights, 55 esquires, and 180 archers: 60 on foot, 120 mounted. Lord Grey, in his 60s, brought 20 men at arms and 60 archers to Henry V's campaigns, and Grey continued to serve overseas under Bedford after the king's death. The aged lord Stourton was a commissioner in Wiltshire, "to urge the king's subjects . . . to supply ships well equipped with men, victuals, and habiliments of war for half a year at their own expense for defense against the king's enemies of France and elsewhere."[34]

Elderly peers had played roles of distinction with Edward III and the Black Prince, and their heirs and successors expected to heed a similar summons to duty in the later stages of the wars. Though men of good birth regularly seem to have taken up arms at 14 or 15 — and we saw in the Scrope and Grosvenor depositions that they were wont to boast about their early prowess — they also stayed in harness forever, given health and strength. Lord Grey was about 63 when he entered into the duties just mentioned,

and Bonville but a year or two his junior when he became lieutenant of
Aquitaine, a thankless task in 1453, the year it all came apart. At least several
elderly peers had served as admiral, though it is not clear how laborious the
post really was. Most distinguished of all the captains was the earl of
Shrewsbury, the only elderly peer to die on the field in France. The last
15 years of his life were virtually the story of the English cause, his death but
the logical conclusion to his service.[35] The Scottish border campaigns
mostly involved men of the north, but again elderly peers with ties north of
the Trent were called to service, often on short notice. Henry Percy, aged
about 61, led the English forces at Homildon Hill in 1402, though the consequences of that day eventually led to rebellion and the long eclipse of the
Percys.

     If warfare at or beyond English borders was waged with the active aid
of old men, we can expect to find them playing their share in the rebellions,
civil dissensions, and organized violence that became a growth industry
through the countryside. Lord Fauconberge, at age 60, was in the van for
Henry VI at Northampton in 1460. The duke of Norfolk fought with Richard III until the 75-year-old peer fell at Bosworth. The earl of Warwick,
disgraced and broken by Richard II when in his late 50s, returned to enjoy
a new day under Henry IV at Shrewsbury in 1403; he was now about 60
and was enjoying a new lease on life. Lord Morley, aged 59, was ordered
to guard the coasts against the French. Scrope of Bolton stood against
Henry VII on behalf of Lambert Simnel at York in 1487; he lived to repent
of his ways and to serve the Tudors on the northern borders while in
his 60s.

     There were others of this group who played their parts in the tur-
moil — and its suppression — that befell the realm after 1399. We have little
reason to think that men in good health ever lost their interest in the martial
duties that were a natural channel for those of their rank. Obligations were
the "flip side" of privilege, the dangers of leading an armed host but part of
the peculiar perquisites of aristocratic rank. Faint hearts may have held men
back at times, but for those so inclined only the real pains of age and the
deathbed kept them from the fray. Of course, we cannot learn from this
kind of survey what proportion of men of arms and archers were on the far
side of 40. The troops raised (in *Henry IV*) by Shallow and led by Falstaff
contained their fair share of the superannuated and the semi-disabled. What
are the links between Elizabethan poetic commentary and Lancastrian recruiting? Certainly Shakespeare's depiction of the levy carries a convincing
ring, and perhaps we can take seriously the view he presents of the mortal

men who came forward to fill a trench.

This glimpse at aspects of public life gives an idea of the diverse services old men of rank might be called on to offer. But this job-specific
approach fails to convey the idea of sustained vitality that might be encompassed within a single career. For this we can turn to some case studies, and
lord Fitzhugh (c. 1358–1425) lends himself with distinction. The last 16 years
of his life are a tale of almost constant service at a prominent and strenuous
level. Beginning in 1410, when in his early 50s, he was a commissioner of
peace with Scotland, constable of England at Henry V's coronation, envoy
to the Council of Constance, a recipient of estates confiscated from Scrope
of Masham after the Southampton plot of 1415, a royal companion in ac-
tions at Harfleur and Agincourt, a leader of the army at Rouen in 1418–19,
and an active participant at the sieges of Melun and Meaux in 1420 and
1422.[36] In addition, he was treasurer of the exchequer from 1417 to 1422,
captain of Falaise in 1422, an executor of Henry V's will, and finally a guardian of the infant Henry VI and a member of the duke of Gloucester's council of regency.

This listing of Fitzhugh's offices, plus a few more minor positions and
favors, makes an impressive tally. When Fitzhugh died in 1425, aged about
66, he was invested with an eminence that little in his early or middle years
had hinted at. Personal friendship with Henry IV and Henry V had probably been the original thrust behind his emergence, and as he served the
throne it became clear that his ability and trustworthiness were in no way
diminished by his advancing years; if anything his usefulness was enhanced
by his ever-growing list of res gestae and years of experience. Seniority and
a commendable record of service rendered strengthened his hand; one job,
well done, led to the next. He must have had considerable reserves of energy to refuel the aging machine. But in his missions in these years he also
had good fortune as he aged; a recent study of his career reminds us that,
"like Henry V, Lord Fitzhugh has been away for three and a half years [in
France], and as a man in his fifties in the fifteenth century he must have
despaired at times of seeing England ever again."[37]

If Fitzhugh presents a striking case for a career that really flourished
after 50, it is not so different except for its exceptional prominence from
that of Thomas, II lord Camoys (1360–1421), and for sustained service few
could match Henry Bourgchier, earl of Essex, with his long stretches, while
an elderly man, as a "hands-on" treasurer. If a man had good health and his
political sun shone, he could go on indefinitely. An assessment of Bourgchier's service as treasurer, in 1455, 1460, and finally from April 1471 for

12 years, shows that his control of the office grew and that he was able to implement his own policies as seniority increased his stature.[38] By his third term he could exact greater profits and demand a freer hand in dealing with state issues. Furthermore, his long term of office was followed by a comparable run for his successor, lord Dynham. Dynham lived from 1434 to 1501 and he served Henry VII from 1486 until the year of his own death. The lesson here, regarding the long reliance on men of age and experience, was presumably not lost on their contemporaries.

There are other sides to the question of public life and public careers, and we shall look at some other questions when other groups are being scrutinized. There is the matter of the relation between the stages of experience and progress through the life cycle. Because of the picture of medieval life as being nasty, brutish, and short, we might assume that people dashed to embrace the full variety of life experiences as quickly and as early as possible. And yet our detailed studies hardly argue in this direction. We are reasonably comfortable with the view that marriage was deferred until people were well into their 20s. This meant that there would always be some considerable fraction of youth dying before and without marriage, as others would marry and produce children but not live to see old age or grandchildren. There were no guarantees about the range of yet-to-be-tested experiences, any more than there were about fertility, or longevity.

An analogous point emerges from a study of the peers. Can we judge whether they — or others of their age — thought they had had a fair innings? or did they go to the grave chafing over a too-quick hand and against rules that cut them off at every turn? What did life bring, and when? A fair number of new peerages went to men well into middle age. For them, at least, an active life that had begun with early service brought its final reward on the farther side of the hill. Some surprises, even for men well beyond the salad days of youth and early maturity, were not out of the question.

We talked about the three Somerset knights whose mobility carried them, when well into their middle years, to peerages. They were not the only men to bask in late-afternoon sunshine. John Wenlock rose to prominence as speaker of Commons and the king's loyal servant and chief butler.[39] He became a Knight of the Garter at 60, a peer of the realm a year or so later. Thomas, I lord Burgh, had been elected to Commons in 1467 and again in 1478; his initial summons as a peer only came in 1487. Different lives and different patterns; Wenlock's tale is a pretty full turn of the wheel compared to the storybook exploits of such precocious young men as William the Marshall or the Black Prince. But there are many rooms in the mansion of aristocracy, and in some at least the elderly were welcome.

If one was almost never too old to take a step forward, conversely it seems one was never so old that everything ahead was necessarily safe and secure. Age alone precluded neither an upward move nor the call to more public service. Among the surprises that advanced age occasionally brought to the feast might be violent death. Of the fifteenth-century peers (summoned 1399–1500), a full 29 percent — 66 men of 225 — died by some form of violence, mostly on the battlefield. Of these deaths, 16 came to men in the 50s, seven to men in their 60s, and two to men who had reached 70. The first Howard duke of Norfolk was a staunch Yorkist, and he died — honorably if foolishly — at Bosworth, aged about 75.[40] Lord Wenlock — he who came to his peerage so late — was about 71 when he fell at Tewkesbury. The earl of Northumberland died at the battle of St. Albans (and he was the son and grandson of men who had also died violent deaths), a Lancastrian casualty of high rank; Bonville died after the second battle there, a Yorkist loss; both men were over 60. The earl Rivers was in his 60s when executed by Edward IV after Edgecot, and Audley of comparable years when he died at Blore Heath. Lord Scales went a different route, lynched by a London mob that took exception in 1460 to his devotion to the House of Lancaster. And somewhat earlier in the century the two Percy brothers, Northumberland and Worcester, had died as a result of the family's break with Henry IV. They had both been well past middle age when drawn to the deep waters of rebellion. We noted the death of Shrewsbury in France. Clearly, while gray hair might earn respect it was not a reliable prophylactic against reprisals.

In a perverse way, violent or unnatural death — whether at the hands of a lynch mob or in the heat of battle — was a tribute to the vigor and the continuity of the threat posed by the old man. Even at age 60 or 65 (or more) he could represent such a serious challenge, and drive it home with such energy, that there was only one sure way to render him harmless, to close the ledger on his debits and credits. Nor was the fifteenth century particularly cold blooded about its elder statesmen. When Henry IV came to the throne men had seen a decade in which a number of elderly peers had either died or had just managed to escape with their heads atop their shoulders. The earl of Warwick, as we noted, had been exiled to the Isle of Man after facing the threat of execution. Lord Cobham had been impeached, and he was only allowed back from Jersey when Bolingbroke reversed the swing of the pendulum. The aged Scrope of Bolton had left Richard II's court in disfavor because of his criticism of the king's policies; in turn, he now had to grovel before Henry IV because of the political sins of his eldest son, the earl of Wiltshire, Richard II's favorite. One was never so old that complete security could be assured just by the weight of one's years.

Death on the field at Bosworth or Tewkesbury is not the kind of activity we associate with old-age behavior. But we know there does not seem to be any such entity as "typical old age behavior." Neither continuing participation, nor retirement and withdrawal, can be termed *the* characteristic behavior. Neither is there much to support any idea that these men and women turned to religion and religious activity.[41] Religiosity or personal religion is a complex of responses and initiatives, some quite routinized, others more individualized and idiosyncratic.[42] When we look for such striking forms of activity as the creation and foundation of regular houses or hospitals and schools, on the part of elderly peers, we come away with little for our efforts. The creation and erection of new institutions by laymen was unusual in the fifteenth century—whether we look at the peers or the bourgeoisie—and beyond a few smallish establishments there were few ventures on a par with Suffolk's mid-century foundation at Ewelme. Few people of any group, let alone those of a particular age bracket, step forward as founders of great magnificence. In so far as there really is behavior we can call the "sociology of endowment," family commitment and local tradition, not age, served to open hearts and purse strings. The wills of the elderly peers bespeak a customary and respectful nod to the church and to pious uses, but not much in the direction of any striking pattern of donation and foundation. Few extremes of behavior or of magnificence are to be found.

In this respect, as in most others, elderly aristocrats were much like other people—noble or common, old or young—except that they moved on a public stage and their faults and virtues, as well as their fortunes and their ages, were writ large on the public consciousness. Age and survival prolonged their public and family roles, but they do not seem to have reshaped them in any arresting fashion. We are what we are, pretty much through the course of the life cycle. Of course, some of us hold on for much longer.

9

Another Case Study: The Bishops

THE PEERS OFFERED mixed returns when their longevity and survival were put under the lens. There were tendencies and examples, to be sure, but uneven life spans and changing circumstances make it hard to generalize about characteristics or ideology that invariably go hand-in-hand with old age. After all, another study could be carried out on peers who died before age 40. To "compare and contrast" we can turn to the episcopate and pose a similar list of questions about careers and old age. By now we are more than ready to accept that there is no single pattern of typical old age behavior or activity. But bishops, by comparison with the hereditary peers, had for the most part to work their way up the great ladder of careerism. For them — perhaps like those new peers from Somerset — success and longevity were, to some extent, linked variables. This also means that the bishops were likely to be, by comparison, an even older universe or population. Except for those few men of aristocratic birth, along with an occasional boy wonder, some years of prior service to both the secular and the ecclesiastical establishment were the customary sine qua non for advancement.[1]

Nor was such service, with the experience and patronage it attracted, accomplished overnight. Accordingly, most men only began their episcopal careers when they were well toward age, and as a group the bishops were considerably older than the peers of a given parliament.

But even survival and upward mobility or career-ladder success are not uni-causal or uni-directional. No matter how talented and well connected one might be at the beginning of a career, if one did not survive a certain number of years one did not live to become a bishop; innumerable young clerics seemed to be on their way when early mortality (or a wrong step) ended the tale. If the climb that eventually brought a select few to a bishopric began in the late teens or early twenties, and if 15 or 20 years of "pre-episcopal" service were the average for the prior career, then we can see that survival to at least 35 or 40 was pretty much a prerequisite for episcopal appointment. These calculations are cut near the minima; many men had many more years behind them. As a group bishops were survivors — whatever else they had in common — and those of 35 or 40 years of age, with 15 years of prior experience, were at the low end of the spectrum when we look at them as a group. Whether they were old men (even at the beginning, let alone at the end) and how active were their oldest representatives are questions to discuss.

There was a general strategy to the forging of an episcopal career, though exceptions to every element and stage of the process are not hard to find. As a group they were well educated, with first or second (or third) degrees from Oxford and Cambridge as fairly standard credentials.[2] Most of the secular clerics who rose to the episcopacy had served lengthy apprenticeships in royal and ecclesiastical administration, and for many the latter field took a distinct second place in terms of priorities. Eventually — for those who comprise our universe of winners — service and good connections might lead to an episcopal nomination. In some instances men then drifted away from their secular roles and concentrated thereafter on spiritual concerns. In most cases, however, the two careers were juggled for some years, though near the end there often was a twilight period in which secular responsibilities were abandoned. It was only in his time of disgrace that Wolsey visited York.

The length of the career or service years of a peer was mainly a function of longevity: he began young, and he then ran, walked, or limped pretty much to the end, whenever that came. The sum of a bishop's career — the combination of pre-episcopal and episcopal years — was shaped by the age at which he entered the church as well as when he left it. Since most of the bishops had academic backgrounds and are readily tracked in Emden's biographical registers, we can usually pick up the date for the first appointment to a benefice or sinecure.[3] Such dates in Table 9-4 below allow us to chart career lengths. When we have the date for ordination we see that it usually comes some few years after the inception of the clerical career. While ordination could come at 21, most men who were seriously on the make had begun to receive nominations to prebends and other positions — livings and sinecures that did not entail a cure of souls — when barely at or even below age 20.

That nominations preceded ordination does not change the overall picture, but it indicates a range of variation on mobility that will be borne out when we turn to cases. John Catterick became a priest in 1398, and in the same year he held his first vicarage and was listed as a magister of Oxford. Likewise, John Carpenter, a rector since 1422, was ordained in 1424 (though he had been a fellow of Oriel College since 1417). Others had to wait a bit. Richard Courtenay, of aristocratic birth and inordinate speed in his ascent of the ladder, held his first living (in absentia) when only nine, although — even with a dispensation — he was not ordained until in his 19th year. John Morton received his bachelor's degree in canon law in 1448, his first living in 1453, his ordination in 1453.

Once within the church, or once ordained, the future career rolls before us as a well paved highroad to success, with a first plateau of the pre-episcopal years and then the heady uplands of the episcopacy. Not everyone, however, was destined for a very long journey. Just as some bishops rose early, so some came to their end while still short of any years that would mark middle, let alone old age. Obviously, a short life meant a short career. Richard Courtenay (1381–1415) received his first benefice in 1392 and became a bishop in 1413; George Neville (1432–76) passed these milestones in 1452 and 1458; Robert Neville (1404–57) in 1413 and 1427; Lionel Wydville (1453–84) became a bishop in 1482. These men were from exalted families and their careers began when they were of shockingly few years. Such early entry into the church might launch a career that actually wound up covering some reasonable number of years (except for Lionel Wydeville) because of the early start rather than because of even average longevity. However, had these aristocratic bishops lived full lives, as did Henry Beaufort, the final tally might well have been most impressive.[4]

Those who did become bishops and survived did very well. They rose from the pack of young Oxford and Cambridge men and of newly ordained priests; they survived the appreciable span of pre-episcopal service; they ultimately reached those years where experience and maturity — along with erudition and political acumen — began to commend them for further advancement and promotion. How long were their total careers? In Table 9-1 we see the distribution, by decades. We have useable starting points for 70 men (from a total of 91). About one third of the bishops had total careers of less than 30 years, with poor Lionel Wydville standing first in the line of the shorter careers, which runs from his 9 to the 28 of William Barrows or William Dudley or the 29 of Robert Hallum. Thus two thirds of the bishops for whom we have information put in 30 or more years, which also means that two thirds of them lived to something like the end of their fifth decade, if not longer. As is often the case with these simple statistics, if we look at the far end — as we did with the peers — we can find impressive evi-

TABLE 9-1.   Length of Bishops' Ecclesiastical Careers, by Decades

Number of bishops	Years					
	<10	10–19	20–29	30–39	40–49	50+
	1	4	17	14	23	11
	1.4%	5.7%	24.2%	20%	32.8%	15.7%

Source: E. B. Fryde, D. E. Greenway, S. Porter, and I. Roy, eds., *Handbook of British Chronology* (London: Royal Historical Society, 1986).

dence regarding the length of service and survival. Almost half our men had careers of over 40 years: one third (32.8 percent) served the church (and other masters) between 40 and 49 years, and one sixth (15.7 percent) for more than 50. Men with 40-year careers were surely close to or beyond 60, at the end, and those with more than a half century of labor would often have gone past 70 or even 80.

Survival or life span is an absolute, whether we can pin it down or not. The two bishops lynched by the disaffected citizenry, William Aiscough and Adam Moleyns, had presumably hoped for further years of service, as of survival. Aiscough had been an MA from Oxford by 1423, and became bishop of Salisbury in 1438. His activity on behalf of the government during Henry VI's majority was extensive, and as the king's confessor he had officiated at Henry's marriage to Margaret of Anjou in 1445. He had a pre-episcopal career of nine years, 12 as a bishop, and he probably was not much over 50 at his death. His loyalty toward the queen and the duke of Suffolk led to such unpopularity that by his death, by a lynch mob in 1450, he was "evil beloved among the commune peple and mikle suspect of meny defautes."[5] Moleyns was a bit younger. His BCL from Oxford came around 1430 and he became bishop of Chichester in 1445. His active role in government also led him into Suffolk's camp, and he was mobbed and put to death on 9 January, 1450 by aggrieved commoners. Reginald Pecock of Chichester was not murdered, but rather forced to resign his bishopric; he seems to have died shortly after he stepped down. When he resigned in September 1458, he had 34 years of service behind him: 26 before he became a bishop, 8 after episcopal nomination. It seems likely that the disgrace and rough treatment of his demotion hardly added to his years, and he was dead by 1460, probably only aged about 55 or a little more.[6]

Men for whom we have information regarding the episcopal career but not the pre-episcopal years have not been included in Table 9-1. We can make some educated guesses for many of the 21 not included, but there is little certainty. Many of them were regulars or mendicants, and the date of their entry into the church is hard to determine. This is the case for Reginald Boulers of Hereford and then of Coventry and Lichfield (8 years as a bishop in the two sees), John Langdon of Rochester (12 years of episcopal service), John Low of (St. Asaph and) Rochester (23 years), Robert Mascall of Hereford (12 years), Thomas Milling of Hereford (18 years), Stephen Patrington of (St. Davids and) Chichester (died in the year of his nomination), Thomas Peverell of Worcester (12 years), Philip Repingdon of Lincoln (20 years), Thomas Spofford of Hereford (34 years), and John Stanbury of Hereford (20 years) are among the men omitted from Table 9-1. That their episcopal careers are slightly below average — 16 years against a general average of 19, though the numbers would be close to even were it not for Patrington's quick exit — indicates that they had been of good age when nominated. What we can piece together concerning their pre-episcopal careers confirms the impression of longish service and the onset of middle age, at least, by the time they were elevated to the episcopacy.

At the far end some bishops' careers were extremely impressive in their longevity; in a few cases this might seem their main claim to fame. Richard Bell was probably well into his 60s when he became bishop of Carlisle in 1478. He had been at Durham College, Oxford, in the early 1430s, prior of Holy Trinity, York in 1441–43, prior of Finchale in 1457–65, and prior of Durham for 15 years before episcopal nomination finally came.[7] This is an extraordinary story of survival and of service. And yet, if Bell was extreme in his pre-episcopal service, it was only by a matter of degree. Reginald Boulers became abbot of Gloucester in 1437, bishop of Hereford in 1451. Though we cannot pick him up before he rose within his monastery, Gloucester was a great house and Boulers presumably moved up on the basis of a proven track record. From his first episcopal appointment — for he was translated to Coventry and Lichfield in 1453 — he only lived for eight years. Other careers also leave few traces but comparable hints of considerable experience.

Robert Mascall, a Carmelite, received his doctorate in theology before he became bishop of Hereford; John Low had been a deacon for 30 years before being nominated to St. Asaph, 41 before his translation to Rochester; Philip Repingdon's ordination preceded his elevation to Lincoln by 35 years, his doctorate in theology by 22. No doubt as a consequence of these long pre-episcopal careers, the regulars were among those bishops who sought the relief afforded by retirement.[8] Some of the men for whom we have inadequate information are those without a record of a university affiliation, and efforts to ferret out the full record of their pre-episcopal service and careerism do not go very far. For these men the length of the episcopate varied considerably. If we are fairly confident about the overall career, and thus of the life span of Thomas Langley (with 31 years at Durham) or Edward Story (35 years at Carlisle and Chichester), we need caution for such men as William Wells (8 years at Rochester), or Alexander Tottington (7 years at Norwich), or John Bottlesham (4 years at Rochester).

The careers of the "forty-year men" give us an entrée into careerism and service at its most sustained and impressive level. The 23 men in this group had ecclesiastical careers that averaged 45.5 years, which means, by extension, life spans that would have taken them at least into their early 60s, if not well beyond. We can look at the relationship between survival and career mobility by comparing the portion of the 46-year career spent in pre-episcopal service with that ensconced in full episcopal dignity. The average span of pre-episcopal service rendered by the 40-year men was 24 years, that of episcopal service about 21 years. The figures for all the bishops (Table 9-1), argue for a roughly even division between the two career segments. For the long survivors, at least, episcopal promotion came when they were probably in their mid- or late 40s, and how long they lasted after that was their own concern. However, the tabular presentation (Table 9-4) indicates that only 11 of these 23 men had careers that were within a decade of even balance between the two halves, and in most cases the discrepant length between the two halves was by more than a decade.

Sometimes the long career was skewed because a man served a shortish pre-episcopal term and then proved to be extremely durable, once promoted. If Cardinal Beaufort is our extreme case (with career segments of 9 and 49 years) we can also see it with Richard Fox (5 and 41 years), John Kempe (12 and 35 years), Edmund Audley (16 and 44 years), and Robert Neville (14 and 30 years). But there are other possibilities. A man might be old and heavy with years and service below the episcopal level, and yet still manage, near the end, to reach a bishopric. John Rickinghall offers an extreme case: 45 years in the church before he became a bishop, only 3 afterward. There are also Robert Gilbert (34 and 12 years), Simon Sydenham (40 and 7 years), William Strickland (32 and 14 years), and Thomas Brouns (31 and 10 years). If these are dramatic examples, it is still of interest to note that few men had the symmetrical career of Thomas Beckington (24 and 22 years) or Richard Clifford (21 and 20 years) or William Grey (23 and 24 years) or Richard Stillington (23 and 25 years). Early advancement and early death were powerful forces, and whether apart or in tandem they made the uncertainties of career advancement but one chapter in the book of the uncertainties of our worldly span.

There are some built-in dangers to this kind of statistical argument. In a world where pre-episcopal careers average 19.6 years, men with 40-year careers had already put in a full span of service *and in addition* proceeded to live a long time after they became bishops. Of the 23 men with 40-49 years of service, 17 had had pre-episcopal service of 20 years or more, running in seven instances to more than 30 years. This is an elaborate way of saying that a long life was a prerequisite to a long career. Many who had already served an above-average apprenticeship were likewise blessed by a good run while on an episcopal throne. The average years of episcopal service for all the bishops is 17.4 years. The 23 40-year men put in, on the average, 21 years. So they ran a bit beyond average in each segment; evidently really long careers were often put together by combining two segments each of which was by itself at or above average length. Of course, deviation from the mean is considerable, and among the 40-year men there are some extremes, noted above.

If the bishops with total careers of 40–49 years give us some idea of how service and survival were linked, what about the eleven men with careers of more than 50 years? The possibility of a pre-episcopal career of average length, subsequently linked to exceptional longevity once raised to a bishopric, seems a likely one for some men. We see it with Edmund Audley, who served 16 years before becoming a bishop, 44 afterward; Henry Bowet, 31 and then 22 years; John Carpenter, 22 and 32; Henry Chichele, 23 and 29; John Hales, 22 and 40; Thomas Kempe, 17 and 39; Edmund Lacy, 17 and 38. Audley, Kempe, and Lacy were a bit below average in the first segment, but not by any great margin.

Other paths lead to the same destination. William Waynfleet had already spent 31 years in the church, between his first rectorship (in 1416) and his nomination to Winchester in 1447. That he managed to live and hold his see until 1486 is another matter, presumably unforseen in the 1440s and 1450s. Henry Beaufort is also exceptional, but his career division of nine pre-episcopal years, 49 episcopal ones is of note.[9] His brief span of early service was what we would expect, given his birth and expectations, but he did live to put in a half-century of service to church and government, a model of survival that poor Lionel Wydville might have envied when his failing health, at an early age, indicated a short albeit glorious rise. At the other end of the queue is Richard Bell, with his long career as a regular cleric. He served his church for about 47 years before being named to Carlisle, and he still was good for another 18 years. Having waited so long, he was not going to let go of the prize once it had finally come.

For the peers two phenomena or patterns of behavior interested us: evidence of sustained activity through life and any indication of what we might characterize as activity peculiar to or commonly associated with the elderly. We came away with a picture that showed diversity and individuality. Secular figures, whether of exalted social status or drawn from the bourgeoisie, had such considerations as family continuity and the link between a man and his heirs to keep in mind when the end drew near. Whether it was the transmission of the duke of Norfolk's worldly position, or the shoemaker at the corner, with his shop and good will, the inheritance and those affected by the accompanying decisions loomed large in the world view of the aged.

Bishops carried a different perspective as part of their intellectual and conceptual baggage. Many a high ranking churchman showed a finely honed sense of family feeling, as we know from the Booth family. But was such family feeling likely to be enhanced or heightened by survival and longevity?[10] While bishops often left family bequests, it is difficult to argue that elderly men outstripped younger ones in any consistent fashion when we look at such behavior. On the other hand, we have alluded to a career pattern wherein a slowing down was to be noted in his secular activities, along with an inclination to turn to spiritual obligations. Unfortunately, ecclesiastical records tend to be fairly obscure concerning personal roles in diocesan administration, and an active record of visitations and adjudications can be built, to a great extent, on the backs of capable subordinates. But this does not rule out the possibility that the absence of precise information about a bishop's later-day activities reflects a slower pace and a diminishing level of involvement.

Among the men who posted long careers and long lives we can find signs of their recognition that body and/or mind did indeed wear out. We looked at the excused absences from the House of Lords and we noted how they intersected with the dates and milestones of careers. Some problems proved to be but temporary, and men returned to full duty. But some were truly entering the terminal phases of their careers by the time the king was moved to exempt them, and for them the morrow would be even quieter,

TABLE 9-2. Bishops Granted Excused Absences from Parliament

Bishop	Pre-episcopal career (years)	Became a bishop	Excused	Died
Lacy, Edm	17	1417	2/1435	1455
Heyworth	—	1419	12/1439	1447
Aiscough	9	1438	7/1445	1450x
Moleyns	22	1445	12/1449	1450x
Beckington	24	1443	6/1452	1465
Lyhert	19	1446	2/1460	1472
Booth, L	17	1457	4/1464	1480
Booth, Wm	31	1447	8/1464	1464
Arundel, J	29	1459	9/1474	1477

Source: John S. Roskell, "The Problem of the Attendance of the Lords in Medieval Parliaments," *BIHR* 29 (1956): 153–204.

marked by greater debility, than the present. The bishops present a comparable tale.

Of the nine men who received excuses, all but Aiscough pleaded some problem relating to health, age, and the strains of service. However, only three of the men—Moleyns, William Booth, and John Arundel—were within five years (or less) of death when they were allowed to withdraw.[11] Lacy had trouble with his shins, whatever that meant in medical terms, but his condition improved and he returned to full service. The others were clearly getting on. Heyworth referred to "ill health and old age," Bekington spoke of "age and infirmity,"[12] Lyhert was moved to mention his "age and long royal service." They were no longer young men, to be sure, and they already had a good generation of public life and service behind them; their complaints had enough merit to be taken seriously. If they were not as far gone as they claimed, their requests for excused absence do testify to some contemporary sympathy for wear and tear. When William Booth sought his excuse he was at the end of 50 years of labors for the northern church, his monarchs, and the Booth family enterprise. But his age was real, his failing condition beyond dispute.

Ill health, of a disabling sort, was hardly to be wondered at by the time we reach the later chapters of some of these long lives. The durations of some careers indicate how many really old men are encompassed by a discussion of the episcopate. Given the proportion of men with 40 and 50 years of service, the bishops are properly be seen as a tough and durable collection, though not all who suffered were among those who endured. George Neville's ill health became serious when he was only about 40, and he died, a young man, though already archbishop of York. There was nothing remarkable about William Grey's problems. His health gave way, at the end of a long career, and shortly before his death he was acknowledged to be beyond much value to his church or his king.[13] John Kempe had a short pre-episcopal career (12 years), but he then began a career of translation from bishopric to bishopric: Rochester in 1419, Chichester in 1421, London that same year, York in 1425, and Canterbury in 1452. His health broke about the time of his final promotion, and a career that included active and courageous opposition to the rebels in Kent in 1450 ran down quickly at the end. He was archbishop of Canterbury for a mere 20 months, and after largely absentee service in York he was able to give almost none at all to his second province. Robert Stillington was in the church for almost 50 years, but he was in considerable trouble in his later years. His proclamation of Edward V as illegitimate won him little popularity at the time, nor did it sit well with Henry VII. He was arrested in 1485 and his old age, as much as anything else, helped procure a pardon.

When we covered the peers we presented some cross sections from various parliaments to gauge how old the peerage was at any given time. We can do this for the bishops, using the parliaments of 1406, 1429, 1453, and 1482, though the material is less precise because career-beginnings, rather than birth dates, are usually the best we can do for starting points. Given the age and experience of the sitting bishops, it is no wonder that excused absences and the cruel teeth of ill health had to be taken into regular account; indeed, we might wonder at how many old men retained their vigor.[14]

John Carpenter had been ordained a priest in 1421 and he had been bishop of Worcester since 1444. Shortly before his death in 1476 he sought permission to resign his office. It had been a long life: he had played a role in Joan of Arc's trial in 1431. Philip Repingdon, once a follower of Wycliffe, had served comparable years to Carpenter, ordained in 1369, a bishop since 1404, now seeking permission in 1419 to withdraw. His efforts were supported, and in February, 1420 Martin V accepted his resignation. His pension was set at 300 marks and then increased to 500 marks, so presumably he lived his last years (until his death in 1424) in comfort. He asked for "burial naked in a sack," in the churchyard of St. Margaret, Lincoln; he was buried, as we would expect, in Lincoln cathedral.[15] Thomas Spofford had been at Oxford by 1397, and abbot of St. Mary, York (1405–21) before

TABLE 9-3.   Years of Total Ecclesiastical Experience of Bishops in Some Fifteenth-Century Parliaments

Parliament	Pre-episcopal	Since episcopal nomination	Total years
1406	21.0 (n = 7)	7.6 (n = 9)	28.6
1429	14.5 (n = 9)	10.1 (n = 14)	24.6
1453	19.3 (n = 13)	10.9 (n = 16)	30.2
1482	20.7 (n = 14)	14.1 (n = 17)	34.8
Averages	19.0 (n = 43)	11.2 (n = 56)	30.2

Based on *Lords Report of the Dignity of a Peer.*

becoming bishop of Hereford in 1421. In 1448—eight years before his death—he too was allowed to resign, with an annual pension of £100. However, he had begun to seek permission for this as far back as 1429, while on a pilgrimage to Rome, and for over a decade he had been rebuffed. In 1433 he begged for special consideration, "par cause d'age come par privez et incurable infirmiteez," and was told to wait until the young king came "to greter yeres of discrecion." In 1438 his plea was because of "corpore debilis ac senio confractis," and the king endorsed his plea to the pope. But the advice from Rome (in 1442) was still that he should "in no wise resigne tyll the world be more stabelished." By that light poor Spofford would still be at Hereford. In 1444 he asked the pope to appoint a suffragan bishop, and finally in 1448 he was allowed to resign, to collect his pension of £100 per annum, and to make way for Richard Beauchamp, a young nobleman who would only be there for two years on his upward climb.[16]

John Stanbury asked to step down from Hereford in 1461, because of age and infirmity, provided he could leave office with a handsome pension. Nothing came of his negotiations, and he stayed in office until his death in 1471. He had been active against west country Lollards around 1470, so perhaps his earlier intimations of mortality had been premature. John Low, feeling the onset of mortal illness, sought to resign in 1465. Though he had royal backing, he died (in 1467) before the pope's letters arrived to arrange the matter. We think of archbishop Chichele as one of the warhorses of the church. And yet he too made inquiries, late in his career, about withdrawal, as he had outlived his contemporaries and his thoughts were turning to his endowments and family benefactions.[17]

Of the men who either inquired about or who actually reached the haven of retirement, four—Repingdon, Low, Spofford, and Stanbury— were regulars. For them diocesan service may always have seemed like a duty they had been called upon to assume rather than a primary career goal. However, whatever the realities of age and health, they were no older, and perhaps no more enfeebled, toward the end, than John Hales, who must have been pushing 80 or 85, or Waynflete, who was a good 85 at his death. And though Waynfleet was not in much evidence in political affairs in his last 15 years, his educational projects are from this twilight period.[18] By way of contrast we can look at the career of Stillington. He was a man who would have been well advised to slow down and to cultivate his pastoral garden. For playing in the politics of Richard III's accession he had to seek a pardon in November 1485, and it was only granted because of his "grete age, long infirmite, and feebleness."[19] Then he chose to dabble in the Perkin Warbeck uprising and he had to take refuge at Oxford. His presence there embarrassed the University, and he spent a year of house arrest at Windsor before he was released to a harmless old age before his death in 1491.

If some men resigned, and others were known to be suffering and fail- ing, the absence of specific information about so many others must indicate that many of them maintained some reasonable level of activity through most of the long career. In terms of service how much could be expected from men as they moved beyond their 60th birthday? As with the secular peers, the answers are mixed; from some, clearly, it was expected and ren- dered. As a group, when their levels of activity are gauged by longevity and survival, these men offer a number of basic patterns. Some would clearly have been destined for still higher things, had they not died too soon. John Catterick may have been close to 30 when he was ordained in 1398. He moved rapidly: bishop of St. Davids in 1414, of Coventry and Lichfield in 1415, and then in 1419 translated to Exeter and dead. He had been active at Constance, a royal proctor in Rome, a diplomat for Henry IV and Henry V, and a crony of Pope Martin V. He surely would have gone well beyond Exeter had he lived another decade or two. William Dudley, later in the century, came from aristocratic family and had academic, political, and diplomatic credentials. He presided over Durham for seven years be- fore his death in 1483 while still but in his mid- or late 40s.

We can impose several patterns for the overall career on those who lasted beyond the milestones of 50 years, and then of 60 and perhaps 70. The most obvious is that of the lives that display a distinct slacking off in the later years, as against those wherein the level of activity was pretty well sustained to the end. Within the first group are a good number of men who exemplify that gradual transfer of focus from the king to the church, a muting of the call to Westminster in lieu of one from the diocese. This latter course is a model that some really did follow. However, it is difficult to unravel the contemporary statements about age and we have little idea of whether the bishops themselves recognized this curve in the career line.

John Arundel was active in the affairs of Oxford and a prominent physician (serving the earl of Warwick and the king) before he became bishop of Chichester in 1459. As well as worrying about the king's chancy health in the 1450s he had spent time negotiating with the Scots. But once he went to his minor see he left few records of much public activity, and the change of government, along with advancing years and scholarly interests, took him completely out of the limelight. Henry Bowet had an even longer career: 31 years in the church before becoming a bishop, 22 afterward. He had been at King's Hall, Cambridge in the 1360s, and was a major ecclesiastical lawyer in Ely in the 1370s. His legal expertise brought him into the Lancastrian circle, and he had been condemned to death in absentia, while on the continent in the exiled Bolingbroke's retinue. It was no surprise when he was named bishop of Bath and Wells in 1404, archbishop of York in 1407. But at York he was a quiet if respectable figure, and both the records of his northern visitations and his own last will bespeak a man satisfied with the conventional definitions of pastoral office. He had left behind the one-time man of affairs and adviser to kings.[20]

A third example of this pattern is provided by James Goldwell, bishop of Norfolk from 1472 to 1499. His training was in canon law, and he had served as Kempe's commissary general and as an apostolic prothonotary. He had also worked for Edward IV and had been registrar of the Order of the Garter. Diplomatic assignments had given him experience with Brittany, Denmark, Poland, France, and Rome (as king's orator, 1468–72). But after his promotion he withdrew from government service, stayed largely in his diocese, and turned his thoughts toward his philanthropic and private projects, for instance, a handsome chantry he founded at Great Chart, Kent, his birthplace and his parents' burial site.[21]

Everyone must have slowed down, to some extent, as age took its toll. But some did so less than others, and they maintained a level of activity and involvement that put them outside the pattern we have been expounding. Richard Clifford probably lived to be about 60. Toward the end, while bishop of London, he played such a prominent role at the council of Constance that he was being mentioned as a possible candidate for the papacy. John Hales lived about 20 years longer than Clifford, and for 10 or 15 years after he became bishop of Coventry and Lichfield (in 1459, when about 50 or a bit more) he engaged in diplomatic work for Edward IV and devoted himself to reforming the administrative apparatus of his cathedral. William Waynfleet may be the champion for longevity and sustained activity, and we have remarked above on the educational and philanthropic projects that occupied his later years.

These bishops are among those for whom reasonably precise dates for the early career can be determined. For some of the regulars, had we fuller data on their earlier contributions, we could probably augment the saga of long, active careers. John Langdon was a monk at Christ Church, Canterbury by 1398, prior by 1404. Before he became bishop of Rochester in 1421 he had been at Constance, and during his 13 years as bishop he remained active; preaching at convocation in 1421 and 1428, a trier of petitions in the parliament of 1431, envoy to France in 1432–34, and at Basel, where death came upon him in September, 1434. He too might well have moved up from his minor episcopal see had he lived. He was hardly flagging toward the end.[22]

The link between age and activity we can label as old-age-specific was of interest when we looked at the secular aristocrats. The key there seems to have been family traditions more than age alone, no matter what form of activity or behavior (or even ideology) we are considering. Episcopal behavior accords with this view. The records reflect terminal concerns, rather than age-specific ones; stages-of-life decisions, not those governed simply by chronology. The various kinds of terminal enterprises — endowing chantries, building educational institutions, scattering gifts — attracted the attention and resources of those who died young or in middle age as well as of the old. The resounding footsteps of approaching death — no matter when heard — were what concentrated one's thoughts, no doubt, just as it focused one's benefactions. In many cases the activities now launched and subsidized toward the end were but the realization of projects contemplated for some years. However, this process whereby good intentions and inspirations only slowly became the solid flesh of buildings and benefactions was one that involved men who died at 30 or 40 as well as those who lasted until 60 or 70. Old age alone does not appear as a great lever for moving pious resolves to the builder's scaffold.

Bishops give us handsome returns when we tally their generosity to ecclesiastical, educational, and charitable recipients. But the issue is not whether they were generous givers and patrons; it is rather whether those who reached old age gave more than those who did not. When, in the course of the life span, were men inclined to subsidize their dreams? Their educational benefactions are easy to cover, and they indicate that mere years of survival offer little guide to philanthropic endeavor.[23] The bishops numbered some significant donors and benefactors among their ranks, and their stories are familiar: Waynfleet with his college and grammar school at Oxford, Fox as the founder of Corpus Christi College at Oxford, Chichele's various foundations and endowments, topped by All Souls College, Rotherham with his northern college, Chichele and Bourgchier with loan chests, Kempe's chantries and colleges, Audley's large gifts of cash, and others of this sort.[24]

The precise dating of the moment of foundation is not always that significant, given the piecemeal and gradualist history of efforts to endow and build. While we can pin down a charter or royal license, it can be set against the protracted process that ran from the first declaration of intent until, so often, some point well beyond the donor's death, when executors finally turned over the needed funds. New foundations were usually the creatures of long periods of concern, and it is hard to determine how much of the interval between the first mention of the project and the opening of the doors, or the distribution of the first alms or scholarships, was due to procrastination by the founder himself, how much due to the realities of this world. The college endowed by Beckington had been of interest to him for a long time; it was only built after his death.[25] Bourgchier's proposed loan chests for Oxford and Cambridge were only fully subsidized when his nephew — his executor on his death in 1486 — died a generation later and left the unfinished business to his own executors. Nor was this snail's pace at all unusual.[26] But it was not the age of the bishops that moved them to implement their schemes, but rather the knowledge of an approaching end.

Again, variation is the keynote as we move to summary and conclusion. A fair number of the 90 or so bishops lived long public lives, and quite a few lived to really advanced ages; survival to 70 and more was hardly exceptional. On the other hand, even among those who lived longish lives the variation in the level and amount of involvement is considerable. Nor were personalized or private activities a more reliable guide to vigor and involvement. Benefaction was not directly related to age, in either positive or negative terms; neither its quantity nor its quality are predictable by any simple numerical standard. Nor, as we can judge, were family ties a reliable guide to many men's behavior. If most bishops had and chose to remember a network of relatives — siblings, nieces and nephews, cousins — most also seem to have been free to decide how many were to be included among their beneficiaries, and to what tune and extent. And in this morass of pre-testamentary and testamentary distribution, of patronage and of affection (or alienation), it rarely seems as though his age was anything but one further factor, and in some cases not one of much significance, in determining why and how things worked out as they did.

Episcopal wills are a subject worth some attention. They are suggestive, and a quick examination indicates that many if not most bishops did take some thought for family, along with servants and colleagues.[27] A will is an exercise in the creative blending of individual choices and socially prescribed channels of benefaction and expression. Age alone, we know, is not likely to have a major impact on a bishop's choices, though old age would leave him with nephews and nieces rather than brothers and sisters, were he inclined in that direction. But the material is awkward when we look for systematic treatment.

Thomas Polton (a regular whose measurable career only runs from 1420 to 1433) remembered a niece, a nephew, a few unidentified relatives, along with his parents' souls.[28] While some men named no kin at all,[29] Roger Whelpdale (bishop from 1413–1423, for a short career; a young man at death?) still had a sister, with her children,[30] and the somewhat older Richard Clifford (1380–1421 in the church) a brother.[31] Stephen Patrington, though a Carmelite, had lots of relatives in mind when he wrote his will.[32] Thomas Bourgchier left his namesake and nephew Sir Thomas jewels and ornaments worth 100 marks, and his kinsman, John Neville, received £100.[33] But Bourgchier was a rich old man; the son, brother, and uncle of peers, and it is unlikely that his behavior was typically clerical, even for the higher ranks. Thomas Langton (a churchman from 1406 to 1437, when he died of the plague) mentioned two sisters and five nephews, a fairly inclusive sweep.[34] But as we said, little of this reveals a pattern or a policy of inclusion, just as there is no reason that think that age per se sharpened, redirected, or altered other predilections.

In some instances bishops, both old and young, worked closely with networks of relatives, within and without the church. Political partnerships, webs of patronage and clientage, and joint efforts in public and private ventures can all be analyzed; relatives, in-laws, retainers, and familiars are identified. Were a complete network possible for our bishops and for the vast circles of men (and women) with whom they inter-acted, we doubtlessly could gain many insights into the workings of national and regional sociopolitical webs. Such families as the Booths, with three bishops in the century and one in the next, are impressive focal points of jobbery and faction. Archbishop Chichele was close to his two brothers as they rode the crests of city office and business, and various nephews and cousins thought — with good reason — to rise in the ecclesiastical hierarchy.[35] Nor were the Booths unique in their family ties within the episcopacy; we also have two Kempes (an archbishop of York and Canterbury and a bishop of London) and two Mortons (Canterbury and Worcester). And if we descend to deans and archdeans, treasurers and chancellors, the tale would be even richer. Thomas Millyng granted three tenements to his brother for a nominal rent and collated his nephew to a living in his cathedral.[36] Nor is there any reason to think this was unexceptional or particularly aggressive.

In such considerations age alone was but a concomitant attribute of career patterns and behavior. However, this can be given a positive guise; *age* was a part of the story. Those who survived longer had — at least for our success stories — that many more years in which to fasten a hold on affairs. A great novel carries more impact than a great short story; a career like that of Thomas Bourgchier (from about 1427 until 1486) or of William Waynfleet (on active service from 1416 until 1486) allows for that many more years of power and that many more years in which to devise, implement, and realize large and complex projects, be they educational benefaction, foreign policy, or a sustained effort to plant a generation or more of relatives into "tenured" positions in the public sector.

Today we try to ask questions in historical inquiries that push us beyond an evaluation of behavior and public activity; how did the bishops see themselves? Can we follow any trail that age and survival may have blazed across their self-consciousness? After all, not only did many of them live to an advanced age, but their own full share of years was atop the hierarchical status that came with high office. Within their diocese bishops could be autocratic and even dictatorial, though their skills as mediators and diplomats were also on frequent display. Did they see themselves as sages, and did age lend an additional dimension to their patriarchal identity?

They rarely left explicit reflections about age or career, at least not much beyond the odd request for release from duties because of old age, long service, and infirmity. Much of the little we have is wrapped in a conventional and formulaic idiom, though that does not argues that it was not a genuine articulation of thought and feeling. Too much weight should not be assigned to Thomas Arundel's testamentary preface: "Ego miserimus et indignissimus peccatur."[37] Nor should we build an edifice of piety

TABLE 9-4. The Bishops, 1399–1485

Bishop	First benefice	Nominated as bishop	Died	Career: Pre- + as bishop
Aiscough, Wm	1429	1438	1450	9 + 12 = 21 [a]
Alcock, J	1461	1472	1500	11 + 28 = 39
Alnwick, Wm	1415	1426	1449	11 + 23 = 34
Arundel, J	1430	1459	1477	29 + 18 = 47
Arundel, Th	1372	1398	1414	24 + 18 = 42 [b]
Audley, Edm	1464	1480	1524	16 + 44 = 60
Barrows, Wm	1401	1423	1429	22 + 6 = 28
Beauchamp, R	1436	1449	1481	13 + 32 = 45
Beaufort, H	1389	1398	1447	9 + 49 = 58
Bekington, Th	1419	1443	1465	24 + 22 = 46
Bell, R	1431	1478	1496	47 + 18 = 65 [c]
Blythe, J	1477	1494	1499	17 + 5 = 22
Booth, John	1452	1465	1478	13 + 13 = 26
Booth, Laur	1440	1457	1480	17 + 23 = 40
Booth, Wm	1416	1447	1464	31 + 17 = 48
Bottlesham, J	—	1400	1404	—+ 4 = ?
Boulers, Reg	—	1451	1459	—+ 8 = ? [c]
Bourgchier, Th	1428	1435	1486	7 + 53 = 60 [d]
Bowet, H	1370	1401	1423	31 + 22 = 53
Brouns, Th	1404	1435	1445	31 + 10 = 41
Bubwith, N	1379	1406	1424	27 + 18 = 45
Carpenter, J	1422	1444	1476	22 + 32 = 54 [e]
Catterick, J	1398	1414	1419	16 + 5 = 21
Chaundler, J	1388	1417	1426	29 + 9 = 38
Chedworth, J	1434	1452	1471	18 + 19 = 37
Chichele, H	1391	1414	1443	23 + 29 = 52 [f]
Clifford, R	1380	1401	1421	21 + 20 = 41
Close, Nich	—	1400	1421	—+ 21 = ?
Courtenay, Ph	1448	1478	1492	30 + 14 = 44 [g]
Courtenay, R	1392	1413	1415	21 + 2 = 23 [h]
Dudley, Wm	1457	1476	1485	19 + 9 = 28
Fitzhugh, Rb	1398	1431	1436	33 + 5 = 38
Fleming, R	1403	1420	1431	17 + 11 = 28 [i]
Fox, R	1482	1487	1528	5 + 41 = 46 [j]
Gilbert, Rb	1402	1436	1448	34 + 12 = 46
Goldwell, Jm	1450	1472	1499	22 + 27 = 49
Gray, Wm	1414	1426	1431	12 + 5 = 17
Grey, Wm	1431	1454	1478	23 + 22 = 45 [k]
Hales, John	1428	1450	1490	22 + 40 = 62
Hallum, Rb	1388	1407	1417	19 + 10 = 29
Heyworth Wm	—	1419	1447	—+ 28 = ?

TABLE 9-4. *Continued*

Bishop	First benefice	Nominated as bishop	Died	Career: Pre- + as bishop
Hill, R	1477	1489	1496	12 + 7 = 19
Kempe, J	1407	1419	1434	12 + 35 = 47[k]
Kempe, Th	1433	1450	1489	17 + 39 = 56
King Oliver	—	1493	1503	— + 10 = ?
Kingscote, J	1446	1462	1463	16 + 1 = 17
Lacy, Edmund	1400	1417	1455	17 + 38 = 55
Langden, J	—	1422	1434	— + 12 = ?[c]
Langley, Th	—	1406	1437	— + 31 = ?[l]
Langton, Th	1473	1485	1501	12 + 16 = 28
Low, John	—	1444	1467	— + 23 = ?[m]
Lumley, Marm	1415	1429	1450	14 + 21 = 35
Lyhert, Walt	1427	1446	1472	19 + 26 = 45
Mascall, Rb	—	1404	1416	— + 12 = ?[n]
Millyng, Th	—	1474	1492	— + 18 = ?[c]
Moleyns, Ad	1423	1445	1450	22 + 5 = 27[o]
Morgan, Ph	—	1419	1435	— + 16 = ?[c]
Morton, John	1453	1479	1500	26 + 21 = 47
Morton, Rb	1458	1487	1497	19 + 10 = 29
Neville, J	1442	1458	1476	16 + 18 = 34[p]
Neville, Rb	1413	1427	1457	14 + 30 = 44[q]
Patrington, St	—	1417	1417	—?[n]
Pecock, Reg	1424	1450	1460?	26 + 10 = 36[r]
Percy, Wm	—	1452	1462	— + 10 = ?
Peverell, Th	—	1407	1419	— + 12 = ?[n]
Polton, Th	—	1420	1433	— + 13 = ?
Praty, R	1422	1438	1445	16 + 7 = 23
Repingdon, Ph	—	1404	1424	— + 20 = ?[c]
Rickinghale, J	1381	1426	1429	45 + 3 = 43
Rotherham, Th	1461	1468	1500	7 + 32 = 39[s]
Russell, J	1461	1476	1494	15 + 18 = 33
Savage, Th	1479	1493	1507	14 + 14 = 28
Scrope, R	1444	1464	1468	20 + 4 = 24
Shirwood, J	1455	1484	1493	29 + 9 = 38
Smith, Wm	1476	1493	1514	17 = 21 = 38
Spofford, Th	—	1422	1456	— + 34 = ?[t]
Stafford, J	1404	1425	1452	21 + 27 = 48
Stanbury, J	—	1453	1473	— + 20 = ?[u]
Stillington, Rb	1443	1466	1491	23 + 25 = 48
Story, Edw	—	1468	1503	— + 35 = ?

(Continued)

TABLE 9-4. *Continued*

Bishop	First benefice	Nominated as bishop	Died	Career: Pre- + as bishop
Strickland, Wm	1368	1400	1414	32 + 14 = 46
Sydenham, S	1391	1431	1438	40 + 7 = 47
Tottington, A	—	1406	1413	— + 7 = ?
Walden, Rog	1374	1397	1406	23 + 9 = 32
Wakeryng, J	1389	1413	1425	24 + 12 = 36
Ware, Henry	1394	1418	1420	24 + 2 = 26
Waynflete, Wm	1416	1447	1486	31 + 39 = 70[v]
Wells, Wm	—	1436	1444	— + 8 = ?
Whelpdale, R	1413	1420	1423	7 + 3 = 10
Wydeville, L	—	1482	1484	— + 2 = ?
Young, R	1390	1404	1418	14 + 14 = 28

a. Killed by a mob. b. Born 1352. c. Regular cleric (Benedictine). d. Born 1410. e. Resigned. f. Born ca. 1362. g. Born ca. 1432. h. Born ca. 1381. i. Born ca. 1378. j. Born ca. 1448. k. In broken health at the end. l. Died of plague. m. Mendicant. n. Carmelite. o. Killed by a mob. p. Born 1432. q. Born 1404. r. Forced to resign his bishopric. s. Born 1423. t. A Regular; he resigned his bishopric. u. A Carmelite; he resigned. v. Born c. 1394.
This table is based on data in Emden, *Biographical Register of the University of Oxford* and *Biographical Register of the University of Cambridge*, and the *Handbook of British Chronology*.

and self-knowledge on the shaky foundation of John Morton's enumeration of saints: "Jesu Christum . . . et beatissime Virginis Marie, sanctorum Petri et Pauli apostolorum, Thome et Christopheri martirum, Sanctarumque Ethelrede, Katerine, atque Marie Magdalene." [38] Such statements tell us no more about exceptional piety than Morton's "putridum corpus meum" talks of Lollard sympathies. Bekington, a man of piety and of experience, ordered an alabaster effigy for his chantry, some 13 years before his death. But he was a realist; the "face (of the effigy) is that of an elderly man." He was 62 when the work was commissioned, 75 when he joined it. [39] Was he vain, or honest regarding the decay of the flesh and the toll of the years? In his will he decreed that funeral expenses "should be moderate, that they shall be rather in the recreation and relief of the poor than in the solace of the rich and powerful." [40]

Clearly, if one had been successful in this world one could well afford an aggressive humility regarding the next. We saw Repingdon's desire to be buried naked in a sack in the churchyard. Farther than noting this rhetorical posturing it does not seem safe to venture. There is little idea of the view that to live to be old was, by itself, a visible and outward indication of a state of grace, as it seemingly had been to the psalmist. But men were not acculturated to express themselves in this fashion in the fifteenth century. What they really felt about surviving so long—or, conversely, about dying young—was just another of the secrets they kept, up to and even beyond the very end.

10

Men and Women of Letters: The Length of Lives and Some Literary Careers

THE PENULTIMATE CHAPTER of a book does not usually need an apologia; it might seem a bit late in the game for disclaimers, for the verbal wrappings of self-protection. Nevertheless, a touch of explanation may be useful here. This chapter is offered in part to provide a lighter approach, and a more random one, to the discussion of old age. While men of letters are not a discrete social group, we know enough about many of them that a look at their lives and patterns of productivity may elucidate some further points about lived experience. Furthermore, as they are among those who transmitted and compounded the lore of their world concerning the stages of life and the onset of old age — topics whose literary treatment helped widen the gulf between lived experience and literary lore — our look at some men of letters seems a fair turn-about.

Peers and bishops are bounded groups, easily identified even from afar. Their career patterns, demography, and outlook (to some extent) can be examined with regard for the boundaries of contemporary society in which they played an integral role. Everyone knew who such men were, and institutions and occasions existed to define and assemble their reification. Peers and bishops were "estates," their lives and careers moved along broad highways under public gaze. To offer comparisons and reflections about old age and the lives and careers of a medley of creative writers and intelligentsia of the late fourteenth and fifteenth centuries is an altogether less comfortable way of aggregating data.

Nevertheless, we do so with the idea such comments will be suggestive regarding how men (and a few women) lived and worked throughout the

course of their lives. How did they perceive themselves and their place in
the chain as they went through the segments of the life cycle? What did they
say about their own lives? If these comments are even more discursive than
those about peers and bishops, we counter by pointing out that we have
not been led, or led astray, by statistics and tables that insinuate a degree of
pseudo-precision. If the universe of peers or the universe of bishops was a
"real" one in late medieval society, we must also remember that prosopography imparts an aspect of substance not necessarily apparent to the lay
perspective.

Though writers and men of letters were not banded together in anything like the convocations of peers and bishops, they were more inclined,
in their professional view of self, to offer the odd autobiographical frag-
ment, as well as the odd reflection about the human condition. Thus a look
at some writers makes us aware of a different side of our concerns: not just
how long people lived and how active their later careers were, but how early
and easily they moved into the kinds of life-career choices we confront today, and whether they reflect what we term self-consciousness. Becoming a
peer, for most of those who made the grade, was mostly a matter of surviving until one's turn came. And for bishops, the episcopal bench was just a
logical career extension — if one were lucky enough. But becoming or being
a writer was a different matter. Some turned this way early, others in their
later years. Writers followed diverse routes of self assertion and career advancement. Their relevant activity, the creation of prose and poetry, was
related to neither youth, middle age, nor old age. Thus writers' lives lead us
to and along different paths, across the terrain, from those of their social
betters.

*   *   *

When Geoffrey Chaucer died in 1400 he should have been a satisfied
if not a happy man, by the traditional criteria of the classical and biblical
view of a full life.[1] He had lived a fairly long time, something approaching
if not quite three score years. He had had a long and successful public career: the House of Commons, comptroller of the customs, clerk of the
king's works, forester of North Petherton, and so on. This was a pretty
impressive resume for a boy who started with but middling level advan-
tages. He seems to have had the usual domestic life, with home and family,
even if many of the details are cloudy; by his death his son Thomas was

already chief butler in the royal household and launched on a career that would eventually see him as speaker of the Commons and father of a daughter who would someday preside over great occasions as the countess of Salisbury and duchess of Suffolk. Furthermore, Geoffrey's own literary efforts had been appreciated, acclaimed, and rewarded, along with his careerism as a civil servant and as a companion to the great and famous. In his last decade he had partially retired from public service, and the literary production that had engaged much of his free time since he first published *The Book of the Duchesse* back in 1369 was only cut off by his death.

There are many gaps in this biography, well documented though it is, just as there is controversy over the order, rate, and design of his literary output. We might spare a few thoughts, in the midst of the certainties and uncertainties about biography and literary output, to consider his longevity and his durability, both as a man and as a writer. His life span, though of significant duration, was hardly remarkable when set against those of some of the peers and the bishops who were his associates at court or in high government service. His deposition in the Scrope and Grosvenor controversy indicates that he carried his years and experience with justifiable pride. But if he was more than average, though hardly a champion in the longevity stakes, how does he stand when we compare him to other writers of his day in terms of life span and sustained literary activity and in the length of the working literary career? Nor is this mere curiosity; Chaucer ran with the literary crowd, as he did with the courtly one, and presumably he exchanged a different form of intimacies and reflections when drinking with writer friends than when his crowd adjourned after testifying to the court of chivalry.

Since the Romantic movement and the likes of Keats, Shelley and Byron, we have been schooled, when we think of the creative process and those who labor on its behalf, to picture the suffering artist who dies young, preferably of consumption in an attic; it is even better if he (or, by then, she) languishes in a foreign country. Such a tragic figure has to be largely neglected and ignored by the doyens of philistine culture until the posthumous "discovery" brings fame, too late for fortune (though the heirs may do very well). And against this view we can hold up an alternate picture — nourished by the "grand old men" of Victorian literature — in which venerable literary figures produce a long string of works devoured in turn by their middle-brow contemporaries, then by their contemporaries' children, and finally by their grandchildren, who awake one morning to peruse the obituary in *The Times*. These were the men who survived into the early

decades of this century and who offered condensations of their wisdom in
the eleventh edition of the *Encyclopedia Britannica*.

These contrary models of literary creation, and of the public's appreciation for the creators, represent polarized analyses of the lives of men and
women of letters: Wilfrid Owen and Isaac Rosenberg keep the pendulum
from swinging over to Tennyson and Hardy, and vice versa. Byron is paired
against Browning, Marlowe against Samuel Johnson, Wilde against Words-
worth. In addition, there is the consideration — beyond mere dates of birth
and death — of when, in the course of the life cycle, did people of letters first
come to their calling? Furthermore, especially when we deal with literature
that antedates the printing press and that emanated from a world where
patronage was a sine qua non for secular writing, is that of how a literary
career was strung with or between activities that served to put bread on
the table?

These are questions we can pose for the late medieval literary scene,
and recent discussions of the concept of vocation encourage us to pursue
them in the context of a discussion of age.[2] To begin we can turn to the
biographical notes in H. S. Bennett's *Chaucer and the Fifteenth Century*, and
his appendix on "Individual Authors" (pp. 264–301) allows us to put a fair
number of writers into three categories: those who died in youth or early
middle age, those for whom we have insufficient data, and those who pretty
surely lived into their fifties or beyond. The first group — the Keatses and
Marlowes — may have been fairly small, though the nature of fifteenth-
century sources probably works to skip over them. But Bennett's second
and third groups are of about equal size: in fact, 29 authors are listed as
having an uncertain life span and 29 seem to have lived to be 50 or more.[3]
Of course, Bennett is not attempting to count *every* possible writer; he gives
us a slice of a much larger (if loosely defined) group, compiled without
explicit bias toward longevity.

The uncertainties of chronology and biography will always be with us.
If neither those who edit for the Early English Text Society nor A. B. Emden, in his registers of Oxford and Cambridge, have been able to close in
on some of the writers of the day, the chances are that we will never go
much farther. In many cases a name and a list of works of reasonable attri-
bution are the end of the line, though in a few cases men and writings now
considered minor might enjoy some vogue among scholars if a fuller story
of the life and literary corpus were forthcoming. However, the history of
culture is not a hunt for buried treasure, but rather an inquiry into how a
segment of society was integrated into the larger fabric. How important

would the otherwise unknown John Gardener be if we could determine whether he was 30 or far beyond that when he wrote the earliest vernacular treatise on gardening? How about the immensely influential Walter Hilton (d. 1396), with his *Scale of Perfection* his only known work? Ritson's old history of English poetry has an intriguing mention of one John Awdelay, "old, blind, deaf"; Robert Baston, a famous poet in his day "who gave his name to 'ryme Baston' "; John Bowyer, canon of Bodmin, who wrote a "dul poem addressed to Jesus Christ"; Rannande, an ironmonger, who in 1457 wrote a "description in rude and barbarous verse on the building of Culhambridge"; as well as George Pilkyngton, supposedly author of "The turnament of Tottenham, or the wooing, wenning, and wedding of Tibbe, the reeve's daughter there."[4] Where are the lost vital statistics of yesteryear, and how much would they add to our view of the life cycle or of the creative process?

But all is not so bleak, and there are numerous well-mapped areas. For roughly an equal number of men of letters from Bennett's pool of authors we have some usable figures regarding life span and longevity, as well as for the date and pace of literary composition. Of his 29 men who reached at least age 50, it seems that a fair number probably approached the neighborhood of 70, including some important figures: Capgrave, Caxton, Fortescue, John Shirley, John Hardyng, Lydgate, Stephen Scrope, and William Way. These data about longevity are no surprise by now, but rather constitute "another county heard from"—an additional group of men who survived and who, had they been brought together at some mythical cocktail party, would have stood as a group with an average life span of the mid-fifties or more. They might also offer some advice and probably a fair number of complaints on the woes of age and the human condition.

A number of our men are fleshed out by adequate biographical detail to put these comments into a more precise perspective. John Gower, Chaucer's friend, lived from about 1325 to 1408. Of good family, he was slightly involved in worldly affairs and eventually came to the attention of the court. His *Mirrour de l'Omme* — begun in 1381 and only finished in the 1390s — was dedicated to Thomas Arundel, archbishop of Canterbury and a powerful member of an aristocratic family. The *Confessio Amantis* was begun at the behest of Richard II and the first version was dedicated to the king (as the second was to Henry IV). Though illness and then blindness cut off his creative activities around the turn of the century, we see a literary career that probably began on the late side and that then ran for about a quarter of a century. In a letter to Arundel, written around 1400, Gower joins the club of those who referred to themselves as, "senex et cecus . . . corpus et egrotum, vetus et miserabili totum."[5]

By the standards of this group the life and career of Thomas Hoccleve offer few mysteries, so broad is the autobiographical thread in his works. As he tells the tale, we have an almost stereotypical progression from wild youth to the unremunerative drudgery of the privy seal office to marriage — after his hopes of ecclesiastical advancement had been dashed — into a penurious and whining old age. Hoccleve turned to the pen early in life and continued at it for some decades. His early writings go back to the turn of the century, and both major and minor poems were forthcoming at regular intervals: The *De Regimine Principus* in 1411, the translated and revised *Regement of Princes* in 1412, the *Address to Sir John Oldcastle* in 1415, the *Dialogue* in 1422. An examination of the dates of patrons and would-be patrons puts 1430 or 1435 as a probable terminal point for his career, though he may have lived for some years beyond this. He was the sort of man to leave the stage, not in a blaze of glory, but with mumbled importunities aimed at still one more potential patron; maybe, with the next poem, he would strike it rich. He also gives details of a serious illness, perhaps a nervous breakdown, as well as how his former friends treated him during and after his bad patch. We can follow him from his recovery from his "wyld infirmyte" until he was granted "such sustenance yearly during his life in the Priory of Southwick, Hampshire, as Nicholas Mokkinge, late master of St Lawrence in the Poultry, had."[6]

Lydgate was probably a bit younger than Hoccleve, having been born in 1370, about fifteen years before he entered the abbey at Bury St. Edmund. He moved through minor orders, was ordained in 1397, went to Oxford, served as prior of Hatfield from 1423 to 1434, and died in 1449 or 1450. He produced *The Church and the Bird* and *The Complaint of the Black Knight* around 1400, and with these he was off and running as a literary figure of some renown. In the course of his ordered life in the cloister, with the encouragement and succor offered by a well-endowed Benedictine house, he produced a steady stream of work. Between 1405 and 1411 he published his *Lyf of Our Lady*, with the prince of Wales as his patron. The *Troy Book* was commissioned in 1412 and completed by 1420, the *Praise of Peace* published in the mid- 1420s. The *Danse Macabre* came after a sojourn in Paris in 1426; the *Title and Pedigree of Henry VI* was commissioned by the king's tutor and guardian, the earl of Warwick, in 1427. In the 1430s he wrote his *Defense of Holy Church* and *The Fall of Princes*. His health and energy held up through the passing years, and in 1445 he more or less completed his career by providing the literary material used in the pageant that celebrated Margaret of Anjou's entry into London prior to her marriage with Henry VI. For much of his working career he was virtually the poet laureate of the House of Lancaster, and the inscription on his tomb at Bury is an indication of contemporary acclaim:

> His jacet Lidyat tumulatus urna
> Qui fuit quondam celebris
> Britanniae fama poesis.

There are many fifteenth-century men who can be classified as writers and authors, or as men of letters and of the literary world, if we use a broad definition of the term. Didactic writers covered the usual range: history, law, religious and mystical expression, theology, sermons, biography and hagiography, travel, and more. Compilers of monastic and urban chronicles, and even of volumes of official or private correspondence, might be considered within our boundaries. A full scholarly census of late medieval literary output — comparable to what John Bale tried to assemble in 1548 in his *Illustrium Majoris Britanniae Scriptorum*, or to Josiah Cox Russell's list of thirteenth-century writers — would probably bring in several hundred names.[7] We can easily choose a few long-lived men, from various avenues of literary endeavor, and see how their lives illuminate some of these themes.

John Trevisa (1342?–1408?; given by Bennett as 1326–1402) was a west country boy who went to Oxford, got himself expelled in 1379 (perhaps because of Wycliffite activity), and became the chaplain and cultural mouthpiece for Thomas, lord Berkeley (1353–1417). Though he was primarily a translator and adapter or reviser, he was a prolific writer for some years, nor did the derivative nature of his work detract from his eminence. He translated the popular *Polychronicon* of Ralph Higden in 1387, with the personal touches and extensions expected in reworking a classic, and he produced versions of Aegidius Romanus' *Regimine Principum*, of Bartholomew Anglicus' *De Proprietatibus Rerum* (done in "the yere of my lord's age 47," which would have been around 1400), and of Vegetius' *De Re Militare* in 1408. He was working up to the end, and if anything the rate of his literary output was increasing, perhaps as he was released from other duties and as his reputation grew.[8]

John Fortescue became chief justice of England in 1442, and he stands as the most memorable common law writer between the heroic figures of Plantaganet history and Sir Edward Coke. To us he offers an extreme example of a writer who produced the bulk of his (extant) literary corpus late in life, probably after he had been writing decisions and law reports for over a generation. Born around 1390 and a governor of Lincoln's Inn by the 1420s, he was a loyal Lancastrian and went into in exile with Queen Margaret after Edward IV's accession.[9] He then labored to justify his partisan loyalty, as well as his country's constitution: his *De Natura Legis Naturae* came in 1461–63, the more important *De Laudibus Legum Angliae* not until 1468–71. Nor was he finished, for he returned to serve the Yorkists — a judge's ultimate loyalty being to the rule of law, not to men or dynasties — and he wrote his *Governaunce of England* in 1471. His exposition of "The Deference Bi Twene Dominium Regale and Dominium Politicum et Regale" did not appear until he was around 80. By now he had a lifetime's experience behind his views, but his recent enforced residence on the continent made him an appropriate expert on why "our system" is better than "their system."

Osbern Bokenham (c.1393–c.1447) was a Suffolk man who lived much of his life as an Austin Friar at Stoke by Clare.[10] He was part of the East Anglian literary establishment, and he wrote at the behest of important ladies of the region: Lady Bourgchier, Katherine Denston, Katherine Howard, and the countess of Oxford.[11] He tells us that he had passed "full yeres, fyfty," before he turned to the composition of *The Life of St. Margaret*, in 1443, and other hagiographic tales — of Katherine, Mary Magdalene, and Elizabeth — came forth in his remaining years. He may have produced a prose translation of Higden's *Polychronicon* and a treatise on the history of the house at Clare. We do not know if he was the Bokenham who became vicar general of the English Austins in 1463: he was probably dead by then. But if all his literary and ecclesiastical activities are to be credited to the one man, he is another example of the late-starting but prolific figure who got going later rather than sooner. Also, like others on this track he found ample reward and appreciation. Once he began to write he pursued his calling with productive zeal for some decades.

Though the men discussed above have been chosen because they lend themselves to our theme, they are typical of the group as surveyed by Bennett, or at least of those whose long lives can be attested. Many others lend themselves for our purposes. There is William of Worcester (1415–1482?), who as Sir John Fastolf's secretary collected material for a history of the

French wars, from 1425–52, and who has left us his *Annales Rerum Anglican*, written in 1468, and his *Itineraries*, covering his travels in 1478 and 1480.[12] He also translated Cicero's *De Senectute*, an interesting choice of text in his circumstances. Or we can turn to John Capgrave, an Austin Friar by 1410 and still alive and writing and able to refer to his own old age in his *Chronicle of England*, dedicated to Edward IV in 1460.[13] We can look at Sir Richard Roos (1410?–1482), who received the patronage of duke Humphrey of Gloucester as far back as 1432 and who was still around to write a prison poem and a lament for the countess of Rivers after 1473, and who lived to remove infelicitous touches from his last version of the Rous Roll.[14]

Nor do even these men exhaust all our possible candidates. Among our authors are figures known by a single work, and yet whose lives clearly seem to have been long ones, before or after the moment of creation. In these cases the link between longevity and creativity is of less interest, as we deal with people transmitting a unique experience or message, whether it came early or late. Julian of Norwich was born around 1342 and lived to about 1416 or beyond. Her *Revelations of Divine Love* was composed, at least in the form which has been transmitted to us, perhaps as late as 1395 or 1400. However, its purpose was to expound on the mystical spiritual lessons she drew from the illness she suffered in early May 1373, "when I was 30 winters old and half." She spent the rest of her long life talking about this climactic week and revising her views of its definitive interpretation.[15] Marjory Kempe is enjoying considerable popularity today, certainly something she never received from her hard-headed contemporaries. She lived from about 1373 to 1440, and her *Book* was not written down by her clerical amanuensis until she was near the end, in the 1430s, decades after her pilgrimage had begun.[16] John Blakman (1410–1484) had been an original fellow of Eton, warden of King's Hall at Cambridge, and a *clericus redditus* at the Carthusian house at Witham before he finally turned, after 1471, to write the *Life of Henry VI*.[17]

Still other figures were engaged in public affairs of some duration and were able to produce literary work. The length of their careers as writers was but a segment of their span of activity. Thomas Walsingham, "the last great medieval chronicler," was a monk at St. Albans by 1364, precentor and *scriptorarius* there from 1380 to 1394, and prior of Wymondham, 1394–97. Toward the end he surrendered his administrative duties and turned to preserving the St. Albans tradition of chronicle-history that went back to the twelfth and thirteenth centuries. He continued Rishanger's *Gesta Abbatum* down to 1393, and then his *Ypodogidma Neustriae* appeared, dedicated to Henry V; its publication in 1420 virtually marked his half-century in the cloister. Thomas Beckington (1390?–1465) was dean of the arches, chancellor of the archbishop of Canterbury, a diplomatic functionary, and bishop of Bath and Wells, 1443–65. His correspondence and the miscellaneous documents generated during his three decades of public life are sufficient to fill two volumes in the Rolls Series plus a volume published by the Camden Society. He has been accorded a left-handed literary epitaph that few others could aspire to: as a writer his "chief importance resides in this introduction of humane values in official epistolography."[18]

* * *

One point that emerges from this survey is that writers of goodly and advanced age — like members of parliament, peers, bishops, men in towns, and all other such groups we have looked at — were hardly rarities. Because our concern is neither with biography nor with literary history and criticism, the intellectual maturation process and the progressive artistic development of the writers is not relevant. However, it is not difficult to pick out some personal-seeming comments, even from men and women much less inclined than Hoccleve to talk about themselves, for views on aging humanity.[19] Many writers are apt to make occasional remarks that are not hard to read as self-revelatory. In his *Compleynt of Venus* Chaucer said, "For elde, that in my spirit dulleth me, hath of enditing al the sotelte, Welnigh beraft out of my remembrance." Capgrave tells us that, "Now is age come, and I want my al that schulde long to a student." From the minor muse of George Ashby (1390–1475) we hear a variation on this theme: "Thaugh I be fallen / in decrepit age / Right nygh at yeres of foure score."[20] But to read specific autobiography into the literary reflections of any writer is risky, and we must walk with extreme caution when we go back five centuries. In part, such statements belong to the general category of detached commentary common to so many cultures and situations. And yet such statements also show that they were indeed aware of and sensitive to the challenges and problems of the life cycle. It is almost as natural to comment about the changes wrought by old age as it is to suffer them.

"Age and achievement" as linked aspects of life offer an interesting dyad. In a standard treatment of these links the data about authors focus on the age at which a masterpiece or famous work was produced, with some concern for the level and duration of sustained productivity.[21] It may sober us to reflect that Jane Austen was 21 when she produced *Pride and Prejudice*, Emily Bronte 29 when she wrote *Wuthering Heights*. On the other hand it should cheer aging academics to learn that Kant worked on *The Critique of Pure Reason* when in his 50s, and that Hobbes (born in the year of the Armada and not dead until 1679) did not finish his *Leviathan* until he was about 63. And in this century a great many of those who pursue literary careers have begun at an early age and—given some modicum of success and financial reward—have simply continued to labor through life, which now often means for four or five decades after their first appearance in print. The careers of a Graham Greene or an Agatha Christie, with apologies for the diversity of taste, are typical ones if we look at twentieth century longevity and vocation.

A different creative pattern and career course emerges for many of our late medieval writers. Literary creation often began, at least in a serious and public way, considerably later in life. Many who eventually reached some plateau of prominence had produced little by age 30, and some had hardly broken into print—to speak anachronistically—until they over 40. While medieval men began political and clerical careers in their mid- or late teens or early 20s, literary ones were only launched at a considerably later date. Almost none of the writers were "professionals" in our sense; they made their way via the church or administrative service or civil service and then—perhaps simultaneously rather than sequentially—sought patrons for their literary endeavor. They were rarely of independent substance, though some aristocrats did turn their hand to "amateur" literary endeavors of some worth.

The patrons who stood behind these writers came largely from the power elite: kings and queens; the dukes of Lancaster, Bedford, Gloucester, Suffolk, and York; the earls of Essex, Oxford, Warwick, Salisbury, Worcester, and Rivers; and significant numbers of the affluent gentry and "squirearchy."[22] Such men and women were not on the lookout for boy geniuses whose talent they could parade on center stage of the intellectual marketplace. Rather, as pillars of the established order themselves, they were likely to offer political and financial support to stable and trustworthy figures who could be relied on to trumpet their own political virtues and values, to speak out on behalf of the status quo and in favor of those so placed by God as to uphold it. Mature writers were a safer bet. Conversely, with the major exception of Wycliffe and his followers, late medieval literature was elaborately personal, its didacticism rarely designed to push for a different arrangement of the world order. Literary expression was not a past time for young radicals (nor for old ones). Nor was it for those who were eager to talk about dying for love. To a great extent it was a vehicle for those with something sober to say, and the flaming pen of youth was rarely at a premium. Sage counsel, from sage men — often of goodly years when they came to write — was a safer, wiser route *and* a better investment — for both patron and poet.

PART IV

SEARCHING
FOR A
CONTEXT

II

Old Age Within and Across Cultures

A GOOD DEAL of this book seems to spring from one disclaimer or another. In the Introduction I asserted that it was not about anything that actually happened. Then I also said, in appropriate chapters, that my goal was to write neither demography nor biography. In the general comments that are brought together here, in lieu of a formal conclusion, I hasten to add that no overall survey of medieval views about old age, or of the stages of life, or of the life of the elderly, will be attempted. There is no precise conclusion to these essays.

Rather, what I offer is an elaboration of themes already treated, a gloss upon observations already made. Old people — recognized as being in some late or final stage of the life course — were common in late medieval society. They were found in all walks of life, some still active and involved and determined to hang on to the very end, others clearly needing to step aside. And for these latter souls their family or social situation sometimes made some form of retirement possible, if not necessarily advantageous, affluent, or honorable. That these assertions would not have been strange or unfamiliar in late medieval English society is perhaps the most telling conclusion of all, one to keep in mind as we wend our way along the final sections of the trail as it leads us past the saws and conventions of wisdom literature and speculation.

What did people in the fifteenth century think about old age and about the aging process? To deal with these questions we shift from behavioral and biographical data to the world of literary and cultural norms. This is always a difficult and uneasy transition, and when our subject is one more treated by the discursive than the behavioral or empirical the shift is even more uncertain. Beyond the difficulty of recapturing the viewpoint of a long-gone world is the whole matter of whether there even is such a creature as *the* viewpoint of that world concerning old age and matters surrounding it. Contemporary discussions were largely dominated by literary and didactic works. As well as taking a look at some of these we will address the question of whether there is any indication that people paid much attention, in life, to what they were told in the vast body of learned discussion so readily available.

In our lives, as we know from personal experience, the world is dealt with through a series of reconciliations of discordant realities, of forgettings and of rememberings, of personal goals and short term agendas that help to brace the ego to deal with matters over which we have no control. As we are wont to say, "we cope." Old age is what one reaches, if and when . . . ; the interpretations attached to this stage of life, be they benign or fearsome, have little effect on it as a natural process that involved flesh, memory, or the tally of birthdays of descendants and the funerals of contemporaries.

If poets lie too much, historians seek to synthesize too much. Insofar as the essays in this study have a common theme, it is that we are hard pressed to offer a common theme comprising that of the human condition *and* incorporating our desire to make sense of the world into which we have come and within which we spend our earthly days. Regarding old age and aging, a lot of people had a lot of different things to say. But life turns out to be like the weather, in this respect, and old age is — depending on our disposition and the circumstances of the moment when we speak or write — either the deepening gloom before dark, or the clear sky that comes when a stormy day has ended and a golden sunset shines upon us.

Some of the material to look at pertaining to the stages of life is familiar enough in the realms of literary history. Indeed, it might well have been the introductory chapter, though I have chosen to put it at the end. It is very intriguing, and it opens real windows into the medieval view of life. On the other hand, literary material is easily taken too seriously by modern students, and a little demotion by a social historian is not such a bad idea. Wisdom literature is often badly out of synch with lived experience, and I worry that many who read the literary materials skip too lightly over this disharmony. Lives are governed by some flickering combination of ideology — received and self-created — and by physical and social realities that are partly open to manipulation but that largely seem to be our destiny.

*   *   *

In the long run, to paraphrase John Meynard Keynes, biology always triumphs; even the hardiest among us age and then die. Nor were all that many, of those who survived birth and early childhood and young maturity (and childbed) even likely to last so as to be numbered among the ranks of the hardiest, of those who proved most stubborn before the scythe of mortality. A recognition of the special needs of and the role played by the aged is pretty close to a universal social constant. Across the face of humanity the aged come in for special concern. But after that little is fixed. In many ways, whether we think of it as a set by quantitative boundaries or simply as the final segment of the life line, the ultimate closure, old age is a relative matter.[1] Studies that offer us a cross-cultural perspective indicate an impressive range in the voices involved in the debate about boundaries and definitions, let alone in the wide variations held for the social role of the aged.

In numerical or arithmetic terms the famous biblical passage may have contained a considerable element of hyperbole in its assertion: "The days of our years are three-score years and ten" (Psalm 90:10). Nevertheless this injunction proved to be one of those turns of phrase that served to establish a norm, or at least a target at which to aim; its counsel has resonated down the centuries as the aphorism of Western wisdom, if not of demography. To reach the years enjoined by the canonical formula was a difficult but not impossible target, and we have seen enough by now to realize that if 70 and 70-plus was not something for the many, it was always one for a few. This held for medieval society, it would seem, whether one moved in ruling circles, at gatherings of patriarchal and extended families, in the many-tiered ranks of aging but hardy clerics, or among the toothless gaffers merely looking for a sunny spot on the village green for an afternoon nap.

If these assertions about an attainable goal hold water, it seems likely that western longevity, at the farther end, was not too different from what it had been in the days of the Old Testament's poetic formulation. After his opening dictum the Psalmist warmed to his task with a gloss: "Or even by reason of strength four-score years. . . . So teach we the number of days, that we may get us a heart to wisdom." Provided that we remember that the focus is on the impressive end of the longevity scale, not on the incidence or rate of achieving this reach, we seem to be on firm ground in talking about the ubiquity of the aged. In addition, we must remember that this longest-lived fraction of the population rested at the top of a demographic pyramid where it is likely that some level of life expectancy that ran to around 50 was the norm for that largish group of men (and women, presumably) who had cleared earlier hurdles and reached 20 or 21.

In this regard northwestern Europe in the fourteenth and fifteenth centuries stood in reasonable comparison to many areas of the third world today.[2] If the numbers hold up, late medieval England was well blessed compared to many societies and cultures that have been tracked by anthropologists and gerontologists. If old age is a universal (for those who last) the actual point in years at which it is biologically and socially manifest, as measured against the moment of birth, is far from a constant. The examination of comparative data still gives a frightening picture of the aging process at its grimmest.[3] As well as quantitative data, the comparative material reveals a wide variation in the role played by the aged, as it does in the treatment — meted out and therefore determined by others — of those who comprised the most senior group in the community. Societies that supposedly were fueled by deference and patriarchy are obviously those in which the aged retain the largest share of perquisites and privileges; the logical extension of the argument is that they actually gained in status, and perhaps in power, by the mere fact of durability and survival. How often this exalted late-day status can be documented in the historical or anthropological records may be a chancy matter, though much wisdom literature and religious teaching (from many cultures and creeds) is designed and expressed to bend the young twigs of the folk in this direction.

In keeping with what we saw regarding the elderly status of so many men of letters, wisdom literature probably reflects the wisdom of the elderly. The Bible is easily combed for useful passages. Though there are verses that certainly cast some doubt on the value and virtue of old age, and some that plead for decent treatment of the elderly, the general tone is that grey hair is worthy of veneration — a visible sign of grace and divine favor — and that it opens the door to devotion and communion with God: "And thou shalt keep His statutes and His commandments . . . that it may go well with thee, and with thy children after thee, and that thou mayest prolong thy days upon the land."[4]

In some societies the realities of survival were always at the door, if not closer. In such cases, as prevailing wisdom would lead us to believe, the aged became marginalized as the ratios between what they could contribute and what they consumed — in time, in resources, and in calories — worked against them. In such a context the logical extension of the issue would be grandma's one-way walk into the woods, or grandpa's winter fishing expedition on the drifting ice floe. How often such solutions were resorted to as a matter of policy and deliberate intervention is also open to question. Like those people who supposedly eat human flesh, or those whose king is ritually killed by the successful challenger, it is likely to be a matter of "the other," best found a bit down the road. Or maybe it is what we all used to do back in the good old days.[5]

Perhaps it is sufficient to note that throughout the world, regardless of differences in climate, in food supplies and nutritional levels, and in varying values placed on life in this world, the unvoiced power of physical breakdown, aided by such helpers as pneumonia, would step in to help with the job. The relative rarity of the aged was not something *caused* by the laws of demography and the actuarial table. They are descriptive and predictive devices and they merely reflect the grim facts of survival; they were formulated in obedience to the cruel dictates of a cruel world.

*   *   *

If the essays and analyses we have offered carry no other lesson, they convey the view that it is difficult and misleading to generalize about the presence of and role of the aged — in any given place or culture, or within any given span of years. But medieval as well as modern theory offered a host of general views and interpretations; we should take them into consideration. The historian, as Marc Bloch said, is in no sense a free man (sic), and we must let the extant materials lead us. Insofar as literary material and passages from drama, philosophy, and poetry re-create life experiences, classical and medieval writing give us a treasure chest of suggestive material. An interest in Greek views of the aged and the values surrounding age is an obvious starting point in a general inquiry.[6] There is an unlimited supply of anecdotes and one-liners, with insight and pithy phrasing, that we can lift from Greek and then from Roman literature.

Diogenes Laertius praised Zeus for carrying old Thales off to die when he had become so feeble that he could attend the games but no longer see them. Lucian thought it appropriate that the Gods spoke in order of age when called to formal counsel by Zeus/Jupiter. Beyond this kind of material quantitative data (about age, survival, and sustained productivity) is easily assembled to argue — much like the medieval data — for the general presence of the aged in most walks of life. Among Greek philosophers — who were clearly men about whom legends were built — we have Carneades living to 85, Cleanthes who at somewhere between 80 and 93 starved himself to death, Diogenes who at 90 may have committed suicide, Isocrates at 98, Zeno who suffered a fatal accident at 98, and a host of others who could have looked back on the Psalmist with a feeling that he was apt to short-change them.[7]

In addition to the numbers offered and the lessons drawn from this material, the vast literary corpus that we have from this reflective and loquacious world draws us to assess the values of classical society regarding the status, the expected behavior, the shortcomings, and the socially redeeming role of the aged. The literary material is so rich and so vast that the difficulty is, here too, in extracting *the* normative view. The very abundance of sources allows us to buttress virtually any position or viewpoint with apt quotations from the texts. We have conflicting views as to whether the aged should be venerated—perhaps because they hold real power—or whether they can be treated with ridicule, the cold shoulder, and even the elbow. As we expect, both positions (and others), located all along the line between the poles of interpretation and partisanship, can be supported, given the choice of favorite literary passages and of stock situations. Or, if we wish, we can set wisdom and homiletic literature, usually in favor of old age and the elderly, against the more hostile and acerbic voice of satire; the stock figures of comedy refuting and neutralizing the hoary patriarchs of the reverential texts.

If we turn to Plato, who spoke in terms of approbation regarding the rule of the aged in his *Republic*, as he did for the Spartan assembly of his own day, we find a generally sympathetic voice. For Plato, as for Cicero, the main thread of the argument about the life course "consists of linking happiness in old age to virtue."[8] But on the other side we can counter by turning to Aristotle, with his musing on how the body wears out, how the old are neither role models nor upright and admirable citizens. The outward decay of the body was but a visible manifestation of a degenerative process that involved the reason, the moral man, and the social man or citizen.[9] As the individual condition, the family, and the polity are joined in one moral and physical continuum, so we extend the tale of physical decay to the dangers posed by the aging patriarch and the rule of gerontocrats. But we are free to spin the wheel again. There is the stately role of Nestor in the *Iliad* or Laertes in the *Odyssey*. Were such presentations accepted as out-weighing the heavy wit and blunt ridicule of the comic dramatists? From Tireseus to Polonius the wisdom of the aged has been presented as a literary device, often meant at the same time to be a counsel of wisdom and a subject of derision and parody.[10]

From the classical and hebraic world onward the debate about the stages of life, plus the elaborate discussions concerning the values attached to its segments and sections, have been a major field of deliberation and contestation, an enduring topic in our musings on the nature and scope of life. But the spice of the quarrel should not make us unduly sanguine about the chances of either resolution or clarification. Late medieval England was, intellectually but one child of and one heir to this long tradition. How was the debate formulated and transmitted so our subjects — learned in some cases, but mainly apt to be schooled in the wisdom of the market place — could absorb it, identify with different views, and be moved by their poetic or didactic reformulation in the language of the day?

We can take a quick look at the transmitted lore on age and the aged, at classical and patristic wisdom about age as measured in years and in the significance of our earthly status. How much of this classical, biblical, and patristic lore was part of the conceptual or practical baggage of fifteenth-century folk is a central question. What people thought, when they turned to stock questions and stock answers about the meaning of life, probably had but limited effect and limited importance in their daily lives. Common sense, with an eye on lived experience, was not always a missing partner in cognition, though it often was a silent one.

Some parts of the transmitted body of literary and intellectual debate do seem to have been of more than passing interest, and in part they might be for the many as well as for the learned few. One question about which the medieval writer or moralist or preacher (or artist or manuscript limner) could pick and choose, from a long list of possible answers, pertained to the basic formulation; was old age "a good thing" or the opposite when set against the backdrop of the entire life? And depending on the answer chosen and the ranks of authorities enlisted for support, what string of causal explanations and consequences — regarding moral, medical, and theological or metaphysical implications — would properly follow?

From a biological or physical viewpoint, old age was inevitable and inescapable. They lived with this truth, probably more closely than we do today. They had to understand how and why a wholly good God had imposed this condition upon fallen humanity; was it part of the punishment we earned by the expulsion from Eden? or was it a more neutral or "natural" aspect of mortal life, simply a logical final chapter to the book wherein each worldly destiny had been writ? The humoral tradition of medicine was able to explain how we grew old and broke down in the process, but the larger "why" was for higher treatment. Would Adam and Eve have been immortal and eternally young, if only? The Fall came so quickly that the "laws of nature" never had much time to assert themselves in a pre-lapsarian world. There were many tales of saints who died young, beside those of saints who died at an extreme age. There were tales of the *puer senex*, the holy child who spoke with the wisdom of an elder of Israel. But virtually nothing has come down about holy men and women exempted from the laws of age and decay (except for the uncorrupted bodies of saints, *after* their deaths).[11]

If the dialogue about the value of old age was primarily theological or moral, it was greatly enriched as literary ammunition and even popular psychology became woven into the discussions. As best we can judge the public "ate it up." Did old age bring patriarchal status and increased authority, wisdom, and even some hope of freedom from sin and temptation? And, if so, did these pluses reach a sum that could offset the obvious loss of power over others and self? A look around the room may have brought the realities of the debate home with little equivocation, but that in no way seems to have diminished the pleasure of the audience.

The classic literary and rhetorical opposition, if we choose to see it in these stage-managed terms, can be presented as one between Cicero and Innocent III. Cicero went to the rostrum first; his *De Senectute* was written about 45 or 44 B.C., when he was 62. In the dialogue, set in 150 B.C., the 84-year-old Cato talks with Scipio Africanus Minor, now 35, and Laelius, now 38. Cicero tells Atticus that he has written the piece in order to "lighten for you and for me our common burden of old age, which, if not already pressing hard upon us, is surely coming on apace."[12] In the dialogue Scipio asks Cato why "old age is never burdensome for you, though it is so vexatious for most old men." Given this opening, Cato explains that the unhappiness most people associate with old age stems from such trivial matters as the loss of physical pleasure, the withdrawal from former circles of activity, increasing physical weakness, and the approach of death. But we should choose, rather, to focus on the compensations and pleasures now available, such as agriculture and horticulture, "in which I found incredible delight . . . not one whit checked by old age." Time and a taste for contemplation have now given Cato the golden years that today we trumpet for "senior citizens," and he concludes by assuring young Scipio that "my old age sits light upon me, and not only is [it] not burdensome, but is even happy."

This treatise has been seen as the "most charming of all Cicero's essays," and tells us more about Roman literature, perhaps, than about counsel to take us through life.[13] Nevertheless the work was among the most popular of Cicero's writings, and it has attracted admirers, if not partisans and allies, through the ages — including, presumably, Caxton.[14] It can stand as the best statement of a widely-voiced theme: Sophocles and Aeschylus had expressed themselves in this vein, and Petrarch in the fourteenth century spoke of (still) worrying, at age 53, about the danger of lascivious thoughts. Eventually, he assured his readers, age delivered a welcome detachment from such worldly and worrisome matters, and by the time he entered genuine old age he had more than made his peace with its rules and regimen.[15]

But Cicero's sanguine and hopeful message does not represent the literary or philosophical mainstream, and the pessimists — or realists, as we choose — generally carried the day. In medieval culture their champion was Lothar dei Signi, Innocent III. In his *On the Misery of the Human Condition* he offered about as dreary a statement on the question of life and age as can be imagined.[16] While old age is but one of the multitude of woes from which there is no escape, it ranks among the most painful and undignified in the long, doleful list. And, by definition, it hits those who survive at the moment when we might think we have qualified, at last, for rest and relaxation rather than for the most harrowing stretch of the journey. No relief for the wicked — as we all must be — and the journey's end, when it finally comes, is welcome if only because the steps immediately before have been so ghastly.

This is morbidity and pessimism at their extreme. We enter life as the product of sin, and it is downhill thereafter. At conception, "the seed conceived is fouled, smirched, corrupted, and the soul infused into it inherits the guilt of sin." Nor is gestation an improvement upon conception: the foetus feeds "on menstrual blood so detestable and impure that on contact with it fruits will fail to sprout, orchards go dry, herbs wither [and] lepers and monsters are born of this corruption." And for those who do reach old age — and note that they are fewer than in the more heroic days of yore, a sign of our degeneracy — there is more. "If anyone does reach old age, his heart weakens, his head shakes, his vigor wanes, his breath reeks, . . . He is stingy and greedy, gloomy, querulous, quick to speak, slow to listen, though by no means slow to anger." Though Innocent wrote the treatise at a time when his career seemed to have reached a dead end, it is hard to suggest that he is just giving voice to personal disappointment. Stark though *On the Misery* seems there is no doubt that a poll of medieval writers and preachers would show him as a guide and a store house of exempla. Nor would the creative writers tilt the balance, as they too were more inclined toward the lugubrious when they summed up the human condition. Cicero was known and read, and respected for the gravity and dispassionate delivery of his stoic wisdom, but the heat of commitment was aroused —

for floggers and for flogged — by the hell fire presentation of sin, suffering, and deterioration that led so properly to our decline into splenetic and impotent old age.

Middle English writers picked up many threads of the fabric, and they were typical in their predilection for the darker shades. Innocent's position was rephrased and echoed in such writings as *Pricke of Conscience* and *The Wretched Engendering*. It was hard to avoid the charm of a great father of the Church who spiced his pages with such tales as that of the mother who ate her own child. With his examples of undeserved suffering (except insofar as we all deserve to suffer), Innocent struck a resonant chord; the pains of old age were the proper repayment for our innate degeneracy. Roger Bacon, who had an interest in geriatric diagnosis and medicine, was also willing to chip in this other vein: "for as much as the fathers are corrupt, they beget children of a corrupt complexion and composition, and their children from the same cause are corrupt themselves; and so corruption is derived from father to son, till abbreviation of life prevails by succession." Our lesser span of years, from the days of the patriarchs and prophets, was a numeric testimonial to our diminishing worth.[17]

*   *   *

The debate between Cicero and Innocent and those who picked up their cudgels was but one of the popular variations of the discussion of age and the life cycle. Perhaps the prize for sustained interest and the number of participants goes to those legions who turned their wit and wisdom to determining the number of stages in the full life line. At a casual level this is familiar; its most memorable phrasing is the schematization of life as a series of stages in the "all the world's a stage" speech of Jacques in *As You Like It* (II, vii). His melancholy version of conventional wisdom runs as follows:

And one man in his time plays many parts,
His acts being seven ages.

And then we move to the relevant portions, the lines that refer to the final two acts of the drama:

And the sixth age shifts
Into the lean and slipper'd pantaloon,

With spectacles on nose and pouch on side;
His youthful hose, well sav'd, a world too wide
For his shrunk shank, and his big manly voice,
Turning again towards childish treble, pipes
And whistles in his sound. Last scene of all,
That ends this strange eventful history,
Is second childishness and mere oblivion,
Sans teeth, sans eyes, sans taste, sans everything.

This was conventional stuff, if rarely so well put.[18] The idea of life as a seven-act drama was just one among many interpretations, and whether Shakespeare was taking sides or whether this scheme just lent itself to his verse is not important here. But we should remember that he had access to a vast and well known-body of views regarding the stages of life, the transitional links or barriers between the stages, and the salient features of each stage. Note that Jacques says nothing about how many years are encompassed within each stage, nor what our aggregate years *should* be at the end; only stages seem of interest.

The divisions of the life course are treated in writings that run from the Talmud and the rabbis and classical authors through Renaissance and early modern formulations. They range from as few as three to as many as a dozen or a score.[19] Those who turned to this matter — and they were many — had considerable latitude to pick and choose their favorite numbers and their pet schemes of explanation. The symmetrical or causative powers of numerology, with those of biological and heavenly and seasonal and humoral and symbolic and trinitarian support, made it likely that whatever number one chose could be supported by an appeal to some principles and data based on observation, metaphysics, and theology. Of course, in all of this speculation and pontification there was virtually no interest in looking at people who happened to be passing in the street or in looking at any of the recorded materials we have had access to.[20] Innocent had remarked that surviving to 60 was now unusual, to 70 a rarity, a heavy dictum in no way borne out by a survey of the life dates of popes from the period.[21]

In the game of pick-and-choose for the number of segments that unlock the secret of life, three, four, seven, and ten were the most popular numbers, though they hardly exhaust the possibilities. Nor did the integers cover gradations or sub-divisions. If one held that life consisted of but three or four stages, then gradations within each stage were likely, whereas if life were composed of a large number of stages then they sufficed to cover the whole. Perhaps guidance as offered by astrologers and physicians, as well as by theologians, helped denote the smaller gradations.

At its simplest, three stages marked the course of human life as laid out in keeping with the master (or The Master's) plan. Horace had pointed his readers in this direction, and his scheme — of youth, maturity, and age — had a simple if pagan symmetry to commend it. It is echoed or restated in much of the literature, as in the *Pricke of Conscience*, with its use of "Begynning, midward, and endyng." The *Parlement of Three Ages* and Chaucer's "Pardoner's Tale" offer further, and familiar, examples. Though too much should not be presumed by fallen man about God's plan, the trinitarian overtones were certainly not least among the reasons to commend this explanatory framework. That the ages of man (and, presumably, of woman, if anyone cared) were shaped to conform to the ruling spheres of Father, Son, and Holy Spirit was not hard to grasp. But we also know — with heresies and chiliastic controversies to hold before us — of the dangers that might result from a rigid adherence to any particular scheme, let alone to its allegorical extensions.

Modern scholarly navigation has charted a course through this sea of diverse opinion. We can sail the waters of literary and intellectual history and see the schools of advocates as they fall into line. They defended their choice — like the trinitarians — by the congruence of their lucky number with a number that was the key to some larger truth.[22] After the tripartite-division school comes, logically enough, those who argued for life as a four-part invention. This division offered strong ties with physiological theory and the humors, as well as with the seasons, the elements, the four divisions of the zodiac, and the principal winds. As Burrow says, the formulation of life as consisting of this number of segments offered "a satisfying scientific explanation for the *cursus aetatis* and also, through the theory of the qualities, with an account of how the order observable in the human microcosm was related to a larger macrocosmic order."[23] A twelfth-century formulation of this view held that our first age ran to 25 or 30, the next to 45 or 50, the third to 55 or 60, and the last until death: youth, maturity, old age, and decrepitude are thus set out. Uneven divisions were evidently not an insurmountable problem.

Though a number of influential thinkers had argued for six stages of life (including Augustine, Isidore of Seville, and Bede), by the twelfth and thirteenth centuries the number seven drew more adherents. The analogy of our life and the seven planets — reflecting and being influenced by plane-

tary and astrological order — was clearly attractive. Vasari tells of a Floren-
tine wall painting that depicted the seven stages of life, each in association
with a cardinal virtue: infancy with charity, boyhood with faith, adolescent
with hope, youth with temperance, manhood with prudence, old age with
fortitude, and decrepitude with justice. Another similitude was with the
seven liberal arts. Other schemes, though never as popular, can be found.
Jewish wisdom literature had advocates of a ten-age scheme, each age to last
for a decade (which by itself is a sanguine comment on patriarchal life) and
each to carry its proper increase of wisdom and holiness. Twelve was getting to be a bulky number, already, but it too had points in its favor as a
systemic explanation of the life line. As we might say in light of Bede's
views — he having variously argued for three, four, and six stages — there
may not have been any overwhelming need to settle on a single position.

This discussion ran through a good deal of writing in the fourteenth
and fifteenth centuries. Thus, for us, some reasonable portion or distillation
of the contested lore can be thought of as part of the cultural and intellectual baggage carried about by people of the day who had any larger body
of popular or literary learning at their command. In a diluted form it was
offered to those who stayed awake during sermons or who, in their bore-
dom on such occasions, looked at the decorations of the church in which
they stood. The material about the stages of life was neither arcane nor
remote. As we read Chaucer to assess how much classical and patristic lore
was common knowledge, in some form or other, so we can think of the
debate on stages of life and age in terms of a similar process of transmission
and reinterpretation. If Chaucer was versed enough in the theories about
ages and humors to write about them with such familiarity and fluency, it
follows that his audience would be able to follow the arguments and understand the allegorical and moral points behind the tale.

Nor is this search for common cultural denominators in Chaucer's audience, or in Caxton's public, or as held by those who watched the drama
cycles pass through the streets a quest for some grail cup of erudition.[24]
Rather, we are delving into what we hold to be a part of the common stock
of knowledge; people were sufficiently informed to be abreast of a particular literary or dramatic or artistic presentation. Whether they cared very
much, or whether they related any theory to the changes in their own life
and body is another matter.

What we find so striking in this issue is the absence of any signs of
awareness, let alone uneasiness, concerning the dissonance between the
transmitted wisdom and the realities of experience brought home by the

numeric sources we used in our early chapters. Individuals, no less than nations or cultures, can accommodate and even integrate articles of belief that seem to outsiders as of questionable validity and that comprise, in toto, an ill-yoked and discordant cultural construct. Seemingly, medieval views about age and the segments of the life cycle were all cobbled up into a *mentalité* that did not voice articulated doubts about the disassociation of traditional wisdom from data at hand.

*   *   *

We have collected different kinds of evidence that, collectively, point toward retirement as an institution and a practice. In this way a few were removed from the work force, with honor served and sometimes with pensions paid. It relieved them of expectations and obligations that were a normal part of an active life, and it allowed (or forced) others to step forward to take their turn. In some instances the need to step aside had to be justified or rationalized, perhaps on grounds of age itself, as with the men excused in London because they were past 70, or of age coupled with disability, as with the clerics whose sad tales were recounted in episcopal registers.

Retirement, much though we have trumpeted its existence and its real if limited applicability, was a dodge against the cruelties of old age, not a remedy for them. The mere idea of a remedy—given the realities of mortality and the premature aging to which so many must have been subject—was pretty much beyond even the realm of fantasy. If nothing could be done to alter or reverse old age, what—beyond retirement and withdrawal—did society offer to those who suffered from this invariably fatal and final condition? If we can do little about old age, what can we do, in societal terms, about the aged? If we are looking to medieval society for a philanthropic outreach, a network of ideological and practical steps toward remediation offered specifically to and for the aged, we are going to deal with data that point in two directions.

Much of the material relating to hospitals and almshouses can lead to the conclusion that the care of the aged was a significant part of a social program. But if we cast our gaze on most of the regulations and founders' instructions it is not difficult to say that the aged, as such, were often among the last to be given specific consideration and the least among those so singled out.[25] When we turn to the world of institutions and of people supported or succored by charity, as we use the term—the world of the "deserving and worthy poor"[26] — we find but little that really argues an attempt to single out the aged, as the aged, for special treatment. Much philanthropy and almsgiving was steered toward the deserving poor, as they were delineated by social structure and hierarchy of parish and town. Much of the money devoted to alms and charity went directly to paupers and the down-and-out; a typical will talks of the ranks of the poor who, it was assumed, would to be available to march in the procession and to attend the funeral.

However, insofar as the aged might have been thought to carry any special cachet that enabled them to move forward in the long queue of the needy and downtrodden, a look at individual expression in wills and at institutional formulations in charters and foundation statements shows that our quest is not going to be an easy one. Whether the plight of the aged was too common to elicit special interest, too disgusting to offer many kudos to those looking for a cause, or simply incorporated into other forms of social benefaction, we cannot say. However, a reading of a large block of philanthropic bequests gives a strong idea of the large number of indiscriminate poor who would always be there when needed. Moreover, this line of ready hands is apart from the ubiquitous fallen women, the healthy supply of unmarried and deserving girls in need of a marriage portion, those in the prisons, and the sick and disabled who are mentioned without details as to gender, medical condition, or age.

But surely the aged were at least among those whose lot was ameliorated by the distribution of charity and the provision of care. And yet we are struck by the way in which they, as a group, are rarely singled out in foundation documents, testamentary bequests, or guild provisions. The standard survey of medieval hospitals shows how definitions and boundaries have been drawn, as the chapters deal with "Hospitals for wayfarers and the sick," "Homes for the feeble and destitute," and "Homes for the insane." Hospitals, as we are reminded, were "an ecclesiastical, not a medical institution . . . for care rather than cure: for the relief of the body, when possible, but preeminently for the refreshment of the soul."[27] They were founded for "sustaining the poor and sick," their cemeteries to hold the "sick poor there dying."[28]

So, whatever they really did, they were not designed as havens for the elderly — except as the latter category of unfortunates was able to tuck itself into the other groups of the "privileged." And yet the times they were singled out, explicitly, are almost the exceptions that reinforce what seems to have been the rule — which probably was to include them without specific mention. The hospital of St. Paul at Norwich was to have "revenue sufficient to maintain fourteen poor men and women, who were decrepit with age, or languished under incurable diseases."[29] The guild of Holy Cross in St. Laurence Jewry gave alms to its members, "in infirmity by reason of mutilation of limbs or because of old age."[30] But usually a founder cared more for "the support of the poor, weak, and sick pilgrims," as was the case with the White Hall at Ilchester, or for "a hundred blind men."[31]

Individualized acts of charity were not much more disposed to single out the aged. Though most wills provided for some generalized form of charitable distribution, here too the old, as a category, rarely figure among those singled out. An expansive will of 1487 lists many types of unfortunates and provides a widely disbursed pittance for many; it offers nothing to those for whom we are most concerned.[32] Gifts and bequests went to "the presoners in the archebisshoppis preson of York . . . To every pore man and woman in masondieus in York and suburbes . . . To xv pore madyns well disposed to mariage . . . 1 beddys to be geven to pore men and pore women in the citee of York and suburbs where the most nede is." A northern will, of 1474, refers to "pore wydowes and other such pore diligent laborers in pore villages," so it must have caught some old women in its nets, if only inadvertently.[33]

We certainly assume the inclusion of some old people among the "72 poor persons, impotent, lying in beds," who were to receive 12 yards apiece of russet cloth.[34] But again, the specification reflects how the poor and downtrodden were categorized. A donor or testator was free to choose his or her own wording, and even generous wills offer us little of direct relevance; a will could cover prisoners, the sick or insane of St. Mary's Bedlam without Byshoppesgate, the poor in Bredestrete ward, and perhaps £1 for the lazar outside the bar of St. George.[35] If a bequest to "the most indigent of poor paralitics" could still miss the elderly, at least Thomas Mokking made sure he hit our mark, in a will of 1427: "26s. 8d. to be distributed among aged poor, blind, cripples, and those unable to work."[36]

I come toward the end of this study with no fixed views about how much late medieval philanthropy was ever directly steered toward the aged. Many of the detailed case studies we have chosen to emphasize this aspect of "traditional life," and tales from villages, manors, guilds, and the like do come down strongly in favor of the view that sometimes, at least, people took care of their own who had grown feeble with age.[37] And yet, when the aged are the topic of central concern, and when the materials that tell the tale of benefaction and of caregiving are laid before us, it is hard to think of the elderly as coming anywhere near a special position in regard to treatment, privilege, or public concern. The final verdict, which is never the one we can claim to have in hand in any historical study, may be as follows: In terms of a over-reaching social policy, to reach the many; Not to Come, Not for Many Years. But in terms of a recognition of special problems for many individuals, a problem that could be ameliorated at least at an individualized or small group level: Sometimes Yes, If Condition and Circumstances were Favorable.

*   *   *

In looking at a small part of the body of medieval speculation about the stages of life, at the positive and negative formulations about the value of old age and the elderly, and at some literary tales that make fun of December-May marriages, we have remarked that most of this material was cast with little interest in or concern for lived experience. The bulk of the reflections about the life line, the norms of age and behavior, and the wisdom pertaining to survival and longevity seem to have been formulated and promulgated as part of a dialogue conducted for many centuries by theologians, writers, artists, and medical theorists. Astrologers and astronomers lent their wisdom, while civil servants who advised princes and bishops did not do so, even if they were busy at the time pensioning off their aging colleagues (though the ever-complaining Hoccleve may be the great exception to this rule). In this gulf between the wisdom of the literary world and the realities of experience — available near at hand to the most casual of observers — we have a striking and persistent instance of cognitive dissonance. What men said about age and the life experience as a cultural construct bore but little relationship to what was going on all around — if anyone had cared to take mundane materials and observations into account. Nor, it is of interest to note, did anyone seem to worry about this gap. The non-integration of wisdom and experience did not pose a problem. In fairness, tunnel vision and a focus on certain pre-selected segments of reality are not peculiar to medieval society.

Today we are prone to enter into debate about the relationship between the world of culture and practice, that of articulated texts and that based on experience and empirical data. Though we accept that the realms of theoretical construction and individualized knowledge are bound together, coupled in a complex and ongoing dialectic of both the tangible and the re-created, it is also our privilege to decide which is the informing partner. If we are hard pressed to say that behavioral patterns as revealed by empirical examination are the prime movers in human society, we are still reluctant to allow structures spun of ideology and discourse to prevail, at least not without a considerable struggle. Jacob and the Angel wrestled all night. How far we are able to stretch our inferences from behavior to world view, let alone to motivation and intention, may be an imponderable, but even imponderables can be pondered, from time to time, with some profit.

The longevity of biblical figures was part of the lore that was transmitted and mulled over. Not only are the ages of the patriarchs stated in quantitative terms, if only to emphasize how our puny standards were below those heroic ones, but fables and moral tales were spun around the allegorical interpretations of the life span. As mythopaeic cannon fodder men played with the idea that Adam had died at 930 (giving away three-score years and ten so King David might live to 70). Abraham had died at 175, on the very day Esau sold his birthright, and he would have lived to 180 except that God cut five years off so the patriarch would be spared having to see more of his grandson's iniquities.[38] Such material was played out for its numerical potential; the York plays depicted Abraham as being 100 at the sacrifice of Isaac: "alde and all vnwelde."

Nor were biography and hagiography oblivious to the duration of life question, though quantitative assessments were sporadic and, in different contexts, apt to carry varying weights. The saint or hero might have a short and dramatic life, while at other times the span ran toward or beyond the biblical prescription. In popular literature and secular biography the portrayal of great age, with the burdens it imposed and the efforts to surmount them, were themes to evoke admiration and sympathy.[39] One might not love the aged merely for their years, but they had the power—by dint of their ability to survive—to make an impression on the public consciousness.

This is certainly piecemeal material. It is introduced now to demonstrate that the questions we looked at above, such as those covering family continuity and career length, were not totally foreign to life as touched, at least in passing, by literary reflection. In the idiom of the day, heroic life spans—contemporary, historical, or literary—could be expanded upon to reveal the links between holy or myth history and the world inhabited by ordinary mortals. A bishop, admittedly with mixed enthusiasm, might accept that members of his team had to retire. They would go to some honorable stretch of pasture, supported by resources and avoid embarrassing the church. And sometimes it was the bishop himself, perhaps reconciled to his old-age by the placebo of a handsome pension. Others also come to this recognition of the toll taken by the years, not just kings and abbots but — at a level below the sources we have utilized — innumerable parents and grandparents in towns, villages, and the countryside.[40]

For all the dominance of literary presentation, quantitative information about ages and years of activity was produced by and for a range of governmental and administrative proceedings. Did men think about the span and quality of life when they were actually engaged in gathering the testimony of old soldiers now in their 70s and 80s and who sometimes claimed years even well beyond these? They must have noted, even if they did not record, the physical appearances that confronted them; what did they think of the garrulousness, the wandering memory, and the failing physical performance while taking the depositions? How much rambling was compressed into the terse locutions of an Inquisition? how many false starts and digressions were part of the leap from oral testimony to written record? It seems unlikely — especially after all the material we have marshaled that argues for the presence and visibility of the aged — that such matters were not part of a day's business, unrecorded though they may have been.

These comments are not a summing up for the prosecution against a contemporary brief for sensitivity. It is not for us to insist upon a harsh reality or to impose informed self-consciousness upon the outlook or mode of expression of late medieval society. Such constructs are rather a reflection of how certain elements, out of the large range of behavioral and conceptual data, get picked up and amplified. And the larger-than-life role given to such constructs helps ensure them of a privileged treatment in subsequent discourse, in the efforts of modern students to reconstruct that society. How much of what I have chosen to talk about would have made sense to them; how much would have been adjudged as missing the point?

The record sources we used above seem to be silent if we are looking for many details of debility and physical and mental incapacity caused or exacerbated by old age. We gained some insights from the descriptions of the common and multiple woes of the old men of London. We know, from records of clerical retirements, of references to the "senile." This subsumes all sorts of old and feeble under the general category of the aged. Details of the decay, the stages and styles of breakdown, are not transmitted, and beyond the pathetic creature of Shakespeare's seventh age there is little to fill in the gaps. In some instances men saw the breakdown of body and mind as inherent in the aging process. We have alluded to the sorry last years of

Edward III and Henry VIII. Was the general veil of silence drawn because of compassion, or because of awe at the mighty being brought low, or out of disgust and indifference? There is little reason to expect much sympathy for those of power and status who lost their way as they aged. Descriptions of aged incompetence and incontinence are abundant in literary presentations and in normative literature but not in biography. Maybe details or case studies were unseemly and, in terms of the moral world and moralization, unnecessary.

In conclusion, if we can hardly paint a rosy picture, we should give some credit where it need not be denied. At least we do not find social currents that worked to sweep the aged aside, to marginalize them because of their exceptional survival. Late medieval England was not a society deeply caught up in the throes of the mass hysteria or calculated social control by means of a witch craze, and it did not seek out the elderly as objects for persecution or social ostracism. How could it: to a great extent, many of those very aged were in positions of power, wealth, and culturally endorsed authority? This stand-off, the unsung triumph of a policy of live-and-let-live, is worth noting, particularly as much of the creative writing could lead to the view that the elderly drew little support or sympathy and were systematically marginalized. If they were not rewarded for the mere fact (or feat) of longevity and survival, let alone venerated for these phenomena, neither were they forced out of the center into the by-ways of meager existence. The aged could hold on to a place in society *if* their resources and networks made it possible. Whether they actually did so, in the majority of cases, is a theme with as many variations as there are case studies. For the most part the biological process marginalized them quite enough; the social process might work in that direction, or it might be a countering force. And, in conclusion, it is heartening to note that we have also seen the way in which some of the elderly were quite capable of pushing back, and pushing pretty firmly at that, for some considerable span of years.

Notes

Introduction

1. The literature on old age is vast, though most of it relates to the modern world. A good general introduction is Robert H. Binstock and Ethel Shanas, eds., *Handbook of Aging and the Social Sciences*, 2nd ed. (New York: Van Nostrand Reinhold, 1985), and James Burren and K. Warner Schare, eds., *Handbook of the Psychology of Aging*, 2nd ed. (New York: Van Nostrand Reinhold, 1985). Joseph T. Freeman, *Aging: Its History and Literature* (New York: Human Sciences Press, 1979), for a quick historical overview, mainly looking at the ideas of the "great white fathers" about age; Mirko D. Grmek, *On Aging and Old Age: Basic Problems and Historic Aspects of Gerontology and Geriatrics* (The Hague, W. Junk, 1958); Gerald J. Gruman, ed., *Roots of Modern Gerontology and Geriatrics* (New York: Arno Press, 1979), for some older articles expecially by Frederick Zeman that helped establish historical gerontology as a field on its own; Leo W. Simmons, *The Role of the Aged in Primitive Society* (New Haven, CT: Yale Univ. Press, 1945: repr., New York, 1970), for much comparative if now outmoded material from an anthropological and ethnographic perspective. Simmons collects material from "among" a vast range of peoples, cultures, and tribes. Many dimensions of the issue are introduced by the article on "Aging" in *International Encyclopedia of the Social Sciences* (New York: Macmillan, 1968), I, 176–202, written by the team of James E. Birren, Yonina Talmon, and Earl F. Cheit. For an older demographic survey, Louis I. Dublin, Alfred J. Lotka, and Mortimer Spiegelman, *Length of Life: A Study of the Life Table*, rev. ed. (New York: Ronald Press, 1949), comparative and historical material in a volume dedicated by its authors to the president of the Metropolitan Life Insurance Company.

2. The pertinent medieval materials are listed below, especially in note 3. For some studies that offer and invite comparisons (despite my own warnings about the danger of looking for similarities from historical contexts that are so different as to tell us little, but that human responses to set problems must operate within fixed parameters): Peter N. Stearns, *Old Age in European Society: The Case of France* (London: Croom Helm, 1977); Stearns, ed., *Old Age in Pre-Industrial Society* (New York and London: Holmes and Meier, 1982); David G. Troyansky, *Old Age in the Old Regime: Image and Expression in Eighteenth-Century France* (Ithaca, NY: Cornell Univ. Press, 1989); Jill S. Quadagno, *Aging in Early Industrial Society: Work, Family, and Social Policy in Nineteenth-Century England* (New York: Academic Press, 1982). For the United States there are studies that look at colonial definitions of the topic and the transition to the modern definition and social response, as well as a great

flood of writings on contemporary social problems: W. Andrew Achenbaum, *Old Age in the New Land: The American Experience Since 1790* (Baltimore and London: Johns Hopkins Univ. Press, 1978); Carole Haber, *Beyond Sixty-Five: The Dilemma of Old Age in America's Past* (Cambridge: Cambridge Univ. Press, 1983); David Hackett Fischer, *Growing Old in America* (Oxford and New York: Oxford Univ. Press, 1978). General comments of interest are in Tamara K. Hareven, "The Life Course and Aging in Historical Perspective," in *Aging and Life Course Transitions: An Interdisciplinary Perspective*, ed. Tamara Hareven and Kathleen J. Adams (New York: Guilford Press, 1982), 1–26. European historians seem to have less trouble with the relatively heartless social view of the elderly than do American historians, who seem to think that a decline in sympathy is part of an "American dilemma" and an indictment of egalitarian society. American historians tend to see the tale of treatment of and respect for the elderly as one of relative decline, from a traditional past in which they were cared for toward a heartless and fragmented industrial society. In fairness, however, no one posits a lost golden age. Growing old was never seen to be a lot of fun. For "the second sex," Peter N. Stearns, "Old Women: Some Historical Observations," *Journal of Family History* 5 (1980): 44–57, p. 44, "Female old age . . . remains as unheeded in the historical literature as it may be in life."

3. Simone de Beauvoir, *The Coming of Age*, trans. Patrick O'Brian (New York: Putnam, 1972; first published as *La Vieillesse* in 1970), not the first major treatment but the one that introduced a wide reading public to its historical as well as its literary dimensions. The recent flood of scholarly work that focuses on the Middle Ages includes (but is hardly limited to) John A. Burrow, *The Ages of Man: A Study in Medieval Writing and Thought* (Oxford: Clarendon Press, 1986), and his "Chaucer's *Knight's Tale* and The Three Ages of Man," in his *Essays on Medieval Literature* (Oxford: Oxford Univ. Press, 1984), 27–44; Michael M. Sheehan, ed., *Aging and the Aged in Medieval Europe* (Toronto: Pontifical Institute of Mediaeval Studies, 1990); Georges Minois, *History of Old Age from Antiquity to the Renaissance*, trans. Sarah H. Tenison (Chicago: Univ. of Chicago Press, 1989); Mary Dove, *The Perfect Age of Man's Life* (Cambridge: Cambridge Univ. Press, 1980); Michael Goodich, *From Birth to Old Age: The Human Life Cycle in Medieval Thought, 1250–1350* (Lanham, MD: Univ. Press of America, 1989). An older study, Samuel Chew, *The Pilgrimage of Life* (New Haven, CT: Yale Univ. Press, 1962), is still of value. The relevant essays in a valuable collection of papers from a 1984 conference, Margaret Pelling and Richard M. Smith, eds., *Life, Death, and the Elderly: Historical Perspectives* (London and New York: Routledge, 1991), will be referred to below.

4. Elizabeth Sears, *The Ages of Man: Medieval Interpretations of the Life Cycle* (Princeton, NJ: Princeton Univ. Press, 1986); Philippa Tristram, *Figures of Life and Death in Medieval English Literature* (New York: New York Univ. Press, 1976), obviously concerned with literature but with an interest in how literary themes and *topoi* carry a visual impact. For a detailed iconographic analysis of one church's visual schematization of life's stages, E. Clive Rouse and Audley Baker, "The Wall-Paintings at Longthorpe Tower near Peterborough, Northants," *Archaeologia* 96 (1955): 1–57. The seven ages of this particular portrayal (infans, puer, adolescens, vir, mediaevus, senectus, and decrepitus) are shown (insofar as they are preserved) in the plates that accompany the article.

5. Minois, *History of Old Age*, looks at the ancient world with some attention. For a detailed if old fashioned treatment, Bessie Ellen Richardson, *Old Age Among the Ancient Greeks* (Baltimore: Johns Hopkins Univ. Pres, 1933; repr., New York: Greenwood Press, 1969).

6. Roger Bacon, *De Retardatione Accidentium Senectutis*, ed. A. G. Little and E. Withington (Oxford: Clarendon Press, 1928); Gabriele Zerbi, *Gerontocomia: On the Care of the Aged*, trans. L. R. Lind, Memoirs of the American Philosophical Society 182 (Philadelphia: the Society, 1988). Lind also includes a translation of Maximianus, *Elegies on Old Age and Love*, 307–36. Lind's bibliography for Zerbi (pp. 337–39) offers some guides to medieval medical literature on age and aging.

7. Josiah Cox Russell, *British Medieval Population* (Albuquerque: Univ. of New Mexico Press, 1948), 182–86; Sylvia Thrupp, *The Merchant Class of Medieval London, 1300–1500* (Chicago: Univ. of Chicago Press, 1948). Thrupp's views are supported by Jennifer I. Kermode, "The Merchants of Three Northern English Towns," in Clough, *Profession, Vocation and Culture in Later Medieval England*, 7–48, esp. 12–16. On the demography of the peerage, T. H. Hollingsworth, *The Demography of the British Peerage*, Supplement to *Population Studies* 18, 2 (1964); J. T. Rosenthal, "Mediaeval Longevity and the Secular Peerage, 1350–1500," *Population Studies* 27 (1973): 287–93; Hollingsworth, "A Note on the Mediaeval Longevity of the Secular Peerage, 1350–1500," *Population Studies* 29 (1975): 155–59, which is mainly on attack on how Rosenthal cast his figures and calculations. I go along with Hollingsworth in this controversy.

8. Georges Duby, "In Northwestern France: The 'Youth' in Twelfth-Century Aristocratic Society," in *Lordship and Community in Medieval Europe*, ed. Fredric L. Cheyette (New York: Holt, Rinehart, and Winston, 1968), 198–209. Also Anthony Esler, *The Aspiring Mind of the Elizabethan Younger Generation* (Durham, NC: Duke Univ. Press, 1966), for one of the few attempts to look at political and social dynamics in terms of generations and age cohorts. David Herlihy, "The Generation in Medieval History," *Viator* 5 (1974): 347–66, a wide sweep and a wealth of suggestions — real vintage Herlihy. On youth-age tension, Antonia Gransden, "Childhood and Youth in Medieval England," *Nottingham Mediaeval Studies* 16 (1972): 3–19, with many examples from secular life and from ecclesiastical settings. In one case (p. 14) three senior monks had to be excused from participating in an arbitration proceeding because of a rupture, piles, and a stroke respectively. For a modern study of these rivalries, Vern L. Bengston et al., "Generation, Cohorts, and Relations between the Generations," in Banstock and Shanas, *Handbook of Aging and the Social Sciences*, 304–38, with a full (if aging) bibliography.

9. Roger Virgoe, "The Earlier Knyvetts: The Rise of a Norfolk Gentry Family, Part II," *Norfolk Archaeology* 41,3 (1992): 249–78. The first part of the family study appeared in *Norfolk Archaeology*, 41,1 (1990): 1–15.

10. Virgoe, "The Earlier Knyvetts," Part II, 250: "John Knyvett had long retired from active involvement in the running of his Norfolk estates and from local government." The quote in the text, below, is from p. 253.

11. This kind of material about age, survival, and three-generation families is common in studies of this sort. For example, in my article on a West Country family: "Sir Richard Choke (d. 1483) of Long Ashton," *Somerset Archaeological and*

Natural History 127 (1984, for 1983): 105–21. Virtually all the recent county and community studies offer relevant material, though different authors devote varying degrees of explicit attention to such matters. Good material is found in but hardly limited to Michael J. Bennett, *Community, Class, and Careerism: Cheshire and Lancashire Society in the Age of "Sir Gawain and the Green Knight"* (Cambridge: Cambridge Univ. Press, 1983); Nigel Saul, *Scenes from Provincial Life: Knightly Families in Sussex, 1280–1460* (Oxford: Clarendon Press, 1986); Saul, *Knights and Esquires: The Gloucestershire Gentry in the Fourteenth Century* (Oxford: Clarendon Press, 1981), especially pp. 106–67; Simon J. Payling, *Political Society in Lancastrian England: The Greater Gentry of Nottinghamshire* (Oxford: Clarendon Press, 1991).

12. Alicia K. Nitecki, "Figures of Old Age in Fourteenth-Century English Literature," in Sheehan, *Aging and the Aged*, 107–16; John A. Burrow, "Chaucer's 'Knight's Tale' and the Three Ages of Man," in his *Essays on Medieval Literature*, 27–48; John V. Scattergood, "Old Age, Love and Friendship in Chaucer's 'Envoy to Scogan,'" *Nottingham Medieval Studies* 35 (1991): 92–101; John M. Steadman, "Old Age and 'Contemptus Mundi' in the 'Pardoner's Tale,'" *Medium Aevum* 33, 2 (1964): 121–30. That a recent study of a closed community says, regarding age composition that, "in medieval Europe anyone over the age of 60 was probably old" is an indication of how accustomed we now are to seeing 60-year-olds in the historical landscape—in contrast to the generalizations of both medieval informants and scholars of not so long ago. The quote is from Barbara Harvey, *Living and Dying in England, 1100–1540: The Monastic Experience* (Oxford: Clarendon Press, 1993), 207. For an opening to the "stages of life" question—dealt with below at length—Henning Kirk, "Geriatric Medicine and the Categorisation of Old Age—The Historical Linkage," *Ageing and Society* 12 (1992): 483–98.

13. Luke Demaitre, "The Care and Extension of Old Age in Medieval Medicine," in Sheehan, *Aging and the Aged*, 3–22, p. 8, saying that the argument for the earliest onset of old age he has encountered—between 35 and 40—is found in Bernard de Gordon: "Senectus seu [etas] consistencie durat a xxxv fere usque ad xl annos" (with the reference being from Vatican Ms Pal 1174, f. 83v).

Chapter 1. Inquisitions Post Mortem as a Window on Old Age

1. Lawrence R. Poos, *A Rural Society After the Black Death: Essex, 1350–1525* (Cambridge: Cambridge Univ. Press, 1991); Poos, "Life Expectancy and 'Age of First Appearance' in Medieval Manorial Court Records," *Local Population Studies* 37 (autumn 1986): 45–52; E. A. Wrigley and R. S. Schofield, *The Population History of England, 1541–1871: A Reconstruction* (Cambridge, MA: Harvard Univ. Press, 1981). As well as Hollingsworth's more technical treatment of the peerage, cited above, his *Historical Demography* (Ithaca, NY: Cornell Univ. Press, 1969) is still of value as a general introduction. I wish to thank Larry Poos for giving these opening chapters a sympathetic reading and for sharing his own work-in-progress with me.

2. Russell, *British Medieval Population*, 175–88, for life tables for secular males, and 186–87 for summary discussion of this material. Also, 189–92 for an attempt to

reconstruct the life tables of the male monastic population. For a recent exchange of views of the value of demographic sources and how we can best trust and interpret them: E. D. Jones, "Going Round in Circles: Some New Evidence for Population in the Later Middle Ages," *Journal of Medieval History* 15 (1989): 329–45; and answered, with some heat, by Mark Bailey, "Blowing Up Bubbles: Some New Demographic Evidence for the Fifteenth Century?" *Journal of Medieval History* 15 (1989): 347–58. Barbara Harvey, *Living and Dying*, 102–39, for a demographic analysis of the community of Westminster Abbey. Her caveat is worth restating: "In population studies relating to small numbers, finding the right benchmark is always difficult" (124). For demography from a physical more than a record basis, Anne L. Grauer, "Patterns of Life and Death: The Paleodemography of Medieval York," in *Health in Past Societies: Biocultural Integration of Human Skeletal Remains in Archaeological Contexts*, ed. Helen Bush and Marek Zvelebil, British Archaeological Reports International Series 567 (Oxford: Tempus Reparatum, 1991), 67–80 for the tables with the relevant data.

3. My approach differs from that of Russell, though obviously his conclusions and mine run in the same direction. His tests indicate that rounding off was as likely to report a younger age as an older one, and the rounding off bias therefore was not skewed and, given a large number of cases, its effect on demographic findings was minimal and self-correcting: Russell, *British Medieval Population*, 109–10. For some other approaches to the question of the weight and power of numbers in medieval thought: Basil Christopher Butler, *Number Symbolism* (New York: Barnes and Noble, 1970); Vincent Hopper, *Medieval Number Symbolism* (Philadelphia: R. Wester, 1978); John Goronwy Edwards, "The Emergence of Majority Rule in English Parliamentary Elections," *Transactions of the Royal Historical Society* 5th ser. 14 (1964): 175–96.

4. Both my argument and much of what has been written in the recent studies of community and county society posit a world in which people knew what was going on around them. K. B. McFarlane spotted this point years ago, when he quoted from the Stonor Letters: "Even the remotest degrees of kinship were kept in mind . . . 'it is reasonable [for] a gentilman to know his pedegre and his possibilyte' and to be upset if a third-cousin acted with 'gret straungenese' towards him." *The Nobility of Later Medieval England* (Oxford: Clarendon Press, 1973), 113.

5. Mary J. Carruthers, *The Book of Memory: A Study of Memory in Medieval Culture* (Cambridge: Cambridge Univ. Press, 1990), an erudite study, mostly devoted to major medieval thinkers; Frances A. Yates, *The Art of Memory* (Chicago: Univ. of Chicago Press, 1966), 50–104 being of most relevance; Jonathan D. Spence, *The Memory Palace of Matteo Ricci* (New York: Viking Penguin, 1983); Bruce M. Ross, *Remembering the Personal Past: Descriptions of Autobiographical Memory* (New York: Oxford Univ. Press, 1991). I discovered, when I became interested in the issue, that the literature on memory is about as extensive as that on old age; for valuable general reflections, see Paul Connerton, *How Societies Remember* (Cambridge: Cambridge Univ. Press, 1989).

6. James Fentress and Chris Wickham, *Social Memory* (Oxford: Blackwell, 1992), with the material here drawn specifically from pp. 7 and 139. The material on oral history also seems pertinent: Jan Vansina, *Oral Tradition: A Study in Historical*

Methodology (Chicago: Aldine, 1961), and *Oral Tradition as History* (Madison: Univ. of Wisconsin Press, 1985), a basic introduction to a vast field.

7. Michael T. Clanchy, *From Memory to Written Record: England, 1066–1307*, 2nd ed. (Oxford: Blackwell, 1993), as the seminal discussion of this transition in medieval England (first published in 1979). Russell, *British Medieval Population*, 92–117, for a discussion of Inquisitions Post Mortem and Proofs of Age that largely vindicates their value for demography. Russell says that where heirs can be traced in subsequent records the ages given in the documents in question seem to be very close to the mark, and that the records are sufficiently reliable to be used when "the law of large numbers" is in operation. Larry Poos and colleagues are working to extend the tracing method and to test it against the teeth of tougher statistical and demographic tests than those available when Russell published his findings; Poos thinks the method may even show that IPMs are perhaps conservative about age (private conversation). Much of the criticism of inquisitions and proofs focuses on their formulaic nature, and the argument against their credibility is presented by R. F. Hunnisett, "The Reliability of Inquisitions as Historical Evidence," in *The Study of Medieval Records: Essays in Honour of Kathleen Major*, ed. D. A. Bullough and R. L. Storey (Oxford: Clarendon Press, 1971), 206–35.

8. As well as the transition from the oral and the communally recollected, at the "producing" end of the process, there is the question of how and why different kinds of administrative proceedings were enrolled or recorded in any particular form or fashion. When — and how early in the process — was it determined that entries on the close and patent rolls would be written on a series of short membranes which were then stitched together until the page reached some 8 or 10 feet? The archaeology of archival development is a topic that would have interested such pioneers of administrative history as T. F. Tout and V. H. Galbraith, though there is no indication that either man turned in an explicit fashion to work in this area.

9. *The Complete Peerage* (*CP*) has many examples of exact information about the hour, as well as the date, of births and deaths. For those of importance, as well as for those of families with a clerical and scribal tradition, recording such matters may have been the custom: Vicary Gibbs et al., *The Complete Peerage*, 12 vols. in 13 (London: St. Catherine Press, 1910–59). For a visual example, Michael K. Jones and Malcolm G. Underwood, *The Queen's Mother: Lady Margaret Beaufort, Countess of Richmond and Derby* (Cambridge: Cambridge Univ. Press, 1992), Plate I (opp. p. 124) for a depiction of the Beaufort Hours, with the entry of Lady Margaret's birth (31 May, 1443).

10. Quoting respectively *Richard II* 1298; *Henry IV* 349; *Henry VII, ii* 172. There are other precise references: *Richard II* 31: "two years on the feast of the Invention of the Holy Cross last," or (*Richard II* 1283), the case of "Richard Talbot, aged 43 weeks, [who] is the son . . . and next heir, and on the day of his death he [the father] had no other son or daughter born legitimately . . . or 47 weeks . . . or 1 year." All references to *Richard II, Henry IV*, and *Henry VII* are to item rather than page numbers.

11. *Richard II* 132; *Henry IV* 540 and 668; *Henry VII, ii* 279. Also, *Henry IV* 717: the son and heir is 21 years and 12 weeks; *Henry VII, ii* 190: a son's son is 21 and of full age; *Henry VII, ii* 576: "aged 20 years complete (annorum perfecte preterito-

rum) 6 January last"; *Richard II* 1054: the son and heir is "19 and more," which is also expressed as "19 years and 27 weeks and 1 day."

12. *Richard II* 48; *Henry IV* 13. Again, comparable material is not hard to find: *Richard II* 318: the son is 19 or 19 1/2 or 21, or, as another document says, "age not known because he was not born in the county"; *Richard II* 484: the son and heir is "12 years and 25 weeks and 6 days," or perhaps he is "14 years and 25 weeks"; *Henry IV* 435, for a brother and heir who is either 50 and more, or 40, or 44.

13. *Richard II* 101.

14. *Richard II* 624, 137, for an example of second cousins as the heirs of an idiot: the line runs from her father's sister's son's children, Joan, 24 years and more, and Agnes, 18 years and more. In *Henry VII, ii* 18–19 we have a genealogy that is puzzling, regarding her "cousins and next heirs." One of those named is 7 and more "and in the king's ward," while another family line pushed a man of 56 and more forward. *Richard II* 243: a third cousin as heir, from a descent traced back to a great grandfather's brother, then down to the brother's great grandson, now aged 40 and more. Is this a little too much to take without a grain of salt? There does not seem to be any way of knowing; presumably, *they* were willing to swallow such information. A comparison of what was needed to prove a case in the courts may give an idea of what materials, though probably in a considerably less formal guise, may have sufficed for an Inquisition.

15. Full citations for *Richard II* and *Henry IV* are given in the list of abbreviations and the bibliography. On the idea that one set of inquisitions is much the same as another, even J. C. Russell, who defends these sources so valiantly, is willing to make concessions: *British Medieval Population*, 103, "This is the way of legal fictions. They are apt to become rather humdrum and without human interest."

16. John Hajnal, "European Marriage Patterns in Perspective," in Glass and Everley, *Population in History*, 110–43. For current thinking with an eye on comparing northern and southern Europe, see P. J. P. Goldberg, "Marriage, Migration, and Servanthood: The York Case Paper Evidence," and Richard M. Smith, "Geographical Diversity in the Resort to Marriage in Late Medieval Europe: Work, Reputation, and Unmarried Females in the Household Formation Systems of Northern and Southern Europe," in Goldberg, ed., *Woman Is a Worthy Wight* (Stroud: Alan Sutton, 1992), 1–15 and 16–59 respectively. On the age of marriage in aristocratic families in early modern times, Sigismund Peller, "Births and Deaths Among Europe's Ruling Families Since 1500," in Glass and Eversley, *Population in History*, 87–100. Goldberg's fuller treatment can now be found in P. J. P. Goldberg, *Women, Work, and Life Cycle in a Medieval Economy* (Oxford: Clarendon Press, 1992), 225–32 (analyzing Zvi Razi's work), and 272–79 for data from York. Goldberg's view supports the idea that the "European marriage pattern" was prevalent in post-plague England, and so does the community study of Cicely Howell, *Land, Family and Inheritance in Transition: Kibworth Harcourt, 1280–1700* (Cambridge: Cambridge Univ. Press, 1983), 221–25.

17. *Henry IV* 594, for the aunt of 60 and more; *Richard II* 418, for a brother of 60; *Richard II* 376, for 2 nephews, sons of 2 sisters, "each of them is 40 years of age and more."

18. *Richard II* 161, for the first cousin. For a second cousin, once removed, and aged 50 years and more, *Henry IV* 1156.

19. For early modern patriarchy, Gordon Schochet, *Patriarchalism in Political Thought: The Authoritarian Family and Political Speculation* (Oxford: Blackwell, 1975).

20. The inquisitions for Yorkshire are simply based on those printed in W. Paley Baildon and J. W. Clay, eds., *Inquisitions Post Mortem Relating to Yorkshire, of the Reigns of Henry IV and Henry V (Yorkshire)* Yorkshire Archaeological Society 59 (1918). Those for Nottinghamshire represent the inquisitions from 1 Henry IV through the accession of Henry VII, taken from the two volumes as published, K. S. S. Train, ed., *Abstracts of the Inquisitions Post Mortem Relating to Nottinghamshire, 1350–1436*, Thoroton Society Record Series 12 (1952), and Mary A. Renshaw, transcr. and ed., *Inquisitions Post Mortem Relating to Nottinghamshire, 1437–1485*, Thoroton Society Record Series 17 (1956) (*Nottinghamshire 1 and 2*). For Lancashire, also covering 1399–1485, Christopher Towneley, Roger Didsworth, and William Langton, eds., *Abstracts of Inquisitions Post Mortem*, 1, 2: Chetham Society, Old Series, 95 and 99 (1875–76)(*Lancashire*). For a guide to some of the other collections in print, see E. L. C. Mullins, *Texts and Calendars* (London: Royal Historical Society, 1958), index.

21. Philippa C. Maddern, *Violence and Social Order: East Anglia, 1422–1442* (Oxford: Clarendon Press, 1992), 32. The context refers to writs of trespass and the possibility of collusive action that could be (and often was) hidden by their formulaic and stilted wording. However, the same shoe fits the present line of inquiry.

22. Dowagers and their households are yet another topic worthy of more study. For an introduction, Rowena E. Archer, "Rich Old Ladies: The Problem of Late Medieval Dowagers," in *Property and Politics: Essays in Late Medieval English History*, ed. Tony Pollard (Gloucester: Alan Sutton, 1984), 15–35; Jennifer C. Ward, *English Noblewomen in the Later Middle Ages* (London and New York: Longman, 1992); Joel T. Rosenthal, *Patriarchy and Families of Privilege in Fifteenth-Century England* (Philadelphia: Univ. of Pennsylvania Press, 1991), 231–46; Kate Mertes, *The English Noble Household, 1250–1600: Good Governance and Politic Rule* (Oxford: Blackwell, 1988), 52–74.

23. *Richard II* 361 and 620.

24. *Henry VII, i* 1165.

25. *Henry VII, i* 1170 and 418.

26. *Henry VII, ii* 121 and 200; *Henry VII, i* 85 and 273.

27. *Henry VII, ii* 188 and 290.

28. *Henry VII, ii* 291, 239.

Chapter 2. Proofs of Age and the Cultures of Attesting to Age

1. Frederick Pollock and Frederic William Maitland, *The History of English Law Before the Time of Edward I*, 2nd rev. ed., intro. S. F. C. Milsom (Cambridge: Cambridge Univ. Press, 1968), II, 640: "the witnesses whom he adduces to prove his full age are examined: that is to say, they are asked how they come to remember

the time of his birth, and they answer with talk of coincidences." On the administrative procedure, E. R. Stevenson, "The Escheator," in *The English Government at Work, 1327–1336, Volume II: Fiscal Administration*, ed. W. A. Morris and Joseph R. Strayer (Cambridge, MA: Mediaeval Academy of America, 1947), 109–67, 131–32, "Was their testimony taken individually or in the presence of one another?" In this chapter I assume that the latter alternative was followed; its socializing consequences do much to explain the details of the material attested. A number of the writings of Sue Sheridan Walker shed light on proofs and their attendant procedures; the most relevant is "Proof of Age of Feudal Heirs in Medieval England," *Mediaeval Studies* 35 (1973): 306–23.

2. Poos, *A Rural Society*, 190–93: "Many of these narratives were somewhat stereotypical, being repeated at different hearings by different witnesses with only minor variations in detail . . . Nevertheless, so long as one is concerned merely with the general plausibility of situations details in their testimonies, particularly where these are less stereotypical, there is no reason to reject unreservedly the notion that the vignettes represent experiences actually drawn from everyday life" (p. 190). Poos talks in general about the value of oral testimony in "Population Turnover in Medieval Essex: The Evidence of Some Early Fourteenth-Century Tithing Lists" in *The World We Have Gained: Histories of Population and Social Structure: Essays Presented to Peter Laslett on his Seventieth Birthday*, ed. Lloyd Bonfield et al. (Oxford: Blackwell, 1986), 1–22. Two articles of value for this discussion are included in *On the Laws and Customs of England: Essays in Honor of Samuel E. Thorne*, ed. Morris S. Arnold, Sally A. Scully, and Stephen S. White (Chapel Hill: Univ. of North Carolina Press, 1981): Charles Donahue, Jr., "Proof by Witnesses in the Church Courts of Medieval England: An Imperfect Reception of Learned Law," 127–58; Donald W. Sutherland, "Legal Reasoning in the Fourteenth Century: The Invention of 'Color' in Pleading," 182–94.

3. Hunnisett, "The Reliability of Inquisitions," 206, on the "artificial nature" of proofs of age. Notes 1, 3, and 4 of p. 206 refer to reviews (mostly over the years in the *English Historical Review*) of published volumes of Inquisitions, reviews wherein the reviewers have cast aspersions on the value of the material as presented in its formulaic fashion. Russell, *British Medieval Population*, 102–4, for a defense of the Proofs.

4. T. A. M. Bishop, reviewing volume XII of the Inquisitions (39–43 Edward III), *English Historical Review* 55 (1940): 328: the "correspondences between the recollections of different juries suggest that jurors were furnished with sets of answers prepared in advance." I wish to thank Simon Payling for enlarging on this idea, in conversation about the sources and the demography of the peerage. Russell, for the defense, *British Medieval Population* 103: "From this report [the very one cited by Bishop] it would seem that such mistakes and falsifications were not condoned by the officials."

5. For an example of the drama—usually the kind one would prefer to avoid—the surrounded daily life, at all social levels, Barbara A. Hanawalt, *The Ties That Bound: Peasant Families in Medieval England* (New York and Oxford: Oxford Univ. Press, 1986).

6. Poos, *A Rural Society*, 282–83, on the links between oral testimony and its

memories, and the reliance on written records, in the context of getting legal and administrative business taken care of a rural setting. Poos endorses Michael Clanchy's distinction between "literate mentality" and "practical literacy," as a guide to the tangle presented by the sources. For a whole range of comments about exact age and when and how and why it came to be part of the regular dialogue of public business and private knowledge, Keith Thomas, "Age and Authority in Early Modern England," *Proceedings of the British Academy* (1975), especially 205–10.

7. Pollock and Maitland, *History of English Law*, II, 640–41, for the observation that the material attested—whatever its weight—is rarely disputed. Sue Sheridan Walker, "Proof of Age," 321, for the astute comment that "no one ever seems to have cross examined jurors to ask how they knew it had been exactly 21 years ago." For an example of an important proof of age that seemed to walk the fine line, that of Richard, Duke of York, *CPR 1429–36*, 207–8 (dated 12 May, 1432): "It appears that according to some of the inquisitions which have been taken after the death of the said earl [of March] the said Duke is of full age, but according to others . . . he is not; and that many of the inquisitions taken after the death of the said duchess [of York] were insufficiently taken or not returned." Since he is acknowledged as already having "done the king good service" he gets the benefit of the doubt and is thereby allowed to take over his lands.

8. Many of the recent studies of county communities emphasize structure. If we go behind structure and look at function or process, we can visualize the kinds of interaction I describe here, the creation of an "event" through the playing out of ritualized roles within a predetermined pattern as it is defined by the social, economic, and political contours of the local community. For some studies that lend themselves to this line of explication, Roger Virgoe, "Aspects of the County Community in the Fifteenth Century," in *Profit, Piety and the Professions in Later Medieval England*, ed. Michael A. Hicks (Gloucester: Alan Sutton, 1990), 1–13; "The Crown, Magnates and Local Government in Fifteenth Century East Anglia," in *The Crown and Local Communities in England and France in the Fifteenth Century*, ed. J. R. L. Highfield and Robin Jeffs (Gloucester: Alan Sutton, 1981), 72–87. For a striking use of a key occasion as the launching point of an analysis of county society and "the social relations of the gentry," it is hard to do much better than Bennett, *Community, Class and Careerism*, 22–40.

9. For an interest on the ritual aspects of public and civic life, Mervyn James, *Society, Politics, and Culture: Studies in Early Modern England* (Cambridge: Cambridge Univ. Press, 1986), especially chapter 1, a reprint of his important 1983 *Past and Present* article; Miri Rubin, *Corpus Christi: The Eucharist in Late Medieval Culture* (Cambridge: Cambridge Univ. Press, 1991); Charles Phythian-Adams, *Desolation of a City: Coventry and the Urban Crisis of the Late Middle Ages* (Cambridge: Cambridge Univ. Press, 1979).

10. I refer to studies that examine the way in which pressure upon the local community did or *did not* lead to a particular result in a parliamentary election: H. G. Richardson, "John of Gaunt and the Parliamentary Representation of Lancashire," *Bulletin of the John Rylands Library* 20 (1938): 175–222; Roger Virgoe, "Three Suffolk Parliamentary Elections of the Mid-Fifteenth Century," *Bulletin of the Institute of Historical Research* 39 (1966): 185–96. For a recent assessment of the

freedom of elections, John S. Roskell, Carole Rawcliffe, and Linda Clark, eds., *History of Parliament: The House of Commons, 1386–1422* (Stroud: Alan Sutton, 1992), I, 55–68.

11. For memories of and intervals and durations as measured in a goodly number of years, and reported to us from a wholly different setting: Claude Jenkins, "Cardinal Morton's Register," in *Tudor Studies Presented to Albert Frederic Pollard*, ed. R. W. Seton-Watson (London: Univ. of London, 1924), 26–74. As in the Scrope and Grosvenor depositions, analyzed below, the clerks talk of their age, their years of service, and their knowledge of the registry process, so the expertise offered from each of these areas combines to give us what seems like a believable and convincing package. P. 30: John Bell, aged 59 and more, "has known the registry in its present place for twenty-four years," and he has worked on the register for 40 years.

12. *Richard II* 124.
13. *Richard II* 180.
14. *Richard II* 181.
15. *Richard II* 68.
16. *Richard II* 124.
17. *Richard II* 124.
18. *Richard II* 68.
19. *Richard II* 351.
20. *Richard II* 180.
21. *Richard II* 351, my emphasis.
22. *Richard II* 351.
23. *Richard II* 350.
24. *Richard II* 401.
25. *Richard II* 352.
26. *Richard II* 181.

Chapter 3. The Scrope and Grosvenor Depositions: More Attestations About Age

1. For biographical information on Richard Scrope, *Dictionary of National Biography* and the *Complete Peerage* (*CP*). Nicholas Harris Nicolas, *The Controversy Between Sir Richard Scrope and Sir Robert Grosvenor in the Court of Chivalry, A.D. MCCCLXXXV–MCCCXC* (*S&G*), 2 vols. (London: privately printed, 1832): the material on the Scrope family has been collected (with documents, especially family wills) in volume II.

2. For a retelling of the affair, with a view that makes Grosvenor both more dignified and a better candidate for the arms in question: R. Steward Brown, "The Scrope and Grosvenor Controversy, 1385–1391," *Transactions of the Historic Society of Lancashire and Cheshire* 89 (1938): 1–22. An older summary is that of J. G. Nichols, "The Scrope-Grosvenor Controversy," *Herald and Genealogist* (1863): 385–400.

3. *S&G*, with the French versions of the depositions published in Volume I: for convenience I have mostly cited his English versions, given in Volume II. The quote is from I, 362.

4. *S&G* I, 359–61. The membranes with these depositions have been badly

torn, and all Nicolas was able to do was list the names and ages. I have just tallied these men, without regard for their partisanship, in the third bracket of Table 3–1. Steward-Brown, 20–22, for a list of all the Grosvenor partisans.

5. Edward Courtenay (1357–1419) XI earl of Devon, was heir to his grandfather's title. The old man, Hugh (1303–77), had dominated the family for many years, and young Edward was presumably just coming comfortably into his own. Nevertheless there is clearly an element of false deference in his protests; the holder of the oldest one-family earldom in the realm could afford to talk this way.

6. We are all in debt to the *annalistes*, though historians are now in denial and say it is time for the winds of change to blow. For some particularly suggestive studies, Emmanuel Le Roy Ladurie, *Montaillou: The Promised Land of Error*, trans. Barbara Bray (New York: G. Braziller, 1978); Carlo Ginzburg, *The Cheese and the Worms: The Cosmos of a Sixteenth-Century Miller*, trans. John Tedeschi and Anne Tedeschi (Baltimore: Johns Hopkins Univ. Press, 1980), and *Ecstasies: Deciphering the Witches' Sabbath*, trans. Raymond Rosenthal (New York: Pantheon Books, 1991); Natalie Zeman Davis, *Fiction in the Archives: Pardon Tales and Their Tellers in Sixteenth-Century France* (Stanford, CA: Stanford Univ. Press, 1987).

7. *S&G* II, 204.

8. *S&G* II, 243.

9. *S&G* II 277, 280.

10. *S&G* II, 354; II, 355.

11. *S&G* II, 333.

12. *S&G* II, 181 for both men.

13. *S&G* II, 244.

14. *S&G* II, 202.

15. *S&G* II, 207.

16. *S&G* II, 210.

17. *S&G* II, 223, 231.

18. Ferrers' testimony was very rich. He spoke of how "the ancestors of the said Sir Richard obtained great praise at the tournaments of Northampton, Guilford, Newmarket, and Dunstable," among their many noteworthy feats and accomplishments.

19. *S&G* II, 295, 319

20. *S&G* II, 216, 329: the arms were displayed at Wensley parish church, but beyond that is just the powerful weight of tradition: "the making of which arms and the name of the donor were beyond the memory of man."

21. *S&G* II, 279, for references to windows that since the time of Henry II had carried the funeral banners of the family; II, 281, for a mention of sealed charters with the relevant arms and information; II, 304, where we learn that "in the old wars in the kingdom of France, and in the new wars also," the arms had been carried and were on display in Skipenbeck church; II, 312, where the deponent says that the arms of Neville, Percy, Clifford, Scrope, et cetera, were in his chamber at home, and that his father said they had been there for 160 years. Anthony R. Wagner, *English Genealogy*, 2nd ed. (Oxford: Clarendon Press, 1972), on the use of the Scrope and Grosvenor depositions for the assembling of family pedigrees in the fourteenth century.

22. For details of Chaucer's involvement, Martin M. Crow and Clair C. Olson, eds. *Chaucer Life Records* (Austin: Univ. of Texas Press, 1966), 370–74. There are also some references to several more articles that deal with the controversy in the notes on pp. 371–72. Derek Pearsall, *The Life of Geoffrey Chaucer: A Critical Biography* (Oxford: Blackwell, 1992) 9–11, primarily on Chaucer's birth date but relying upon and discussing the Scrope and Grosvenor testimony.

23. *S&G* II, 317.

24. *S&G* II, 323.

25. *S&G* II, 325, 372.

26. *S&G* II, 161, 264, 265.

27. *S&G* II, 259. The faulty memory belonged to Robert, lord FitzPayne, now aged about 65. He had himself been armed (i.e., borne arms) in the various places to which he referred, wherever they had been.

28. *S&G* II, 425. Thirlewalle said that his father had lived to be 7 score and 5, by which he presumably meant 75. He had been armed for 69 years. Clearly, even an attempt to be precise, let alone convincing, breaks down against the obstacle of such memories.

Chapter 4. Three-Generation Family Links and Inquisitions Post Mortem

1. Peter Laslett, *The World We Have Lost*, 2nd ed. (New York: Scribner, 1971), 103: "You could not with any confidence expect to see your grandchildren in the world we have lost." For another case study that found little about grandparent-grandchild links within families, and would therefore seem to support Laslett, Jennifer C. Ward, "Wealth and Family in Early 16th Century Colchester," *Essex Archaeology and History* 21 (1990): 110–17. On the other hand, there is some tradition among medievalists of concentrating on the strength of three-generation family links. Marc Bloch talks of their role in transmitting the lore: *The Historian's Craft*, trans. Peter Putnam, intro. J. R. Strayer (Manchester: Manchester Univ. Press, 1954), 40–41, and in "Mémoire collective, tradition, et coûtume," *Revue de Synthèse Historique* 40 (1925): 73–83; Rodney Hilton, in the context of the transfer of property and the value that surrounded this critical step, in *The English Peasantry in the Later Middle Ages* (Oxford: Clarendon Press, 1975), 29: "The importance of grandparents in a period when people achieved early maturity, early marriage (probably), and early death, should not be underestimated."

2. The European marriage pattern has been discussed in the notes above. For aristocratic marriage, Sigismund Peller, "Births and Deaths Among Europe's Ruling Families Since 1500," in Glass and Eversley, *Population in History*, 87–100, with data on marriage (88–90) and on old age (98–99); T. H. Hollingsworth, "A Demographic Study of the British Ducal Families," in Glass and Eversley, *Population in History*, 354–74: especially Table 18, p. 365, on mean age at marriage; Lawrence Stone, *The Crisis of the Aristocracy, 1558–1641* (Oxford: Clarendon Press, 1965), 589–671, fig. 20 (654) on age at first marriage, 1540–1659.

3. The longevity of women is a lesser topic, the existence of grandmother-

grandchild links often buried by the disinterest of the sources. There were clearly more such links than grandfather-grandchild ones, thanks to a number of demographic factors, could we but uncover a larger proportion of the whole story. Were they warmer and more nurturing links? For all that, we cannot be certain about the value placed on ties between the patriarch/grandfather and his direct descendants. Wider surveys, less culture-bound to European culture, report data that are not as firmly positive: Stephen G. Post, "Infanticide and Geronticide," *Aging and Society* 10 (1990): 317–18, with particular interest in when the "severely demented elderly" are considered voiceless and as such can be considered as having "ceased to exist." Also Anthony P. Glascock, "By Any Other Name, It Is Still Killing: A Comparison of the Treatment of the Elderly in America and in Other Societies," in *The Cultural Context of Aging: Worldwide Perspectives*, ed. Jay Sokolovsky (New York: Bergin and Garvey, 1990), 43–56.

4. Geoffrey R. Elton, *England Under the Tudors* (London: Methuen, 1954), 5: "It was unfortunate that Edward III lived too long and had too many children." Also, "the blood of Edward III ramified through too many veins." Of course, against this picture of Malthusian progression was the reality, pointed out by Elton, that Edward the Black Prince had but one son, and that son no sons in his turn. For contemporary laments on the woes of a realm with an old and feeble monarch, Mary Aquinas Devlin, ed., *The Sermons of Thomas Brinton, Bishop of Rochester, 1373–89*, Camden Society 3rd ser. 85–86 (1954), I, 60–66. W. M. Ormrod, *The Reign of Edward III* (New Haven, CT: Yale Univ. Press, 1990), 38: "In 1377 some may have been less kind in their comments about a rather pathetic old man whose indolence and incapacity had jeopardized the welfare of the realm," a view Ormrod supports by references to satirical and hostile doggerel of the day. Also, with the judgmental approach of an older generation, James H. Ramsay, *The Genesis of Lancaster* (Oxford: Clarendon Press, 1913), II, 67–68: [Edward was] "a man of the sensuo-athletic type, morally weak, easily led . . . in his latter days the well-disposed writers could not help deploring the painful sight of a monarch worn out with sensuality and sunk in sloth."

5. Elaine Clark, "Some Aspects of Social Security in Medieval England," *Journal of Family History* 7 (1982): 307–20, and "The Quest for Security in Medieval England," in Sheehan, *Aging and the Aged*, 189–200: these are the major contributions to an important topic dealt with, if only briefly, below. This area of study is further supported by the work of Richard M. Smith, "The Manorial Court and the Elderly Tenant in Late Medieval England," in Pelling and Smith, *Life, Death, and the Elderly*, 39–61. Lutz K. Berkner, "The Stem Family and the Developmental Cycle of the Peasant Household: An Austrian Example," *American Historical Review* 77 (1972): 398–418. For a good essay, with a lengthy bibliography, covering most aspects of the family as the topic of historical discussion, Michael Mitterauer and Reinhard Sieder, *The European Family: Patriarchy to Partnership from the Middle Ages to the Present Day*, trans. Karla Oosterveen and Manfred Horzinger (Oxford: Blackwell, 1982), 179–226 for a bibliography that covers the medieval family and the presence of the aged there, among other topics.

6. Though it is dangerous, if tempting, to make points from the entries — found or not found — in an index, there is no reference to grandparents in the classic

introduction to the study of children in history: Philippe Ariès, *Centuries of Childhood: A Social History of Family Life*, trans. Robert Baldick (New York: Knopf, 1962). Neither are there relevant index entries in two current books that help explicate the role of children in medieval society: Shulamith Shahar, *Childhood in the Middle Ages*, trans. Chaya Galai (London: Routledge, 1990), with much to say and pushed by an anti-Ariès perspective regarding the identity and worth of childhood and children; Barbara A. Hanawalt, *Growing Up in Medieval London: The Experience of Childhood in History* (New York and Oxford: Oxford Univ. Press, 1993). Hanawalt's index does cite the "ages of man literature" and, of course, there are many kinds of entries on parents and parenting.

7. *Richard II* 524; *Yorkshire* 139; *Lancashire* 70; *Henry VII, i* 754. For a reference to the son of a deceased son, now married and aged 18 and more, *Henry IV* 622.

8. *Henry VII, ii* 77; *Richard II* 188; *Henry IV* 578; *Henry IV* 1116; *Richard II* 1137. Also, *Henry VII, ii* 21, for a son's son who was 21 and, lest there be any doubt, was explicitly labeled as being "of full age."

9. *Richard II* 193; *Lancashire* 99; *Nottingham* II, 41. And for more of (pretty much) the same: *Richard II* 666; *Henry IV* 395; *Yorkshire* 162; *Nottingham* II, 85; *Henry VII,i* 390 and 865.

10. *Henry VII, i* 488.

11. *Henry VII, ii* 550, 444.

12. *Henry VII, ii* 227.

13. *Henry VII, i* 801; *Richard II* 1014. Presumably the dead daughters had been older than their surviving siblings. Also, *Henry VII, ii* 610, 591 (where the aggregation of heirs consisted of a daughter of 36 and now a widow, one of 34 and married, one of 22 and married, and a daughter of a dead daughter, unmarried and 17). *Henry IV* 1127: a widow was survived by a daughter of 40, a widow; a daughter of 30 and married; a daughter of 26 or 24 or 28, and married; a daughter's son, now 22 and more and married. The widow's husband, we are told, had "died long ago."

14. *Richard II* 1137.

15. Two lines of scholarly inquiry seem relevant, though their convergence is not always easy to establish. One is the general line of economic-demographic inquiry, still well presented by John Hatcher, *Plague, Population, and the English Economy, 1348–1530* (London: Macmillan, 1977). The other pertains to replacement rates and family continuity of specific families or as reported by local, county, and community studies, as cited above. Of particular importance, Lawrence R. Poos and Richard M. Smith, "Legal Windows onto Historical Populations: Recent Research on Demography and the Manor Court in Medieval England, " *Law and History Review* 2 (1984): 128–52, where the material on replacement rates in other recent studies is sifted and evaluated. For an example of demographic material commanding attention in a work not deliberately slanted in this direction, Edwin B. DeWindt, *Land and People in Hollywell-cum Needingworth* (Toronto: Pontifical Institute of Mediaeval Studies, 1972), 190–91.

16. As in *Henry VII, i* 975: the son of the dead man's son, aged 30 and more, is identified as "his cousin and heir, viz, son of John his son." This was not uncommon; often the brief genealogy tells us who the "cousin" was, but we only can be certain in those cases where detailed and circumstantial genealogical material is piled

up so as to reveal that a burden of clarification could be imposed on those who testified or those who recorded—whether the impetus for clarification came from their own choice or was imposed from above.

17. *Richard II* 1106.

18. *Henry IV* 212, 430.

19. *Richard II* 449. Lady Cromwell's heirs are reported as her son John's son John's son William, now 7 and more and "in the king's ward." Her other heir was her brother Constantine's daughter Elizabeth's son John's son, William Knyvett, now 6 and more.

Chapter 5. Three-Generation Family Links and Last Wills and Testaments

1. In many instances the factor of insanity or idiocy pushed an heir out of the line of succession, and numerous Inquisitions deal with this contingency: *Henry VII, ii* 85: the son (now aged 58 and more, and supposedly in line to inherit) "is and from the time of his birth was an idiot and natural fool." Keith Thomas refers to "the accepted legal dictum that an idiot was someone who could not count up to twenty or tell his own age": "Age and Authority," 206.

2. I acknowledge the advice of the late Don Queller, given in personal comment after I read a paper on grandparents. He said I should stop saying "affect" and simply talk about whether there is evidence that people loved each other—in whatever form they expressed such matters in a late medieval idiom and in whatever fashion we choose to interpret their speech and emotions.

3. *Henry VII, ii* 541: a landholder had died on 31 January, 20 Henry VII (1505). His first son then died on 15 February of that year, that is, 16 days later. So the heir to the land was a second son, aged 10 and more, as attested in an inquisition held the following 8 September.

4. *TE* iv, 62.

5. Though all who work with late medieval wills, even in the most casual fashion, are aware of their shortcomings as a source, these difficulties are summarized with noteworthy precision by Clive Burgess, "Late Medieval Wills and Pious Convention: Testamentary Evidence Reconsidered," in Hicks, *Profit, Piety and the Professions in Later Medieval England*, 214–33 (with 14–18 for the succinct consideration of wills).

6. *TE* 3, 277. *SMW* 221: "I bequethe to the child in my wife's wombe, if God fortune hit to have cristendome and live, 5 marc, what it commyth to full age." If the child died, there was another daughter already on the scene: she would inherit her share when she came of age or when she married or when her mother died. Presumably the first event would trigger the process. Also, *SMW* ii, 34: "And the child with which my wife is pregnant."

7. *Sharpe* 391.

8. *TE* 4, 125.

9. *TE* 2, 237. After the flip-flopping regarding the unborn grandchild, the will

moves on to a bequest to "William ye son of Bertyn," the said William being a son's son.

10. *TE* 2, 28. *SMW* 272, seems a pretty clear case of no grandchildren, at least not yet: "bequests to son Nicholas and "to the heyres of his body lawfully comyng . . ."

11. *Henry VII, ii* 58, where his son's son, now 13 and more, is his "cousin and next heir." *Henry VII, ii* 32, where the "cousin and next heir" is identified as "William . . . son of John, son of Thomas, his elder brother," that is, his great nephew, now 15 and more.

12. *TE* iv, 274. *TE* iv, 211: Elizabeth Fitzwilliam's daughter was Katherine Skipwith, and there is little reason to doubt that "Margaret Skipwith, filiae meae spirituali" was Katherine's daughter. Also, *SMW* 23 and 364.

13. *TE* iv, 131.

14. *Sharpe* 558–59. Her brother comes in for a small bequest but at least carries no derogatory status-identifier. This bequest to the girl, with its passing reference to her dual role as servant and close kin, tells a whole story about the probable fate of children, even members of the nuclear family, who had to rely on the labor-force decisions of surrogate parents (or, no doubt, of natural parents). It is not that the granddaughter was used as a servant that is worth much note, but rather that in her grandfather's will her domestic situation was given as her primary identification, her ties of blood as a secondary one. A different research agenda might be able to shed light on generational interaction within households, as is hinted at for a later period; Richard Wall, "Work, Welfare, and the Family: An Illustration of the Adoptive Family Economy," in Bonfield et al., *The World We Have Gained*, 261–94. There is (287–88) suggestive material on the role of illegitimate grandchildren as domestic servants.

15. *TE* iv, 180.

16. *TE* iv, 97.

17. *Sharpe* 552.

18. *Chichele* 151. Also *Chichele* 624, where a godchild's child is remembered: "Item lego Willelmo filio Johannis Burnell filiolo meo, xl d."

19. *TE* i, 181.

20. John Nichols, ed., *A Collection of Wills* (London, 1780: repr. New York: Kraus Reprint, 1969) 145–73. The quote is on 158.

21. *Sharpe* (full reference in the bibliography); he calendared the wills with what is probably a heavy hand. It is likely that a reading of the manuscript material would give us a richer yield. Ernest F. Jacob, in editing *Chichele's Register*, transcribed the entire volume. Thus a distinction I read as indicating fifteenth-century behavior as bespeaking class and culture may actually rest more on a twentieth-century editorial convention.

22. The York wills (*TE* in the abbreviations), and those for Somerset (*SMW*) are mixes of documents, drawn together for their regional interest, rather than as the material of a single register or repository. They have been used for their substantive value but not tallied for their proportion of three-generation clauses.

23. *TE* i, 269. *TE* i, 335: "Willielmo filio Willielmo fillii mei vj marcas et unum

lectum." This was more generous than most, though we know so little about comparative sizes of estates, personal property, the weight of other claimants, and other such considerations that would be needed were comparisons regarding who got what even thinkable between wills.

24. *TE* ii, 276, 70.

25. *TE* iv, 109.

26. *TE* iv, 204. The tenement in Thornton, by Bradford, was but "newly byldyd."

27. *TE* ii, 156.

28. *SMW* 320.

29. *TE* iii, 183.

30. *TE* ii, 21.

31. *TE* iv, 62. *SMW* 381: "I bequeth to the 4 childrenne of the said Alis Thies, and everich of theym syngularly, 3s. 4d." *SMW* 389: "Item, to the 4 children of the said Champneyes and my doughter, oon pipe of woode [woad] that is to say to Thomas, Richard, Anne and Isabell, evenly to be devided bitwene them."

32. *Chichele* 3.

33. *TE* iv, 170; *TE* ii, 36: a testator's son had four children, each enriched by their grandfather, respectively: the first son received 10 marks, the next child (a daughter) 100 shillings, then a son came in for 100 shillings, and finally a married daughter was listed for 5 marks. *SMW* 127: "to my son . . . and to Edith his wife . . . to each of their children (cuilibet proli eorundem), 20s."

34. *TE* ii, 48.

35. *TE* iv, 243.

36. *TE* iv, 184.

37. *TE* iv, 198. Also, *Chichele* 519: "Item lego Roberto, Ricardo filiis et Beatrici filie predicti Thome Knolles filii mei," plus instructions on the guardianship of the grandchildren.

38. *TE* iii, 185.

39. *TE* ii, 192.

40. *Sharpe* 553. There are three grandchildren mentioned: for none of out three to survive would be a grim prospect.

41. *Chichele* 519.

42. *TE* ii, 48; *TE* ii, 192; *SMW* 241.

43. *TE* iv, 96. This may well have been a mother-in-law, perhaps from any one of the testator's four marriages. The second reference is from *TE* iii, 62: the testator a canon of York. To generalize from very few cases, clerics were apt to leave bequests to relatives of the preceding generation, that is, to the kin whom they had known best before life in the Church led them into different orbits.

44. *SMW* 39.

45. *SMW* 58, 100.

46. *TE* i, 174. *TE* ii, 10: "in custodia dominae Johannae matris uxoris meas."

47. *Chichele* 176; *TE* iii, 61–63; *SMW* 12. Also *Chichele* 392, 450.

48. *TE* iii, 197.

49. *TE* iii, 257.

50. *TE* i, 343.

51. *TE* iv, 127.

52. *Chichele* 165.

53. James Gairdner, ed., *The Paston Letters* (London: Constable, 1895), III, 285–87. A number of other grandchildren are remembered. I have looked at the three-generation relations of this endearing family, with particular reference to Agnes and Margaret, in a paper (forthcoming) in a volume on "Medieval Mothers" edited by Bonnie Wheeler and John Carmi Parsons.

54. *TE* iv, 166.

55. *TE* iv, 127: he went on to discuss a bequest to his mother, made so she would pray for his soul: "to gyf me hir dayly blessyng, and yt sche wold forgyf me all trespasses and fowts don be me to hir syn I was born of hir wome, as sche wold be forgeven afor God."

56. *SMW* 291.

57. *TE* iv, 184.

Chapter 6. Three-Generation Family Links and Some Aristocratic Genealogies

1. The genealogical material is taken from *CP*. Because this great reference work was compiled and published between 1910 and 1959, scholarly standards improved and we are able to see a steady movement, as the volumes were published, toward more rigorous editorial and demographic inquiry. Thus in succeeding volumes there is greater skepticism regarding dates (particularly of birth), which means in effect that peers whose names appear towards the beginning of the alphabet are treated in a more credulous fashion that those who appear in the second half of the 13-volume set. This is an odd form of historiographic discrimination, dictated by the alphabet, and it militates against above-average longevity from about the letter K or L onward.

2. Rowena E. Archer, "Rich Old Ladies: The Problem of Late Medieval Dowagers," in *Property and Politics: Essays in Later Medieval English History*, ed. Anthony J. Pollard (Gloucester: Alan Sutton, 1984), 15–35; Joel T. Rosenthal, "Aristocratic Widows in Fifteenth-Century England," in *Women and the Structure of Society*, ed. Barbara J. Harris and Jo Ann K. McNamara (Durham, NC: Duke Univ. Press, 1984), 36–47, 259–60; Carole Rawcliffe, *The Staffords, Earls of Stafford and Dukes of Buckingham, 1394–1521* (Cambridge: Cambridge Univ. Press, 1978), passim. To compare English data with some from the Continent, A. Bideau, "A Demographic and Social Analysis of Widowhood and Remarriage: The Example of the Castellany of Thoissey-en-Dombes, 1670–1840," *Journal of Family History* 5 (1980): 28–43; Heath Dillard, *Daughters of the Reconquest: Women in Castilian Town Society, 1100–1300* (Cambridge: Cambridge Univ. Press, 1984), 96–126.

3. The passion this quarrel inspired should send a long-lasting message to the historical profession. We can pick up the exchange with R. H. Tawney, "The Rise of the Gentry, 1558–1640," and "A Postscript," first published in the *Economic History Review* (1941 and 1954 respectively) and reprinted in *Essays in Economic History*, ed. E. M. Carus-Wilson (London: Arnold, 1954), 173–214. For the "other side" and

coming toward the end of the issue, J. H. Hexter, "The Myth of the Middle Class in Tudor England" and "Storm over the Gentry," in his *Reappraisals in History* (Evanston, Ill.: Northwestern Univ. Press, 1961), 71–162, and "Lawrence Stone and the English Aristocracy," in *On Historians* (Cambridge, MA: Harvard Univ. Press, 1979), 149–226.

4. McFarlane, *The Nobility of Later Medieval England*, 172–76; Rosenthal, *Patriarchy and Families of Privilege*, 102–36.

5. J. Enoch Powell and Keith Wallis, *The House of Lords in the Middle Ages: A History of the English House of Lords to 1540* (London: Weidenfeld and Nicolson, 1968).

6. F. Sandford, *Genealogical History of the Kings and Queens of England* (London, 1707).

7. As in note 4 above, McFarlane, *The Nobility of Later Medieval England*, 142–76. I have followed this lead but tried to amplify some of the material in *Patriarchy and Families of Privilege*, Part I. The general issue of replacement rates, especially in rural society, is treated by Sylvia L. Thrupp, "The Problem of Replacement Rates in Late Medieval England," *Economic History Review* 2nd ser. 18 (1965) 101–19.

8. For London merchants, Thrupp, *The Merchant Class*, 191–206: "In any event, it is obvious that the class could not have maintained its numbers without outside recruiting" (206).

9. But this is an unusual case, the only one of its sort in the annals of the medieval peerage. John de la Warre had succeeded to the peerage, as his brother's heir, in 1371. Despite two marriages he died sine prole in July, 1398, by which time his younger brother Thomas was a priest (having received a dispensation in 1363 to be ordained when he had reached age 20). Thomas was summoned to Lords from 1399 through 1426. On his death his half-sister's son, Reynold West (1395–1420) was summoned as lord de la Warre (from July, 1427 through September 1449). Reynold left sons and the peerage of de la Warre passed, for good, into the West family (as we tally patriarchal lines).

10. John, IV lord Harrington (1984 or earlier-1408) was at least 22 when his father (Robert, III lord, 1356–1406) died. John died in France, and his widow Elizabeth, daughter of the earl of Devon, married William, lord Bonville (x.1461: father of her niece's husband). Elizabeth lived until 1471, when she died without any children.

11. For violent death among the peers and its affect on aristocratic families, *Patriarchy and Families of Privilege*, Part I, with some effort to present statistical and tabular material on these families. For some thoughts about the demographic "privileges" of the upper classes, Russell, *British Medieval Population*, 117: "The food of the nobility and gentry may have been too rich and the skill of the medical profession is open to exaggeration." For a recent study that links diet and health, Barbara Harvey, *Living and Dying in England*.

12. M. T. Martin, ed., *The Percy Chartulary*, Surtees Society 117 (1911), though the material only relates to lands, as we might imagine; family matters, whatever weight they carried, did not figure in the compilations of such documentary collections.

13. Other cases are not too different. Edward Courtenay, earl of Devon (1357–1491) was 17 when his aged grandfather, Hugh, X earl, died (1303–1377). Edward lived until his son's son, Thomas, XIII earl of Devon (1414–58) was 5. Here it was the old man's impressive longevity—into his mid-70s—that made the linkage possible.

14. Another family that demonstrates the pattern of long lives alternating with short. While William died at about 73, his father had been a young man (1356–1388) and his grandfather had likewise come nowhere near his allotted span (1333–1371).

15. The father of the two men, Hugh (b. 1447 or earlier, d. 1488), was at least 10 years old when his grandfather's second wife, Margery Clifton, died (in 1456). However, it is not likely that ties between a young heir and a step-grandmother were apt to be close, unless they lived in the same household.

16. Thomas Wright, ed., *The Book of the Knight of La Tour Landry*, EETS 33 (1868), 89–90.

17. T. C. B. Timmins, ed., *Chandler's Salisbury Register*, Wiltshire Record Society 39 (1983), 403.

18. *Henry IV* 345–46. This was more memorable because Isabel's father was already dead by the time of her birth.

Chapter 7. Retirement, for Some, at the End of the Road

1. Georges Minois, *History of Old Age*, passim. Though Minois does not offer much by way of systematic treatment of his many themes, his comments are perceptive and a guide to a wealth of contemporary material. The section (245–47) specifically devoted to retirement in the late Middle Ages and Renaissance is subtitled, "Retirement: The Idea Catches On."

2. In some of the literary and homiletic presentations old age was seen as a moral fault, a shortcoming. Pre-lapsarian man would not have aged; therefore aging was a mark of our diminished condition, even if individuals were not at fault for the universal stigma. This no-win approach was a favorite of Innocent III: we will discuss his *On the Misery of the Human Condition* below.

3. Unfortunately for our discussion, Gabriele Zerbi's *Gerontocomia* is medically directed and its focus is on ways of coping with the physical onset of age; it has much less interest in social and collective aspects of aging.

4. This approach will be considered below in the final chapter. The collection edited by Michael Sheehan, *Aging and the Aged in Medieval Europe*, gives a capsule view of the diversity of medieval sources and of modern scholarly approaches.

5. As quoted by Sylvia Thrupp, *The Merchant Class of Medieval London*, 195. This topos of exaggeration about age was a common one. Creighton Gilbert, "When Did Man in the Renaissance Grow Old?" *Studies in the Renaissance* 14 (1967): 7–32; 11, for a complaint by Pietro Aretino on how "old age is slowing down my wits, and love, which ought to stimulate them, is putting them to sleep," voiced when Aretino was 40 or 45. Gilbert continues with a quote from Erasmus, who was about 40 when he penned his dreary lesson: "In man alone, at once, after the sev-

enth / Five-year-span, and that hardly complete, / Dried-up old age tires the body's strength, / Nor is that enough, but before / The speeding life has turned the tenth five-year-span / It does not fear to attack / The immortal part of man, brought from heaven" (12).

6. Osbern Bokenham, *The Legendys of Hooly Wummen*, ed. Mary Serjeantson, EETS o.s. 206 (1938), lines 187–91. For a recent treatment of Bokenham, *A Legend of Holy Women*, trans. Sheila Delany (Notre Dame,IN: Notre Dame Univ. Press, 1992). Bokenham is of particular interest because he affects to worry—perhaps as just a literary convention—about the onset of senility and the loss of powers: p. 29 (of Delany's translation), "But I fear to begin so late, lest people ascribe it to dotage. For I know full well I am advanced in age, and my life's term fast approaches."

7. *CP* iv, 20. He enlarged upon his woes, lumping together the complaints brought on by "myne age, debilite, disease of the gowte, and my leg which troubleth me very sore."

8. *CPL X, 1447–54* 212.

9. *CPL X, 1447–54* 107; also, 159, for another instance of "seventy years old and impotent."

10. *CPL IX, 1431–47* 374, 494. Elizabeth Makowski, "The Conjugal Debt and Medieval Canon Law," *Journal of Medieval History* 3 (1977): 99–114. These questions receive thorough treatment in James Brundage, *Law, Sex, and Christian Society in Medieval Europe* (Chicago: Univ. of Chicago Press, 1987).

11. At 35 one had begun to face up to the need for more sober behavior; this was when one was to abandon the youthful passion for the dance and the tournament, and when one began to contemplate a retreat from court life: John W. Draper, "Shakespeare's Attitude Towards Old Age," *Journal of Gerontology* 1 (1946): 119. Draper provides references to Elizabethan translations and rephrasings whereby the general reader of the day could dip into the body of classical and medieval lore that carried the traditional (and tedious) wisdom about age.

12. As explicated in Joseph T. Freeman, "François Ranchin: Contributor to an Early Chapter in Geriatrics," *Journal of the History of Medicine* 5 (1950): 422–31.

13. J. Livingston Lowes, "The Prologue to *The Legend of Good Women*, Considered in Its Chronological Relations," *PMLA* 20 (1905): 783–84. Men were at least a bit better off than women, for the latter could begin the long slide as early as 25 or 30; "vint et cinq ans dura ma jeune fleurs, mais a trente ans fu ma couleur muee."

14. Chaucerians have played with the question of whether one could be considered old at 35 or whether one had until 50: Brook Forehand, "Old Age and Chaucer's Reeve," *PMLA* 69 (1954): 984–89. Monasteries, taking their lead from The Rule, recognized the special problems of the aged, in a general way; specific cases will be touched on below. Timothy Fry, ed., *The Rule of Saint Benedict in English* (Collegeville, MN: Liturgical Press, 1982), passim: chapter 37 tells of how "human nature itself is inclined to be compassionate toward the old and the young." Also, Isabelle Cochelin, "*In senectute bona*: pour une typologie de la vieillesse dans l'hagiographie monastique des xiie et xiiie siècles," in *Les Âges de la vie au Moyen Âge: Actes de colloque du Département audits Médiévales de l'Univ. de Paris-Sorbonne et de l'Univ. Friedrich Wilhelm de Bonn, 16–17 mai, 1990*, ed. Henri Dubois et Michel Zink (Paris:

Presses de l'Université de Paris-Sorbonne, 1992).

15. John Smyth of Nibley, *The Lives of the Berkeleys*, ed. J. Maclean, for the Bristol and Gloucester Archaeological Society, 3 vols. (1883). Smyth talks of how, led by Psalm 90, we can think in terms of "ten times seven or seven times ten." As to the willingness of lord Berkeley to conform to such larger schemes in the universe; "and that this lord . . . should over live his brother Marques twice seven years, and one seven months. As though all their circumferences were closed in that number of seasons" (174–75).

16. *CCR, 1405–09* 361–62.

17. *Calendar of Miscellaneous Inquisitions vii (1399–1422)*, #319.

18. *CPL X, 1447–54* 525.

19. Margaret McGregor, ed., *Bedford Wills Proved in the Prerogative Court of Canterbury, 1383–1548*, Bedfordshire Historical Record Society 58 (1979), 43–44.

20. G. Poulett Scrope, *A History of Castle Combe, Wiltshire* (London: privately printed, 1852), 279: Scrope's comments on the inroads of time, delivered to his elderly stepfather, Sir John Fastolf, seem reasonable: "And now, seth it is soo that the natural course off kynde, by reuolucion and successyon of lx yeres growyn vpon yowe, at this tyme of age and febleness, ye comen abatyng youre bodly laboures": Stephen Scrope, *The Epistle of Othea*, ed. Curt Buhler, EETS 264 (1970), 121. Scrope tells the elderly Fastolf that, in view of his age, it is time to abandon "exercysing off dedis of cheuallrie," and to turn instead (in a Ciceronian vein) to "contemplacion of morall wysdome and exercisyng gostly werkyys." For Fastolf's last days, Colin F. Richmond, *The Paston Family in the Fifteenth Century: The First Phase* (Cambridge: Cambridge Univ. Press, 1990), 249–59. Richmond argues that, while Fastolf was clearly feeling the effects of his considerable age, he was active and in control of his complicated affairs, at least in fits and starts, up until his death (at which point he was probably aged 75 or thereabouts).

21. As quoted, *CPL* xi, 568. Lord Scrope had been absent from sessions of parliament because of bad health: *PPC* vi, 181–82.

22. Josiah Cox Russell, "How Many of the Population Were Aged?" in Sheehan, *Aging and the Aged in Medieval Europe*, 119–27.

23. If we wish to begin with an understatement concerning the post-work phase of the life cycle, we can consider the idea that "retirement is a demotion in the work system": Marvin Sussman, "An Analytical Model for the Study of Retirement," in *Retirement*, ed. Frances M. Carp (New York: Behavioral Publications, 1972), 29–73 (quote on p. 29). For a discussion of formative stages in the development of private retirement policies in the nineteenth and twentieth centuries (in the United States), W. Andrew Achenbaum, *Old Age in the New Land*, especially Part III, "Contemporary Old Age in Historical Perspective."

24. As with most other favors and perquisites of the world, the balance was predetermined in favor of those who entered the game with a winning hand: "the relationship between work and prestige within a culture is a very potent determinant of the nature of retirement," Margaret Clark, "An Anthropological View of Retirement," in Carp, *Retirement*, 129.

25. J. J. Scarisbrick, *Henry VIII* (Berkeley: Univ. of California Press, 1968), 484, on the king's decline: "Henry's bullock body was a magnificent piece of natu-

re's handiwork and, for the first thirty-five years of his life, had served him better than anyone sprung of such unpromising stock, exposed to so hazardous a thing as Tudor medicine and addicted to such dangerous sports as he was, could reasonably have expected." Pp. 484–88 on the king's health and loss thereof, pp. 491–96 on his death. Contemporaries were aware of the slide from athleticism to near-senility, though they had to be careful in their comments. It was observed that Henry "waxed heavy with sickness, age and corpulence of body, and might not travel so readily abroad, but was constrained to seek to have his game and pleasure ready and at hand," quoted from *Acts of the Privy Council*, in David Thomas, "The Elizabethan Crown Lands: Their Purposes and Problems," in *The Estates of the English Crown, 1558–1640*, ed. R. W. Hoyle (Cambridge: Cambridge Univ. Press, 1992), 82. Michael Prestwich, *Edward I* (Berkeley and Los Angeles: Univ. of California Press, 1988), 556–58, for the last days of another active and long-lived monarch.

26. Dante, *Inferno*, III: "Last of all / I recognized the shadow of that soul / Who, in his cowardice, made the Great Denial" (lines 55–57), trans. John Ciardi (New York: New American Library, 1954). Of the parties in this sordid business in 1294, Celestine V had been born in 1215 and was therefore well beyond what might have been considered a reasonable and proper age for retirement when he abdicated, not that such a consideration was of any relevance in this context. Even Boniface VIII, the young Benedict Gaetani and the villain of the piece, had been born in 1234.

27. Elizabeth Sears, *The Ages of Man*, figs. 86–92 for depictions of the wheel of fortune and of the wheel of life. Relevant material is scattered throughout Samuel Chew, *The Pilgrimage of Life* (New Haven, CT: Yale Univ. Press, 1962).

28. John S. Roskell, "The Problem of the Attendance of the Lords in Medieval Parliaments," *Bulletin of the Institute of Historical Research* 29 (1956): 153–204.

29. *CPR 1429–36* 453.

30. *CPR 1436–41* 362.

31. *CPR 1446–51* 558; also Thomas Rymer, *Foedera*, ed. A. Clarke, F. Holbrooke, and J. Caley, 4 vols. in 7 pts (London, 1741), V, ii, 41 (for an excuse from 18 June, 1452).

32. *CPR 1446–52* 297. Rymer, *Foedera* V, ii, 20 (dated 9 December, 1449). Since Moleyns was lynched by a mob on 9 January, 1450, it is not useful to speculate as to whether he would have recovered sufficiently to come back to work at an acceptable level of strength and application. He did not.

33. *CPR 1452–61* 642. Roskell says that Moleyns wanted to be free to follow up his vows to go on pilgrimage (p. 204).

34. *CPR 1461–67* 341. Booth may have been ill for some time before the excused absence; the writ was issued at Chancery on 10 August, 1464 and he died on 12 September of that year.

35. James H. Wylie, *History of England Under Henry the Fourth* (London: Oxford Univ. Press, 1896; repr. New York: AMS Press, 1969), III, 132.

36. *CPR 1452–61* 645.

37. *CPR, 1461–67* 72, 213.

38. *Langley* #701 (III, 69–70).

39. "Now falle to greet age and poverte . . . and being for his said service never

yet recompensed ne rewarded; it plese youre highe and excellent grace . . . as it shal plese you with youre most gracious almesse," from "The Petition of Thomas Hostelle," quoted in Douglas Gray, *The Oxford Book of Late Medieval Verse and Prose* (Oxford: Clarendon Press, 1985), 35–36.

40. *CCR 1399–1402* 21.

41. *CCR 1461–68* 43.

42. Maddern, *Violence and Social Order*, 150, on an old hand in local government now being dropped from a peace commission at age 64. Though this might not sound punitive, Maddern says "it was unusual for a man to be dropped . . . especially if he were an energetic magistrate, whatever his age." Regarding pensions for early modern servants of the state (and again, dealing primarily with men of minor status in public affairs), Joan R. Kent, *The English Village Constable, 1580–1642* (Oxford: Clarendon Press, 1986), 254.

43. Jennifer Kermode, "Urban Decline: The Flight from Office in Late Medieval York," *Economic History Review* 2nd ser. 35 (1982): 179–98: the juicy quote is on p. 192. In Coventry, in 1472, 30 old men swore regarding the rights to a common: "In asmoche as for oure gret ages be liklyhode wee may not long abyde in this erthely lyfe [as they were all 60 and above]": Charles Phythian-Adams, *Desolation of a City: Coventry and the Urban Crisis of the Late Middle Ages* (Cambridge: Cambridge Univ. Press, 1979), 93.

44. Phythian-Adams, *Desolation of a City*, 192–93.

45. *Letter Book K* 6. In an evocative passage, Sylvia Thrupp, *London Merchants*, 224, on the "leisured section" of urban society, composed mostly of "elderly merchants in retirement," wealthy widows, and married women.

46. *Letter Book K* 86–87. The Statute of Laborers of 1351 exempted those of 60 and more from its strictures: Larry Poos pointed this out to me, and it is part of the general discussion of age and retirement by the editors, Pelling and Smith, *Life, Death, and the Elderly*, 5–13.

47. *Letter Book I* 24, 59, 94, 347, 307, 309, 386, 109; *Letter Book L* 159, 237; *Letter Book I* 139: "owing to bodily infirmity and more particularly deafness"; *Letter Book I* 87: "owing to paralysis and other infirmities"; *Letter Book H* 442: "in as much as the state of his legs prevented him from walking without great pain."

48. *Letter Book I* 103, 271.

49. *Letter Book H* 405.

50. *Letter Book K* 228.

51. P. H. Cullum, *Cremetts and Corrodies: Care of the Poor and Sick at St. Leonard's Hospital, York, in the Middle Ages*, Borthwick Papers 79 (York: Univ. of York, 1991). For more on this subject: Peter Heath, ed., *Bishop Geoffrey de Blythe's Visitaitons, c. 1515–1523*, Staffordshire Record Society iv, 7 (1973); xlvi–vii; P. L. Hull, ed., *The Cartulary of Launceston Priory*. Devon and Cornwall Record Society n.s. 30 (1987), passim. The question of whether corrodies were primarily a form of old-age strategy or whether they just opened a house's door for paid boarders, regardless of their age and affluence, is not readily answered. In addition to the citations given above: Ian Keil, "Corrodies of Glastonbury Abbey in the Later Middle Ages," *Somerset Archaeological and Natural History Society* 108 (1963–64): 111–31; Barbara Harvey, *Living and Dying*, 207–8 (with a warning against assuming corrodians to

have been aged and necessarily going into retirement), and 239–51 (for an appendix of Westminster corrodians); Eleanor Searle and Barbara Ross, eds., *The Cellarer's Rolls of Battle Abbey, 1275–1513*, Sussex Record Society 65 (1967), 15–16. For the general issue of aging ecclesiastical personnel, Robert N. Swanson, *Church and Society in Late Medieval England* (Oxford: Blackwell, 1989) on a clerical population that perhaps ran around 33,000 (30–64), on pensions (56–58); "A crucial stage in any cleric's life was old age. Resignation documents often make the point that, unless given a pension, the quondam incumbent would be reduced to beggary" (63–64). Also Peter Heath, *The English Parish Clergy on the Eve of the Reformation* (London: Routledge and Kegan Paul, 1969), 146–86; A. Hamilton Thompson, *The English Clergy and Their Organization in the Later Middle Ages* (Oxford: Clarendon Press, 1947), 117–20, 241–42 (where some illuminating documents are published). The most relevant detailed treatment I have found is that of Nicholas Orme, "Suffering of the Clergy: Illness and Old Age in Exeter Diocese, 1300–1540," in Pelling and Smith, *Life, Death, and the Elderly*, 62–73.

52. A. Hamilton Thompson, ed., *Visitations of Religious Houses in the Diocese of Lincoln* Canterbury and York Society 24, 29 (1919–1927: repr. London, 1969), II, 380.

53. Hull, *The Cartularly of Launceston Priory*, #271, where the corrodian's horse was to receive, "each night yearly a botel of oats a sufficient hay for the same horse" [which he had brought with him], exactly like what the prior's own esquire had for his animal. Also #330, where in addition to 4 loaves of daily bread, 2 gallons of the best beer and wine on Sundays and feast days, 2 dishes of fish when fish was eaten, lodging for two horses, 40 pounds of candles a year for his room, etc; there was to be, for the corrodian, "lodging for two greyhounds and reasonable food for them."

54. R. T. Timson, ed., *The Cartulary of Blyth Priory*, Thoroton Society Record Series 27–28 (1973), lxxxvii. The retirement had been "on account of old age and infirmity," and it stipulated that when the prior left the house he was to have "all things necessary when going from home." Also, cvi, where two corrodies had been purchased, one to cease on the death of the purchaser, the other to run through his wife's death. The expectation seems to be that he would die first; perhaps he was much older or already in poor health.

55. Thompson, *Visitations*, I, 158. Since the dean could not "undergo the burthens that lie upon him, he therefore prays that in his relief the other canons who are strong may visit the sick of the parish."

56. Thompson, *Visitations*, II, 272; II, 276, where "the chamberlain says that, what for the abbot's old age and his infirmities and those of the prior and the sub-prior's simpleness, religious discipline is well-nigh dead." At Markby Priory, when the old prior was turned out to pasture, he was accorded very comfortable treatment: "an honest lodging with a fire-place and a privy," plus as much bread and beer as two canons would receive, and 4 marks a year for raiment, and more of this ilk: II, 224. For a mid-fourteenth-century monastic election, where the new incumbent was "prevented by age and weakness" from going to Rome except by way of a proxy, Dorothy M. Owen, ed., *John Lydford's Book*, Historical Manuscripts Commission, Joint Publications 22 (London, HMSO, 1974), #55.

57. *Rede* 164. The priest was to receive a pension of 12 marks per annum; 312:

the rector of Singleton was to get 10 marks as his annual pension, in quarterly installments: he was "broken by old age"; 25–26 the rector of Bignor was pensioned off at 8 marks a year, now needed "by occasion of his bodily infirmity and senile age."

58. Joan Greatrex, ed., *The Register of the Common Seal of St. Swithin, Winchester*, Hampshire Record Society 2 (1978), 326, 107, for an inspeximus of 1449 that touches many bases: "Out of the bishops' fatherly concern for the retiring rector in his weakness . . . and for the priestly order to avoid being held in disgrace and its ministers to avoid censure, it is necessary to provide some support." The *Register* offers other items of interest: 103, 177, 179, 187, 222, 292, 402 (where there was an obligation for the corrodian to train boys), and 507.

59. *Chichele* IV, 105: his condition was "non propter tua demerita sed certis ex causis nos ad hoc racionabiliter . . . considerantes tamen labores diutinos quos circa dicti prioratus negocia hactenus senectutui pio compacientes affectu."

60. *CPL IX, 1431–47* 406–7; *CPL VIII, 1427–47* 196.

61. *CPL VII, 1417–31* 456.

62. *CPL XV, 1492–98* 718.

63. *CPL XV, 1492–98* 905.

64. *Repingdon* I, 297–98.

65. *Langley* I, 160–61.

66. *Lacy* II, 202–3: "tanta adversa valetude vesatus ac corporis sui debilitacione gravatur, eciam paralasium . . . infirmitatem . . . et nimiam senectute quia nonagenarius est." Once again we learn that the church had more than one motive for concern; the lay administrator of the property had allowed the rectory house to fall into disrepair and the woods had been felled but not replanted.

67. *Rede* 24. The text talks of "fama publica ac facti notoriatate."

68. *Rotherham* 907, 682.

69. *Lacy* III, 188.

70. *Chichele* III, 317–18.

71. *CPL, XIII, 1471–84* 446.

72. *Langley* V, 115.

73. *Rotherham* II, 968.

74. *Lacy* III, 188: the retired incumbent had stepped down because of old age, weakness, and blindness.

75. *Rede* 25–26. Paying on the installment plan is not an invention of the modern consumer society: Christopher Harper-Bill, ed., *The Register of John Morton, Archbishop of Canterbury, 1486–1500*, Canterbury and York Society part 148, vol. 75 (1987), #502: the 10 marks pension was to be paid in four installments — at Michaelmas, Christmas, Feast of the Annunciation, and Nativity of St. John Baptist, "or within 13 days of each feast." This was pretty much the standard pattern.

76. For more on the theme of shame, as a motivating force in the world of pension-granting T. C. B. Timmins, ed., *The Register of John Chandler, Dean of Salisbury, 1404–17*, Wiltshire Record Society 39 (1983), #563: The life pension of £20, payable quarterly, was "to spare him from poverty in consideration of his long and diligent ministry." Arnold Judd, *The Life of Thomas Bekynton* (Chichester: Moore and Tillyer, 1961), 130: "The bishop would not have him forced, in his old age and

weakness, to beg for the necessities of life, to the disgrace of the clerical order," and he ordered a pension of £5 per annum. On Bekynton's policy regarding pensions, Judd, 116, 127 (for a pension to a dean of Wells, now "blind and decrepit").

77. *Rede* 254, 263.

78. *Lacy* II, 201–2.

79. *Chichele* IV, 163–64.

80. *CPL XV, 1492–1498* 518.

81. The significant research for rural England has been done by Elaine Clark, especially in her "Some Aspects of Social Security in Medieval England," though others have remarked for many years on the way agreements were made whereby the older generation passed the land on but sought to protect itself: Henry S. Bennett, *Life on the English Manor* (rev. ed. Cambridge: Cambridge Univ. Press, 1956), 253–54, covering a widow's contract with her sons, plus a father-son agreement; George C. Homans, *English Villagers of the Thirteenth Century* (New York: Russell and Russell, 1960), 154–59, citing literary material as well as manorial records. Homans noted that "the time when the change is made is an anxious one." For a comparative dimension on peasant strategies, Lutz Berkner's article, cited above, in the *American Historical Review*, covering the Austrian stem family and its arrangement for taking care of the elderly as the working generations rolled over. Peter Laslett, "The History of Aging and the Aged," in *Family Life and Illicit Love in Earlier Generations: Essays in Historical Sociology* (Cambridge: Cambridge Univ. Press, 1977), 174–213, on the very limited social pressures to take care of the aged. Judith M. Bennett, *Women in the Medieval English Countryside: Gender and Household in Brigstock Before the Plague* (New York: Oxford Univ. Press, 1987), 61, 149 on the rural poor and the options to a life of labor for the aged. The valuable comments by Richard M. Smith in *Life, Death, and the Elderly* have been cited above.

82. Geoffrey Templeman, ed., *The Records of the Guild of the Holy Trinity, St. Mary, St. John the Baptist, and St. Katherine of Coventry*, vol. II (Dugdale Society, 1944) the guild would help a member "no longer capable of work by reason of illness, accident, or old age" (45); a widow was helped, "by considering the great age, nede, & pouerte that she is ynne" (45).

83. David Herlihy, "The Generation in Medieval History."

Chapter 8. Careers and Case Studies of the Peers

1. From estimates of their aggregate numbers we can try to calculate an age curve for the clergy: Josiah Cox Russell, "The Clerical Population of Medieval England," *Traditio* 2 (1944): 177–212; Heath, *The English Parish Clergy on the Eve of the Reformation*, 183–86. For a recent estimate of clerical population, with an interest in the aged clergy, Swanson, *Church and Society in Late Medieval England*, 30–36, 56–62.

2. Maurice Keen, *English Society in the Later Middle Ages, 1348–1500* (London: Penguin Books, 1990), 33–47 (for the countryside), 78–90 (for the towns and cities).

3. There are references to age and stages of life and the life cycle, as they are pertinent in a look at the careers of "white collar" professionals in many of the essays in Clough, ed., *Profession, Vocation, and Culture in Late Medieval England*.

4. Woodburn O. Ross, ed., *Middle English Sermons*, EETS o.s. 209 (1940), 23.

5. Thomas F. Simmons, ed., *Lay Folks Mass Book*, EETS o.s. 71 (1879), 131; also, p. 34, in a general enjoinder for prayers on behalf of "Oure sib men, and oure wele-willandes / Oure frendes, tenandes, & sermandies, / Olde men, childer & alle wymmen, / Marchandes, men of craft, & tilmen."

6. Juan Ruiz, *The Book of Good Life*, tr. Rigo Mignani and Mario Di Caesare (Albany: SUNY Press, 1970), 143.

7. This quote, from John Miller (1735–1801) appears in E. E. Evans-Pritchard, *A History of Anthropological Thought*, ed. Andre Singer (New York: Basic Books, 1981), 21. Also, Mabel Day and Robert Steele, eds., *Mum and The Sothesegger*, EETS o.s. 199 (1934), 55, "Semely a sage as I sawe there / I saw not sothely sith I was bot / An olde auncyn many of a hunthrid wintere."

8. The material is readily drawn from Roskell et al., *The History of Parliament: The House of Commons, 1386–1421*. The generosity of Rawcliffe and Clark enabled me to use the material, before publication, in the offices of the History of Parliament Trust, Tavistock Square, London. I wish to indicate a special debt for their help and their encouragement when this study was in a totally inchoate state.

9. This is a result of the much higher survival rate for the records of county and royal government than for those of town government and urban life. The constituency analyses in Volume I of the *History of Parliament* give details regarding what can be known about lost names and lost men. Though virtually all constituencies have some gaps, those of boroughs are often sadly deficient even in members' names and identities.

10. For the constituency analysis of the Somerset men, *History of Parliament*, I, 585–89; for that of Bristol (listed under the county of Gloucestershire), I, 403–7. The individuals, of course, appear in Volumes II–IV, by alphabetical listing. Somerset and Bristol have been arbitrarily chosen; there is no reason to think — and this is based on a survey of all four volumes — that they are unusual in regard to any of the issues dealt with here.

11. Without wanting to inflate the ages of those we look at, we should still see many of the dates as representing the minimum span of public life. Some men only make their appearance in the recorded historical record when they emerge as members of Bristol's common council, where our tally begins. They presumably had made some mark, no longer traceable, before the first one unearthed by the *History of Parliament* research team. Many of the entries in the *History* talk about unusually long careers, early appearances in public life, and sustained appearances when quite elderly.

12. For some of the references in the *History of Parliament* to demographic considerations for a constituency, I, 264 (Berkshire); I, 276 (Buckinghamshire); I, 293 (Cornwall), I, 340 (Devon), among many others.

13. These are the *Fasti Parochiales*, published by the Yorkshire Archaeological Society, Record Series: I, ed. A. Hamilton Thompson and Charles T. Clay, 1933,

YAS 85; II, ed A. Hamilton Thompson and Charles T. Clay, 1943, YAS 107; III, ed. N. A. Lawrence, 1967, YAS, 129; IV, ed. Norah K. M. Gurney and Charles T. Clay, 1971, YAS, 133; V, ed. N. A. H. Lawrence, 1985 (for 1983), YAS 143.

14. *Fasti*, III, for the data on Folkton, Lowthorpe, and Rudston.

15. The volume of *Fasti* analyzed is IV, covering the Deanery of Craven.

16. *Fasti*, IV, 3 (for William Blase), 9 (for Addingham).

17. *Fasti* IV, 52.

18. *Fasti* IV, 76.

19. The material on the abbots is from Browne Willis, *An History of the Mitred Parliamentary Abbots*, 2 vols. (London, 1719) 7–8.

20. Willis, *Mitred Abbots* 27.

21. The impressive run of long careers that helped launch Cluny in the tenth and eleventh centuries may be unique in the annals of western monasticism: by the time Maiolus (954–994) or Odilo (994–1048) died they must have outlived virtually all their birth-cohort contemporaries who were in high ecclesiastical offices.

22. Willis, *Mitred Abbots* 31–32.

23. Willis, *Mitred Abbots* 72, 79–80.

24. Willis, *Mitred Abbots* 106–7, 149–50, 216–18.

25. The material, in more detail and covering the second half of the fourteenth century as well as the fifteenth, is presented in Joel T. Rosenthal, "Old Men's Lives: Elderly English Peers, 1350–1500," *Mediaevalia* 8 (1982): 211–37.

26. David Herlihy, "The Generation in Medieval History," 395.

27. Table 8-1 is the same as that in "Old Men's Lives," 235, except that the latter covers the cohort of peers born before 1325 and making a parliamentary appearance after 1350, plus the cohort of peers born 1326–50. Where no specific reference is given for biographical material on a peer, the source is *CP*. For material on aristocratic longevity in a later period, Peller, "Births and Deaths Among Europe's Ruling Families Since 1500."

28. Sylvia Thrupp, *The Merchant Class of Medieval London* 194–95.

29. Philip Greven, *Four Generations* (Ithaca, NY: Cornell Univ. Press, 1970), 26–27, for the demography of the early settlers of Andover, Massachusetts.

30. John Demos, *A Little Commonwealth: Family Life in Plymouth Colony* (New York: Oxford Univ. Press, 1970), 192–93. However, life in the northeastern colonies may have been atypically healthy; it compares most advantageously with life in an area farther south: Daniel B. Smith, "Mortality and Family in Colonial Chesapeake," *Journal of Interdisciplinary History* 8 (1978): 403–27. For a more recent look at old age in the North American colonial world, Laurel Thatcher Ulrich, *A Midwife's Tale: The Life of Martha Ballard Based on Her Diary, 1785–1812* (New York: Knopf, 1990), 309–45, covering Ballard's last years. Though Ballard survived to 77, the diary reveals the heavy toll exacted by old age: physical disability, loss of earning power and independence, and a good deal of psychological and personal anomie.

31. W. L. Warren, *Henry II* (Berkeley: Univ. of California Press, 1973), 626. For Edward III, in addition to the material cited above, we get a comparable view of a royal old age in May McKisack, *The Fourteenth Century* (Oxford: Clarendon Press, 1959), 270, "We know, too, that his private life was not austere and that his

dissipations took heavy toll of his middle years; for he was not yet sixty when he fell into premature senility." For a variation in the theme, we have the austere Henry VII; see S. B. Chrimes, *Henry VII* (Berkeley and Los Angeles: Univ. of California Press, 1972). Henry spoke of failing eyesight by 1501 (313) and there was a general decline from 1506 onwards (313); he was "utterly without hope of recovery" by 24 March, 1509 (314). He died on 21 April; Chrimes says that we should not believe the precision of Gairdner's 1889 diagnosis of the king's last illness.

32. Ralph A. Griffiths, *The Reign of Henry VI* (Berkeley: Univ. of California Press, 1981), passim, for comments about the turnover in the composition of the king's council and of the changing age profile of the advisors as men came and went.

33. James Gairdner, ed., *Letters and Papers Illustrative of the Reigns of Richard III and Henry VII*, London, Rolls Series 24 (1861), 7.

34. *CPR 1461–67* 37.

35. Hugh Talbot, *The English Achilles: The Life and Campaigns of John Talbot, 1st Earl of Shrewsbury* (London: Chatto and Windus, 1981), 165–71; Anthony J. Pollard, *John Talbot and the War in France, 1427–1453* (London: Royal Historical Society, 1983), 1: He was "erroneously believed to be eighty years old (he was approximately sixty-six). . . . For him it was the end of fifty years of warfare and a large part of a lifetime devoted to the forlorn struggle."

36. A. Compton Reeves, *Lancastrian Englishmen* (Washington, DC: University Press of America, 1981), 65–138, for a full biographical treatment.

37. Reeves, *Lancastrian Englishmen*, 105.

38. Linda Clark, "The Benefits and Burdens of Office: Henry Bourgchier (1408–83), Viscount Bourgchier and Earl of Essex, and the Treasurership of the Exchequer," in Hicks, *Profit, Piety and the Professions in Later Medieval England*, 119–36.

39. John S. Roskell, "John, Lord Wenlock of Someries," *Bedfordshire Historical Record Society* 38 (1958): 12–48.

40. Michael J. Bennett, *The Battle of Bosworth* (New York: St. Martin's Press, 1985), passim: 114, on the earl of Oxford's particular disinclination to be merciful towards the elderly duke of Norfolk. Local quarrels, family memories, and probably a good sprinkling of personal animus all made for a merciless outcome.

41. David O. Moberg, "Religiosity in Old Age," *Gerontologist* 5, 2 (1962): 78–87, 111–12. Moberg argues that religious attitudes become strong with age, but that "ritualistic behavior outside the home tends to diminish with increasing age" (86). Bradley C. Courtney, Leonard W. Poon, Leonard Martin, Gloria M. Clayton, and Mary Ann Johnson, "Religiosity and Adaptation in the Oldest-Old (Centenarians)," *International Journal of Aging and Human Development* 34 (1992): 47–56. For a case study that shows a strong positive correlation between age and a strong impulse to be a founder and benefactor, David K. Maxfield, "A Fifteenth-Century Lawsuit: The Case of St. Anthony's Hospital," *Journal of Ecclesiastical History* 44 (1993): 199–223.

42. Colin F. Richmond, "Religion and the Fifteenth-Century English Gentleman," in Dobson, *The Church, Politics and Patronage in the Fifteenth Century*, 193–208.

Chapter 9. Another Case Study: The Bishops

1. Richard G. Davies, "The Episcopate," in Clough, *Profession, Vocation and Culture in Later Medieval England*, 51–89, with the statement that sums up the desiderata for success: "The ideal candidate, such as George Neville, combined all: 'blood, virtue and cunning'" (56–57).

2. Joel T. Rosenthal, *The Training of an Elite Group: English Bishops in the Fifteenth Century*, Transactions of the American Philosophical Society 60, 5 (Philadelphia: American Philosophical Society, 1970): 12–19; Davies, "The Episcopate"; A. B. Emden, *A Biographical Register of the University of Oxford to A.D. 1500* (Oxford: Oxford Univ. Press, 1957–59; A. B. Emden, *A Biographical Register of the University of Cambridge to A.D. 1500* (Cambridge: Cambridge Univ. Press, 1963); T. H. Aston, "Oxford's Medieval Alumni," *Past and Present* 74 (1977): 3–40; T. H. Aston, G. D. Duncan, and T. A. R. Evans, "The Medieval Alumni of the University of Cambridge," *Past and Present* 86 (1980): 9–86.

3. Though we all rely on Emden's findings, there are obviously many problems in his work. For a critique, Malcolm Burson, "Emden's *Registers* and the Prosopography of Medieval English Universities," *Medieval Prosopography* 3, 2 (1982): 35–51.

4. Beaufort's long life is now thoroughly examined, Gerald L. Harriss, *Cardinal Beaufort: A Study of Lancastrian Ascendancy and Decline* (Oxford: Clarendon Press, 1988). For a bleak summation of the final stages: "In his last years Beaufort had no view of the future of his society. The future which he had striven for in his early career was crumbling before his eyes. His present concerns were to ensure his physical comfort, advance his family, and reward those who had served him faithfully" 355).

5. Quoted by Emden, *Oxford* I, 16.

6. Pecock's life is likely to remain an enigma: Vivian H. H. Green, *Bishop Reginald Pecock; A Study in Ecclesiastical History and Thought* (Cambridge: Cambridge Univ. Press, 1945), and Charles W. Brockwell, Jr., *Bishop Reginald Pecock and the Lancastrian Church* (Lewiston, NY: Edwin Mellen Press, 1985).

7. R. Barrie Dobson, "Richard Bell, Prior of Durham (1464–78) and Bishop of Carlisle (1478–95)" *Cumberland and Westmorland Archaeological Society* n.s. 65 (1965): 182–221. This thorough study shows how Bell (like the rabbit in the popular television battery advertisement) just kept going and going. At 46 he failed to become prior of Durham, "foiled by his failure to win the support of the senior Durham monks" (198). When he finally became bishop of Durham, at age 70, he was unable to secure consecration from his metropolitan, Lawrence Booth, "in view of the age and illness" of Booth (211). Bell was the only bishop of Durham to resign between 1246 and 1946, leaving when he was around 85 for a retirement that has left no trace in the records.

8. The list of excused absences that Roskell presents ("The Problem of the Attendance of the Lords, 210–13") includes a few abbots: abbot of Westminster, excused 6/1347, for 2 years, for conventual business; abbot of Cirencester, excused for life, 2/1350, because of age and infirmity; abbot of Malmesbury, excused from

next parliament, 1/1351; abbot of Gloucester, excused for life, 3/1352 (and he resigned in 1377); abbot of Evesham, excused for life, 1/1375 (and he died, 10/1379); abbot of Gloucester, excused for life, 3/1383 (lived until 1412); abbot of Bury St. Edmunds, excused 10/1383 for conventual affairs; abbot of Glastonbury, excused 7/1386, for life (and dying, 1420). All of these excuses were issued between the mid- and late four-teenth century, and only a few went to men who were worn out by old age. The declining importance of even major abbots at a session of parliament is probably the most important single factor behind the willingness to present and then to accept these petitions for absence.

9. Hardly a record admired by all who have considered the facts: Thomas Fuller, *The Worthies of England*, ed. P. Austin Nuttall, 3 vols. (London: T. Tegg, 1840; repr. New York: AMS Press, 1965), II, 25: "Having been bishop of Lincoln and Winchester fifty years, yet was he so far from being weaned from the world, he sucked the hardest (as if he would have bit off the nipples thereof) the nearer he was to his grave."

10. For the Booth family, in more detail, Joel T. Rosenthal, *Patriarchy and Families of Privilege*, 145–51, and Ernest Axon, "The Family of Bothe (Booth) and the Church in the 15th and 16th Centuries," *Transactions of the Lancashire and Cheshire Antiquarian Society* 53 (1938): 32–82.

11. A. Compton Reeves, on the idea that Moleyns was sent into de facto exile, on the grounds that his pro-government policies were so strong that he had become a political liability: *Lancastrian Englishmen*, 243. On a similar treatment meted out to Bishop Lumley, because of his unpopular partisanship on behalf of (or loyalty to) Cardinal Beaufort, R. L. Storey, "Marmaduke Lumley, Bishop of Carlisle, 1430–1450," *Transactions of the Cumberland and Westmorland Antiquarian and Archaeological Society* n.s. 55 (1955): 112–31.

12. Arnold Judd, *The Life of Thomas Bekynton*, for Beckington's high level of activity (119), and a look at his itinerary, which shows him to be slowing down (at least as far as the extant records cover the tale) in the years after 1459 (149–52).

13. Emden, *Oxford*, referring to Henry Wharton's *Anglia Sacra* I, 672–73.

14. Richard G. Davies, "The Attendance of the Episcopate in English Parliaments, 1376–1461," *Proceedings of the American Philosophical Society* 129, 1 (March, 1985): 30–81. In addition to the bishops referred to here, Davies cites material about the problems of Henry Bowet (36) and Edmund Lacy (40).

15. Emden, *Oxford*; *CPL VI (1404–15)* 95–96, 449; *CPL VII (1417–31)* 116.

16. A. T. Bannister, ed., *Registrum Thome Spofford, Episcopi Herefordensis, A.D. MCCCCXXII–MCCCCXLVIII* Canterbury and York Society, 23 (1919), 165–67, 232–33, 251–52, 258–59; *CPL X (1447–55)* 42.

17. E. F. Jacob, *Archbishop Henry Chichele* (London: Nelson, 1967), 87–99, for an extensive discussion of the archbishop's many educational and philanthropic activities. Beckington's benefactions are treated, Judd, *Life of Thomas Bekynton*, 162–67.

18. R. S. Stanier, *Magdalen School: A History of Magdalen College School, Oxford* Oxford Historical Society n.s. 3 (1940), 13–15.

19. William Campbell, ed., *Materials for a History of the Reign of Henry VII*, 2 vols., Rolls Series 60 (1873–77), I, 172–73.

20. For Bowet's inventory, *TE* III, 69–85; for his visitations, A. Hamilton Thompson, "Documents Relating to the Visitations of the Diocese and Province of York," in *Miscellanea II*, Surtees Society 127 (1916), 152–210.

21. Francis Blomefield, *An Essay Towards a Topographical History of the County of Norfolk* 11 vols. 2nd ed. (London and Norwich, 1806–1810), III, 539–42.

22. A. T. Bannister, *Registrum Thome Millyng, Episcopi Herefordensis, A.D. MCCCCLXXIV–MCCCCXCII* Canterbury and York Society 26 (1920), for evidence of sustained activity until the end.

23. Helen Jewell, "English Bishops as Educational Benefactors in the Later Fifteenth Century," in Dobson, *The Church, Politics, and Patronage in the Fifteenth Century*, 146–67; Joel T. Rosenthal, "Lancastrian Bishops and Educational Benefaction," in Barron and Harper-Bill, *The Church in Pre-Reformation Society*, 199–211.

24. The studies referred to in note 23 cover these and many other foundations and pet projects.

25. George G. Perry, "Bishop Beckington and King Henry VI," *English Historical Review* 9 (1894): 261–74.

26. E. W. Parkin, "The Medieval Origins of Wye College," *Archaeologia Cantiana* 102 (1985): 213–17, for John Kempe's long involvement. He proposed the establishment of the college as early as 1432, but did not "bring his plans to fruition" until 1447.

27. Though they are small studies, about the only systematic attempts to work with episcopal wills are Joel T. Rosenthal, "The Fifteenth Century Episcopate: Careers and Bequests," in *Sanctity and Secularity: The Church and the World*, ed. Derek Baker, Studies in Church History 10 (Oxford: Blackwell, 1973), 117–27, and "Lancastrian Episcopal Wills: Directing and Distributing," *Medieval Prosopography* 11, 1 (Spring 1990): 35–84.

28. *Chichele* 485–95.

29. Nicholas Bubwith, in *Chichele* 298–302, and Philip Morgan, in *Chichele* 530–31, are among such bishops.

30. *Chichele* 237–40.

31. *Chichele* 224–25.

32. *Chichele* 133–35.

33. Leland L. Duncan, ed., "The Will of Thomas Bourgchier, Archbishop of Canterbury, 1486," *Archaeologia Cantiana* 24 (1900): 244–52.

34. C. Eveleigh Woodruff, ed., *Kent Sede Vacante Wills*, Kent Archaeological Society, Record Branch 3 (1914), 105–10.

35. For the Chichele family as an enterprise, comparable if smaller in reach than the Booth family, Rosenthal, *Patriarchy and Families of Privilege*, 145–50; for biographical material on the archbishop's brothers, Thrupp, *Merchant Class*, 330–31, and now in more detail, Roskell et al., *History of Parliament*, II, 560–64, with articles on Robert and William.

36. Bannister, *Millyng's Register*, i–ii. He was a good administrator, even if largely a bishop of Hereford in absentia.

37. Woodruff, *Kent Sede Vacante* 81.

38. Woodruff, *Kent Sede Vacante* 85.

39. Alfred C. Fryer, "Monumental Effigies in Somerset, part ix," *Somerset Ar-*

chaeological and Natural History 69 (1923): 14–16, and plates vii–viii. Judd, *Life of Thomas Bekynton* 167–69, for a description of the tomb.

40. *SMW* I, 202. Some bishops had even grander futures once they were beneath their tombs: Edmund Lacy's burial spot became a minor pilgrim site, until bishop Haynes stopped talk of miracles and healing there: G. R. Dunstan, "Some Aspects of the Register of Edmund Lacy, Bishop of Exeter, 1420–55," *Journal of Ecclesiastical History* 6 (1955): 37–47 (with the specific reference, 41–42).

Chapter 10. Men and Women of Letters: The Length of Lives and Some Literary Careers

1. There is probably reason to suspect that this rosy view of the full life was probably not the one actually held by Chaucer in his last decade. There are several discussions of the gray years: Sumner Ferris, "Chaucer, Richard II, Henry IV, and 13 October," in *Chaucer and Middle English Studies, in Honour of Rossell Hope Robbins*, ed. Beryl Rowland (Kent, OH: Kent State Univ. Press, 1974), 210–17, and George G. Coulton, *Chaucer and His England* 8th ed. (New York: Russell and Russell, 1957), 64–71 (with a variety of quotations to support the idea of a lugubrious old age). On Chaucer's age, O. F. Emerson, "Chaucer's Testimony as to His Age," *Modern Philology* 11 (1913–14): 117–25, and Hazel A. Stevenson, "A Possible Relation Between Chaucer's Long Lease and the Date of His Birth," *Modern Language Notes* 50 (1935): 318–22. Recent work is summarized in the entries for Geoffrey and Thomas Chaucer in the *History of Parliament*, II, 518–23, 524–32 respectively. Geoffrey's birth date is given as c. 1343. Letters patent that he received in 1398 spoke of "urgent and arduous affairs of the king," and he was at Henry IV's coronation in the autumn, 1399. Thomas's dates are given as c. 1367–1434. He was one of the leading non-aristocratic figures in the early days of the Lancastrian dynasty. For a recent look at Chaucer's last days — and presented without revisionist views — see Derek Pearsall, *The Life of Geoffrey Chaucer*, 273–77.

2. J. A. Burrow, *Medieval Writers and Their Work: Middle English Literature and Its Background, 1100–1500* (Oxford: Oxford Univ. Press, 1982), and Clough, ed., *Profession, Vocation, and Culture in Later Medieval England*, are both suggestive.

3. Henry Stanley Bennett, *Chaucer and the Fifteenth Century* (New York: Oxford Univ. Press, 1974) 264–301. Bennett's list of men is clearly neither inclusive nor systematic; its miscellaneous nature, if anything, commends it for the hit-or-miss path I am trying to follow in this chapter, since Bennett was not presumably searching for longevity.

4. Joseph Ritson, *Bibliographica Poetica* (London: Printed by C. Roworth for G. and W. Nicol, 1802), 43–110.

5. John H. Fisher, *John Gower, Moral Philosopher and Friend of Chaucer* (New York: New York Univ. Press, 1964), 65. In Gower's case there was justice in such complaints (because of blindness and general decrepitude), and he was allowed either a marriage of convenience or the services of a permanent housekeeper for his last years. Fisher puts Gower's birth around 1330; by 1377 Gower indicated that he

wished to use what time was left for his literary efforts and moved toward what we might consider as semi-retirement.

6. Henry S. Bennett, *Six Medieval Men and Women* (Cambridge: Cambridge Univ. Press, 1955), 90, 69–99 for Hoccleve in general, and Jerome Mitchell, "The Autobiographical Element in Hoccleve," *Modern Language Quarterly* 28 (1967): 269–84, for an explicit discussion of the question, and a fuller treatment in his *Thomas Hoccleve, c. 1368–c. 1430* (Urbana: Univ. of Illinois Press, 1968). A recent view, not very complimentary to Hoccleve as an author, reminds us that "Jerome Mitchell notes . . . Hoccleve's sole attraction for compilers of Middle English anthologies rests in the autobiographical elements embedded in a handful of his poems," Malcolm Richardson, "Hoccleve in His Social Context," *Chaucer Review* 20 (1986): 313–22 (quote 313). Also A. Compton Reeves, "Thomas Hoccleve, Bureaucrat," *Medievalia et Humanistica* n.s. 5 (1974): 201–14. The material in now gathered into a short study that combines an interest in biography and career with literary output; John A. Burrow, *Thomas Hoccleve*, Authors in the Middle Ages 4 (London: Variorum, 1994).

7. John Bale, *Illustrium Majoris Britanniae Scriptorum* (London, 1548). Russell, *Dictionary of Writers of Thirteenth Century England* offers a model of a biographical survey that has not been emulated for later centuries.

8. David C. Fowler, "John Trevisa, Scholar and Translator," *Transactions of the Bristol and Gloucestershire Archaeological Society* 89 (1970): 99–108. Fowler suggests that Trevisa may have gotten into trouble as an Oxford undergraduate for being part of the team working on the Lollard translation of the Bible. Ralph Hanna III, "Sir Thomas Berkeley and His Patronage," *Speculum* 64 (1989): 878–916, for more on west country patronage, translation, and literary activity.

9. Sir John Fortescue, *The Governance of England*, ed. Charles Plummer (Oxford: Clarendon Press, 1885), 68–73, for the latter stages of Fortescue's life.

10. Osbern Bokenham, *Legendes of Hooly Wummen*, ed. Mary S. Sarjeantson, EETS 206 (1938), xiii–xxiv. The problem is put to us squarely: "Nothing is known of the life of Osbern Bokenham except what is stated in and can be gathered from his writings and the manuscripts in which these are extant" (xiii). Bennett, *Six Medieval Men and Women*, 96, quotes Bokenham: "Death hath at my gate, drawn up his cart to carry me hence." But Bennett sagely adds, "We need not take all of this too seriously."

11. The local literary and cultural scene is examined in Samuel Moore, "Patrons of Letters in Norfolk and Suffolk, ca. 1450," *PMLA* 27 (1912): 188–207, and *PMLA* 28 (1913): 79–105.

12. J. H. Harvey, ed., *Itineraries of William Worcester* (Oxford: Clarendon Press, 1969).

13. Cyril L. Smetana, *The Life of St. Norbert by John Capgrave, OESA (1393–1464)* Studies and Texts 40 (Toronto: Pontifical Institute of Mediaeval Studies, 1977), 7–11 on Capgrave's life and the dating of his works. There is a treatment of his travel literature: C. A. Mills, ed., *John Capgrave: Solace of Pilgrims*, with introductory note by H. M. Bannister (London and New York: H. Froude, 1911), xi–xiii.

14. Ethel Seaton, *Sir Richard Roos, c. 1410–1482: Lancastrian Poet* (London:

Rupert Hart-Davis, 1961), and Charles Ross, ed., *John Rous: The Rous Roll* (Gloucester: Alan Sutton, 1980).

15. Paulo Molinari, *Julian of Norwich: The Teaching of a Fourteenth Century English Mystic* (London and New York: Longmans, Green, 1958), 11–12 for Margery Kempe's visit to Julian.

16. B. A. Windeatt, tr. *The Book of Margery Kempe* (Harmondsworth: Penguin, 1985), 29–30, for a "suggested chronology." Margery Kempe has now become a growth industry, though most of the current work is concerned with her feminist self-consciousness. In some ways it is peculiar to consider Margery as a writer, since the interesting issue of her status, as one who dictated her own life story, is worthy of more elaborate and sympathetic treatment than it has received. For a useful and dispassionate biographical presentation, Anthony E. Goodman, "The Piety of John Brunham's Daughter, of Lynn," in *Medieval Women*, ed. Derek Baker (Oxford: Blackwell, for the Ecclesiastical History Society, 1978), 347–58.

17. Roger Lovatt, "John Blacman, Biographer of Henry VI," in *The Writing of History in the Middle Ages: Essays Presented to Richard William Southern*, ed. R. H. C. Davis and J. M. Wallace-Hadrill (Oxford: Clarendon Press, 1981), 415–44. For the royal biography, Montague R. James, tr. and ed., *Henry the Sixth: A Reprint of John Blacman's Memoir* (Cambridge: Cambridge Univ. Press, 1919).

18. Roberto Weiss, *Humanism in England during the Fifteenth Century*, 2nd ed. (Oxford: Blackwell, 1957), 74.

19. There is a discussion of this problem: George Kane, *The Autobiographical Fallacy in Chaucer and Langland Studies* The Chambers Memorial Lecture (London: University College, London, 1965); A. C. Hughes, *Walter Hilton's Directory to Contemplation* (Rome, 1962), 8, for the view that Hilton is "deliberately impersonal."

20. Ashby also refers to those writers, "wrytyng to theyr sygnet full fourty yere, as well beyond the see as on thys syde": Mary Bateson, ed., *George Ashby's Poems* EETS e.s. 76 (1899), 75. For a long lesson on the wisdom of the elderly, from his "Dicta Philosophorum": "Trust neuer to your owne wytte, ne in Counseil / But of aged men in discrecion / Being experte of thrify antiquaite." There are other snippets that can be offered: John M. Bowers, ed., *The Canterbury Tales: Fifteenth-Century Continuations and Additions* (Kalamazoo, MI: Medieval Institute Publications, 1992), 15 (from Lydgate's Prologue to the *Siege of Thebes*): "I answerde my name was Lydgate / Monk of Bery, mygh fyfty yere of age / "Come to this toune to do my pilgrimage, / As I have ahight, I ha thereof no shamme!"

21. Harvey Lehman, *Age and Achievement* (Princeton, NJ: Princeton Univ. Press, for the American Philosophical Society, 1953), and Lehman, "The Production of Masterworks Prior to Age 30," *The Gerontologist* 5, 2 (1965): 24–29, 48; Wayne Dennis, "Creative Productivity Between the Ages of 20 and 80 Years," *Journal of Gerontology* 21 (1966): 1–8: mostly a list of works produced, by decades of life, by academics and artists. It is comforting to learn that scholars hold up, in terms of the quality of later works, better than do artists. Ernest F. Jacob was impressed by the late-authorship issue when he talked about Pecock: "Reynold Pecock, Bishop of Chichester," in his *Essays in Later Medieval History* (Manchester: Manchester Univ. Press, 1968), 1–34. When Pecock was in his early or mid-60s (around 1457) he said

he would only answer for what he had written in the last three years. There is also solace for lesser folk in learning that Tycho Brahe, the greatest visual observer in the history of western astronomy, said, regarding astronomical observations he made at 50: "Those I call the observations of my manhood, completely valid and absolutely certain, and this is my opinion of them:" Marie Boas, *The Scientific Renaissance, 1450–1630* (London: Collins, 1962), 112. That Brahe may have been wrong in his assessment of his own contributions is a different problem.

22. On patronage and men of letters, V. J. Scattergood and J. W. Sherborne, eds., *English Court Culture in the Later Middle Ages* (New York: St. Martin's Press, 1983), and Richard Firth Green, *Poets and Princepleasers: Literature and the English Court in the Late Middle Ages* (Toronto: Univ. of Toronto Press, 1980).

Chapter 11. Old Age Within and Across Cultures

1. For a recent discussion of when old age begins, Henning Kirk, "Geriatric Medicine and the Categorisation of Old Age—The Historical Linkage," *Aging and Society*, 12 (1992): 152–56. Herbert C. Covey, "The Definitions of the Beginning of Old Age in History," *International Journal of Aging and Human Development* 34 (1982): 325–37. Covey looks at such medieval heavies as Isidore of Seville (who dated old age from 70, as well as arguing for the six-stage division of life) and Avicenna (who had four divisions of the life line, and began his last at 60).

2. On the "demographic crisis" of Europe after the Plague, David Herlihy, "The Generation in Medieval History"; John Hatcher, *Plague, Population and the English Economy, 1348–1530*; James L. Bolton, *The Medieval English Economy, 1150–1500* (London: J. M. Dent, 1980), 214–20, 258–61 for the post-plague condition of towns and countryside. For a study that argues for continuity, William J. Courteney, "The Effect of the Black Death on English Higher Education," *Speculum* 55 (1980): 696–714.

3. For a general treatment of the elderly around the "undeveloped" or "third" world, Leo W. Simmons, *The Role of the Aged in Primitive Society*, and summarized by Simmons in his "Aging in Pre-Industrial Societies," in *Handbook of Social Gerontology*, ed. Clark Tibbits (Chicago: Univ., of Chicago Press, 1970), 62–76. For a case study of a culture in which the elderly have high status and commensurate privileges, Dennis Werner, "Gerontocracy Among the Mekromoti of Central Brazil," *Anthropological Quarterly* 54 (1981): 15–27; p. 19 shows tables that correlate age with influence. Also in the vast literature, Jay Sokolovsky, ed., *The Cultural Context of Aging: Worldwide Perspectives* (New York: Bergin and Garvey, 199) with various essays relevant to this treatment.

4. *Deuteronomy* 4: 40; for other passages in this vein, *Psalms* 91: 16; *Deuteronomy* 5: 16, 11: 21, 22: 7; *Proverbs* 16: 31, 10: 27; *Isaiah* 65: 20. For a less sanguine view, *Psalms* 71: 9; *Ecclesiastes* 12; *Job* 12: 12. This is clearly a topic of perennial interest: Louis A. Krause, "Old Age in the Bible and Poetry," *Annals of Internal Medicine* 36 (1952): 152–56; Frank N. Egerton, "The Longevity of the Patriarchs: A Topic in the History of Demography," *Journal of the History of Ideas* 27 (1966): 575–84.

More tales, and many more biblical verses, are covered in Sabine Baring-Gould, *Legends of Old Testament Characters* (London, 1871), I, passim.

5. William Arens, *The Man-Eating Myth: Anthropology and Anthropophagy* (New York: Oxford Univ. Press, 1979). The chances are that the older anthropological literature on the ritual killing of kings, so central to *The Golden Bough*, would likewise prove elusive were we to ask hard questions about when and where.

6. The classical material is drawn mainly from Minois, *History of Old Age from Antiquity to the Renaissance*, 43–76 for Greece, 77–112 for Rome. Also, Richardson, *Old Age Among the Ancient Greeks*, for a treatment with a considerable focus on art and inscriptions.

7. Minois, *History of Old Age*, 55–56. The table in Richardson, *Old Age Among the Ancient Greeks*, 215–22, is even longer. Richardson's catalogue of inscriptions (277–360) arranges the subjects of the inscriptions by age, running from 22 children who died while less than one year to 24 men and women of over 90. Since Richardson's book is an old study, a revised version of such an analysis, in light of evidence uncovered in the last 60 years (plus our statistical and archaeological sophistication regarding who was buried with an inscription, etc.) would offer an instructive contrast in both methodology and demography.

8. Minois, *History of Old Age*, 59.

9. Minois, *History of Old Age*, 60–62: Aristotle is characterized as being "pitiless" toward the aged, thinking that after 50 it was all downhill. Unlike the lofty role reserved in Plato's *Republic* for those of many years, the best they can do in Aristotle's view is to serve in priestly functions that in classical antiquity were more commemorative than sacerdotal.

10. We should keep in mind the flexibility of age—when comparing chronology to role—and the way in which one's functions help determine the grid of "social age." For example, John W. Draper, "Shakespeare's Attitude Towards Old Age," argues that Polonius, probably just in his 40s or 50s (judging in part by his children's ages: young adulthood for Laertes, early maturity for Ophelia), was still deemed to be a competent prime minister and that much of the behavior that made his appear so elderly was appropriate to a wise minister when dealing with the next generation.

11. Robert Kastenbaum, "The Age of Saints and the Saintliness of Age," *International Journal of Aging and Human Development* 30 (1990): 95–118.

12. Cicero, *De Senectute, De Amicitia, De Divinatione*, tr. William A. Falconer, Loeb Library (Cambridge, MA: Harvard University Press, and London: William Heinemann, 1979).

13. Moses Hadas, *A History of Latin Literature* (New York: Columbia Univ. Press, 1952), 134. Also, Albert R. Chandler, "Cicero's Ideal Old Men," *Journal of Gerontology* 3 (1948): 285–89.

14. W. J. B. Crotch, ed., *The Prologues and Epilogues of William Caxton* EETS o.s. 176 (1928), 41–44: "How Caton exhorteth & counseilleth olde men to be Ioyeful, and bere pacyently olde age when it cometh to them" (41). Crotch also prints Wynken de Worde's obituary on (old) Caxton: "which hath be translated oute of Frenche into Englisshe by William Caxton of Westmynstre late deed and fynyshed at the last daye of hys lyff" (cxxiv).

15. James D. Foltz, "Senescence and Renascence: Petrarch's Thoughts on Growing Old," *Journal of Medieval and Renaissance Studies* 10 (1980): 207–37. Petrarch began by agreeing with Augustine on the idea of six ages of the world and, consequently, six segments of human life, and he grew verbose and philosophical as he waxed old: "Young men want to prolong their years and pleasures, while the old hope to obtain respect and deference" (226). Age as the gateway to contentment was a line of thought that always attracted some support among the intelligentsia: Charles Trinkhaus, *Adversity's Noblemen: The Italian Humanists on Happiness* (New York, 1940: repr. New York: Octagon Books, 1965), 75–76.

16. The most convenient version is Lothario dei Segni (Pope Innocent III), *On the Misery of the Human Condition*, tr. M. M. Dietz, ed. Donald R. Howard (Indianapolis, IN: Bobbs-Merrill, 1969), though the serious scholarly treatment is Innocent III (Lotario dei Segni), *De Miseria Condicionis Humane*, ed. and tr. Robert E. Lewis (Athens: Univ. of Georgia Press, 1978). Howard provides a scholarly discussion and notes on Lothario's quotations and allusions. He argues that this acerbic treatise should be read as a serious statement, not merely an academic exercise on the fleeting value of human life — as some apologists have tried to portray it. J. Livingston Lowes, "The *Prologue to the Legend of Good Women*," talks of Innocent's "still more dismal treatise" (790). George R. Coffman, "Old Age from Horace to Chaucer: Some Literary Affinities and Adventures of an Idea," *Speculum* 9 (1934): 244–77, for the view that the treatise is not generally typical of Innocent's writing, but stands as the work of "a recluse, an ascetic, a misanthrope . . . a Jeremiad with pity omitted" (254). Coffman deals with the *Pricke of Conscience* and contends that it was the major literary vehicle whereby Innocent's ideas were transmitted into fourteenth century English vernacular writing (262–66). Coffman's article contains a great deal of relevant information about the literary transmission of the ideas that marked the negative school of thought about age.

17. The Bacon quote, from the 1683 translation (*The Cure of Old Age*), is given in Richard L. Grant, "Concepts of Aging: An Historical Review," *Perspectives in Biology and Medicine* 6 (1963): 443–79, 465. The title page of the 1683 translation of Bacon's work is reproduced in Joseph A. Freeman, "The History of Geriatrics," *Annals of Medical History* n.s. 10 (1938): 324–35. For a modern scholarly edition of the Bacon text, Roger Bacon, *De Retardatione Accidentium Senectutis*, ed. A. G. Little and E. Withington (Oxford: Clarendon Press, 1928).

18. For an elaborate discussion of Shakespeare's possible sources and literary analogues, Horace H. Furness, *As You Like It: A Variorum Edition*, 12th impression (Philadelphia: Lippincott, 1918) 121–28; Richard Knowles and Evelyn J. Mattern, *As You Like It: A New Variorum Edition* (New York: Modern Language Association, 1977) 130–37. John A. Burrow, *The Ages of Man* 52–52, for a brief summary of sources and analogues. Also of interest are R. H. Bowers, "A Medieval Analogue to *As You Like It*, II, vii, 137–66," *Shakespeare Quarterly* 3 (1952): 109–12; Herbert C. Covey, "A Return to Infancy: Old Age and The Second Childhood in History," *International Journal of Aging and Human Development* 36, 2 (1992–93): 81–90.

19. The literature on this issue is fairly elaborate, concentrating as it mostly does on the various theories advanced in literature, in pictorial representations, and in medical and humoral theory. For good introductory treatments, a very old work

is still of surprising value and interest: J. W. Jones, "Observations on the Origin of the Division of Man's Life into Stages," *Archaeologia* 35 (1853): 167–89, covering Hebrew and Byzantine as well as classical and medieval discussions; Samuel Chew, *The Pilgrimage of Life*; Samuel A. Small, "The *Iuventus* Stage of Life," in *Philologica: The Malone Anniversary Studies*, ed. Thomas A. Kirby and Henry B. Woolf (Baltimore: Johns Hopkins Univ. Press, 1949), 235–38. The medieval dexterity with numerology is covered in Vincent F. Hopper, *Medieval Number Symbolism*, now amplified by Anne Higgins, "Medieval Notions of the Structure of Time," *Journal of Medieval and Renaissance Studies* 19, 2 (1989): 227–50, pp. 238–48 on the periodization of history and of human life. For an eight-stage depiction of the life cycle, Carleton Brown, ed., *Religious Lyrics of the XVth Century* (Oxford: Clarendon Press, 1952; repr. of 1939 ed.), "This world is but a daye," with its elaborate divisions of life into morrow-tyde, myde-morrow daye, vnde-day, mydday, nonne, myd-vndernone, ewynsong, and "now ys this day commn to be nygt." For a scheme of six stages of twelve years per stage, as accepted de facto in urban life, Charles Phythian-Adams, *Desolation of a City*, 180.

20. Martin Crow and Clair Olson, *Chaucer Life Records*, 371, for the account of how Chaucer was walking down Fridaystrete in London when he just happened to notice the arms of Sir Robert Grosvenor hanging from an inn window.

21. Minois, *History of Old Age*, for material presented in tabular fashion: the (short) ages of Merovingian rulers (146); early papal survival (152); attested age of witnesses at canonization ceremonies (172); a list of St. Louis' ancestors who lived to age 60 and beyond (199). These presentations are intriguing but often less than convincing. Paul E. Dutton, "Beyond the Topos of Senescence: The Political Problems of Aged Carolingian Rulers," in Sheehan, *Aging and the Aged*, 75–94: 92, 94 for the statistical material.

22. In addition to the (older) authorities listed above, the main source of this exposition is Burrow, *The Ages of Man*. Comparable material is treated in Dove, *The Perfect Age of Man's Life*, 16–25; Michael Goodich, *From Birth to Old Age*, 59–81; Elizabeth Sears, *The Ages of Man*: the index references in this study lead the reader to divisions of the life cycle by three stages, by four, five, six, seven, eight, ten, and twelve, with many illustrations to show depictions of the schemes; Philippa Tristram, *Figures of Life and Death in Medieval English Literature*, 77–94. An overview, not concentrating on medieval data, is found in Daniel J. Levinson et al., *The Seasons of Man's Life* (New York: Knopf, 1978), and a recent debate, Roland S. Guyot, "A New Theory About the Ages of Man," and Thomas R. Cole, "Comments on Roland S. Guyot's 'A New Theory About the Ages of Man'," *International Journal of Aging and Human Development* 36, 2 (1992–93): 91–98, 98–101 respectively. Comprehensive discussions, starting from the literature of the day, are found in Thorlac Turville-Petre, "The Three Ages of Man in *The Parlement of the Three Ages*," *Medium Aevum* 46 (1977): 66–76, and Beryl Rowland, "The Three Ages of *The Parlement of the Three Ages*," *Chaucer Review* 9 (1974–75): 342–52.

23. Burrow, *Ages of Man* 13. Pythagoras was the father of this school of thought, and the Pythagoreans saw four as "the root and source of eternal nature" (14). Ovid had Pythagoras talking in this vein in book XV of the *Metamorphoses*: "Do you not see the year assuming four aspects, in imitation of our own

lifetime?" For a medieval presentation of seven, Albert Way, ed., *Promptorium Parvulorum*, Camden Society o.s. 25 (1863–65), 7: the "vij ages" being infancy, to age 7;
puerica, to 14; adolescentia, to 29; juventus, to 50; gravitas, to 70; senectus, "que
null terminatur termino; [and then] senium etc ultima pars senectutis. Septima erit
in resurrectione finali."

24. Paul Strohm, "Chaucer's Audience," *Literature and History* 5 (1979): 26–
41; "Chaucer's Fifteenth Century Audience and the Narrowing of the Chaucer Tradition," *Studies in the Age of Chaucer* 4 (1982): 3–32; "Chaucer's Audience(s):
Fictional, Implied, Intended, Actual," *Chaucer Review* 18 (1983–84): 137–45.

25. Miri Rubin, *Charity and Community in Medieval Cambridge* (Cambridge:
Cambridge Univ. Press, 1987), for a recent and general discussion that touches on
all kinds of unfortunates, outcasts, and the marginal, along with the remedies for
their ills as offered by a wealthy town, noting kindly and well-subsidized treatment
of the aged master of a hospital (132); how the aged were *not* among those granted
indulgences because of individual need (264–69).

26. Brian Tierney, "The Decretist and the 'Deserving Poor'," *Comparative
Studies in Society and History* 1 (1958–59): 360–73.

27. Rotha M. Clay, *The Mediaeval Hospitals of England* (London, 1909: repr.
New York: Barnes and Noble, 1966), xvii–xviii for a general assessment of hospitals'
roles. Also, "The majority of hospitals were for the support of infirm and aged
people" (15). Rubin, *Community and Charity*, 148–236, for the hospitals of the town
of Cambridge; such as, the Hospital of St. John the Evangelist, a major institution,
looking to "the sick and weak" (137ff.).

28. *Cartulary of the Hospital of St. Thomas the Martyr, Southwark (Stow Ms. 942)*,
ed. P. L. Hull (privately printed for the Governors, 1932), #11 and #95. Also Catherine Jamison, *The History of the Royal Hospital of St. Katherine by the Tower of London*
(London: privately printed, 1952), passim.

29. Francis Blomefield, *An Essay Toward a Topographical History of the County
of Norfolk*, 2nd ed., 11 vols. (London and Norwich: 1806–10): iv, 432.

30. Edith Rickert, ed., *Chaucer's World* (New York: Columbia Univ. Press,
1948), 352.

31. William Dugdale, *Monasticon Anglicanum*, ed. J. Caley, H. Ellis, and
B. Bandinel, 6 vols. in 8, (London: 1817–30), 703 (for Elsing); and Dugdale, on
Whittington's Hospital, quoting the charter: "personis illis miserbilibus providere,
quibus penuria paupertatis." In talking about the Neville foundation at Well, "unum
hospitale pro certis hospitalitatibus pauperum, et infirmorum, et aliis caritatis
operibus . . . pauperum miserabilium personarum sustentationem" (654).

32. *TE* iv, 29: the will is that of John Carre, written 6 November 1487. The
interest in setting out such elaborate provisions is fairly common: each bed given
away was "to have a new coverlet, a new mattresse, ij new blanket, ij new shetes,
price of every bedd xiij s. iiij d. Summa, xxxiij li., vj s., viij d."

33. Philip E. Jones, ed., *Calendar of the London Plea and Memoranda Rolls,
1458–82* (Cambridge: Cambridge Univ. Press, 1961), 104: this will is also given, *TE*
iv, 202. For a typical example of a generous will that manages to pay no explicit
attention to the elderly: "money to be disposid for the wele of my soule; that is to
say to the exhibicion of pure chylder apte to lerne at scole, pore maydens well dis-

posyd to mariagis, and to wayes or briges, broken or hurte to the neusance or niuer-
ties of Crystin people, amendynge and reparinge" (202).

34. *SMW* I, 404–5.

35. J. R. H. Weaver and Alice Beardwood, eds., *Some Oxfordshire Wills, 1393–
1510*, Oxfordshire Record Society 39 (1958), 29. The will is that of Thomas Beamond,
written on 12 August, 1457.

36. Weaver and Beardwood, *Some Oxfordshire Wills*, 14: a will of 1 October,
1427.

37. Studies that emphasize the positive and caring aspects of medieval society
include Marjorie K. McIntosh, "Local Responses to the Poor in Late Medieval and
Tudor England," *Continuity and Change* 3 (1988): 209–45: life cycle poverty inten-
sified between 1465–1530, and society (though still on a voluntary basis) moved to
deal with it; "Local Change and Community Control in England, 1465–1500,"
Huntington Library Quarterly 49 (1986): 219–42. For studies of guilds and hospitals — many of which offer data supporting the view of heightened social concern,
Caroline M. Barron, "The Parish Fraternities of Medieval London," in Barron and
Harper-Bill, *The Church in Pre-Reformation Society*, 13–37, pp. 26–27 for a compari-
son, as possible, between intention and implementation. Also Frances M. Page,
"The Customary Poor Laws of Three Cambridge Manors," *Cambridge Historical
Journal* 3 (1930): 125–33; H. J. Westlake, *The Parish Gilds of Medieval England* (London: Society for Promoting Christian Knowledge, 1919), 138–238, for appendix on
the Gild certificates of 1389; Geoffrey Templeman, ed., *The Records of the Guild of the
Holy Trinity, St. Mary, St. John the Baptist, and St. Katherine of Coventry* Dugdale
Society 19 (1944), 152–57; Canon Jackson, "Ancient Statutes of Heytesbury Almshouse," *Wiltshire Archaeological and Natural History Magazine* 11 (1869): 289–302:
the "seke pouer, feble, and impotent" were to be admitted, if they could be taken
care "of by their fellows," but "no leepre be admytted or putte unto the saide hows
and if anyone turns out to be leprous and a threat to othere, [he was] to be soberly
removed," though he was to be cared for, for life, in another location. For typical
entries about guild members' obligations towards the aged and the indigent, Toulmin Smith and L. Toulmin Smith, eds., *English Gilds*, EETS o.s. 40 (1870), 5, 9;
Francis W. Steer, "The Statutes of Saffron Walden Almshouse," *Transactions of the
Essex Archaeological Society* n.s. 25 (1955–56): 160–221; J. Durkan, "Care of the Poor
in Pre-Reformation Hospitals," in *Essays in the Scottish Reformation, 1513–1625*, ed.
David McRoberts (Glasgow: Burns, 1962), 116–28, though the charitable/medical
aspects of the institutions are not the main thrust of this study.

38. Baring-Gould, *Legends of Old Testament Characters*, I. One Muslim legend
relates that Abraham chose to die at 200 because the specter of an angel who visited
him and who himself was already 202 was too decrepit to contemplate (I, 236).

39. References from literature are easy to find. In the *Song of Roland*, The Sara-
cen said, "Great is my amazement / At Charlemagne, who is hoary and white-
haired; / To my knowledge he is more than two hundred years old": Glyn Burgess,
tr., *The Song of Roland* (New York: Penguin Books, 1990), 46. On the last days of
St. Louis, Frank Marzials, tr., *Memoirs of the Crusades* (London: J. M. Dent,
1908), 320.

40. I was pleased to learn, in reading an essay I did not see until my views were

well formulated, that Nicholas Orme came to a similar view of the church and the dimensions of its social outreach: "The Church . . . did not develop successful policies and measures for dealing with all its clergy. They grew infirm and old, as they lived, in various different surroundings, individually and in communities, in a complexity with which the authorities could not cope. It is another demonstration that the Church was not in practice the centralized effective body that people often thought (and think) it to be": "Sufferings of the Clergy," 71.

Bibliography

PRIMARY SOURCES

Archer, Margaret, ed. *The Register of Bishop Philip Repingdon, 1405–19*. Lincoln Record Society 57–58, 74 (1963 –).

Bacon, Roger. *De Retardatione Accidentium Senectutis*, ed. A. G. Little and E. Withington. Oxford: Clarendon Press, 1928.

Baildon, W. Paley and J. W. Clay, eds. *Inquisitions Post Mortem Relating to Yorkshire of the Reigns of Henry IV and Henry V*. Yorkshire Archaeological Society 59 (1918).

Bale, John. *Illustrium Majoris Brittanniae Scriptorum*. London, 1548.

Bannister, A. T., ed. *Registrum Thome Spofford, Episcopi Herefordensis, A.D. MCCCCXXII–MCCCCXLVIII*. Canterbury and York Society 23 (1919).

———, ed. *Registrum Thome Millyng, Episcopi Herefordensis, A.D. MCCCCLXXIV–MCCCCXCII*. Canterbury and York Society 26 (1920).

Barker, E. E., ed. *The Register of Thomas Rotherham, Archbishop of York, 1480–1500*. Vol. 1. Canterbury and York Society, 69 (1976).

Bateson, Mary, ed. *George Ashby's Poems*. EETS e.s. 76 (1899).

Bokenham, Osbern. *The Legendys of Hooly Wummen*, ed. Mary Serjeantson. EETS o.s. 206 (1938).

———. *A Legend of Holy Women*, trans. Sheila Delany. Notre Dame, IN: Notre Dame University Press, 1992.

Bowers, John M., ed. *The Canterbury Tales: Fifteenth Century Continuations and Additions*. Kalamazoo, MI: Medieval Institute Publications, 1992.

Brown, Carleton, ed. *Religious Lyrics of the XVth Century*. Oxford: Clarendon Press, 1952; repr. of 1939 ed.

Burgess, Glyn, trans. *The Song of Roland*. New York: Penguin, 1990.

Calendar of Inquisitions Post Mortem xvii (15–23 Richard II). London: HMSO, 1988.

Calendar of Inquisitions Post Mortem xviii (1–6 Henry IV), ed. J. L. Kirby. London: HMSO, 1987.

Calendar of Miscellaneous Inquisitions vii (1399–1422). London: HMSO, 1987.

Calendar of Inquisitions Post Mortem, Henry VII. 2 vols. London: HMSO, 1898–1915.

Calendar of Papal Letters, 1362–1498. London: HMSO, and Dublin, 1902–1986.

Calendar of the Close Rolls, 1377–1509. London: HMSO, 1914–63.

Calendar of the Patent Rolls, 1377–1509. London, HMSO, 1895–1916.

Campbell, William, ed. *Materials for a History of the Reign of Henry VII*. 2 vols. London: Rolls Series 60 (1873–77).

Cartulary of the Hospital of St. Thomas the Martyr, Southwark (Stow Ms. 942), ed. P. L. Hull. London: Privately printed for the Governors of the Hospital, 1932.

Cicero. *De Senectute, De Amicitia, De Divination*, trans. William A. Falconer. Cambridge, MA: Harvard University Press, and London: Wm. Heinemann, 1979.

Crotch, W. J. B., ed. *The Prologues and Epilogues of William Caxton*. EETS o.s. 176 (1928).

Crow, Martin M. and Clair C. Olson, eds. *Chaucer Life Records*. Austin: University of Texas Press, 1966.

Day, Mabel and Robert Steele, eds. *Mum and the Sothesegger*. EETS o.s. 199 (1934).

Deedes, C., ed. *The Episcopal Register of Robert Rede, Bishop of Chichester, 1397–1415*. 2 vols. Sussex Record Society 8, 10 (1908–10).

Devlin, Sister Mary Aquinas, ed. *The Sermons of Thomas Brinton, Bishop of Rochester, 1373–89*. Camden Society 3rd ser. 85–86 (1954).

Dugdale, William. *Monasticon Anglicanum*, ed. J. Caley, H. Ellis, and B. Bandinal. 6 vols. in 8. London, 1817–30.

Duncan, Leland L., ed. "The Will of Thomas Bourgchier, Archbishop of Canterbury, 1486." *Archaeologia Cantiana* 24 (1900): 244–52.

Dunstan, G. R., ed. *The Register of Edmund Lacy, Bishop of Exeter, 1420–55*. 5 vols. Canterbury and York Society 60–63, 66 (1963–72).

Fortescue, John. *The Governance of England*, ed. Charles Plummer. Oxford: Clarendon Press, 1885.

Fry, Timothy, ed. *The Rule of St. Benedict in English*. Collegeville, MN: Liturgical Press, 1982.

Gairdner, James, ed. *Letters and Papers Illustrative of the Reigns of Richard III and Henry VII*. London: Rolls Series 24 (1861).

———, ed. *The Paston Letters*. 3 vols., London: A. Constable and Co., 1895.

Gray, Douglas, ed. *The Oxford Book of Late Medieval Verse and Prose*. Oxford: Clarendon Press, 1985.

Greatrex, Joan, ed. *The Register of the Common Seal of St. Swithin, Winchester*. Hampshire Record Society II (1978).

Gurney, Norah K. M. and Charles Clay, eds. *Fasti Parochiales, 4*. Yorkshire Archaeological Society 133 (1971).

Harper-Bill, Christopher, ed. *The Register of John Morton, Archbishop of Canterbury, 1486–1500*. Canterbury and York Society, part 148, vol. 75 (1987).

Harvey, John H., ed. *Itineraries of William of Worcester*. Oxford: Clarendon Press, 1969.

Heath, Peter, ed. *Bishop Geoffrey de Blythe's Visitations, c. 1515–1523*. Staffordshire Record Society iv, 7 (1973).

Hull, P. L., ed. *The Cartulary of Launceston Priory*. Devon and Cornwall Record Society n.s. 30 (1987).

Innocent III (Lothario dei Segni). *On the Misery of the Human Condition*, ed. Donald R. Howard; trans. Margaret M Dietz. Indianapolis, IN: Bobbs-Merrill, 1969.

——— *De Miseria Condicionis Humane*, ed. and trans. Robert E. Lewis. Athens: University of Georgia Press, 1978.

Jackson, Canon, ed. "Ancient Statutes of Heytesbury Almshouse." *Wiltshire Archaeological and Natural History Magazine* 11 (1869): 289–302.
Jacob, Ernest F. and H. C. Johnson, eds. *The Register of Henry Chichele, Archbishop of Canterbury, 1414–43.* 4 vols. Oxford: Oxford Universty Press, 1938–43.
James, Montague R., trans. and ed. *Henry the Sixth: A Reprint of John Blacman's Memoir.* Cambridge: Cambridge Unviersity Press, 1919.
Jones, Philip E., ed. *Calendar of the London Plea and Memoranda Rolls, 1458–82.* Cambridge: Cambridge University Press, 1961.
Lawrence, N.A., ed. *Fasti Parochiales, 3 and 5.* Yorkshire Archaeological Society 129 and 143 (1967, 1985).
Lords Report on the Dignity of a Peer. Volume 4 and appendices. London: printed for The House of Lords, 1829.
Martin, M. T., ed. *The Percy Chartulary.* Surtees Society 117 (1911).
Marzials, Frank., trans. *Memoirs of the Crusades.* London: J. M. Dent, 1908.
Maximianus. *Elegies on Old Age and Love,* In Zerbi, *Gerontocomia,* 307–36.
McGregor, Margaret, ed. *Bedfordshire Wills Proved in the Prerogative Court of Canterbury, 1383–1548.* Bedfordshire Historical Record Society 58 (1979).
Mills, C. A., ed. *John Capgrave: Solace of Pilgrims,* intro. H. M. Bannister. London and New York: H. Frowde, 1911.
Nichols, John, ed. *A Collection of Wills.* London, 1780: repr. New York: Kraus Reprint, 1969.
Nicolas, Nicholas Harris, ed. *The Controversy Between Sir Richard Scrope and Sir Robert Grosvenor.* 2 vols. London: Privately printed, 1832.
Owen, Dorothy M., ed. *John Lydford's Book.* London: Historical Manuscripts Commission, Joint Publications, 1974.
Raine, James and James Raine, Jr., eds. *Testamenta Eboracensia, I, II, III, IV.* Surtees Society 4, 31, 45, 53 (1836–69).
Renshaw, Mary A., transcr. and ed. *Inquisitions Post Mortem Relating to Nottinghamshire, 1437–1485.* Thoroton Society, Record Series 17 (1956).
Rickert, Edith, ed. *Chaucer's World.* London: Oxford University Press, 1948.
Ross, Woodburn O., ed. *Middle English Sermons.* EETS o.s. 109 (1940).
Ruiz, Juan. *The Book of Good Lives,* ed. Rigo Mignani and Mario A. Di Caesare. Albany, NY: SUNY Press, 1970.
Rymer, Thomas. *Foedera,* ed. A. Clarke, F. Holbrooke, and J. Caley. 4 vols. in 7 pts. London: Rec. Comm., 1816–69.
Scrope, Stephen. *The Epistle of Othea,* ed. Curt Buhler. EETS 264 (1970).
Searle, Eleanor and Barbara Ross, eds. *The Cellarers' Rolls of Battle Abbey, 1275–1513.* Sussex Record Society 65 (1967).
Sharpe, Reginald R., ed. *Calendar of the Wills Proved in the Court of Hustings, A.D. 1258–A.D. 1688.* 2 vols. London: J. C. Francis, 1889–90.
———, ed. *The Letter Books of London, H, I, K, L.* London: J. E. Francis, 1907–12.
Simmons, Thomas F., ed. *Lay Folks Mass Book.* EETS o.s. 71 (1879).
Smetana, Cyril L., ed. *The Life of St. Norbert by John Capgrave, OESH (1393–1464).* Toronto: Pontifical Institute of Mediaeval Studies, Studies and Texts 40, 1977.
Smith, Toulmin, and Lucy Toulmin Smith, eds. *English Gilds.* EETS o.s. 40 (1870).

Steer, Francis W. "The Statutes of Saffron Walden Almshouse." *Transactions of the Essex Archaeological Society* n.s. 25 (1955–56): 160–221.

Storey, R. L., ed. *The Register of Thomas Langley, Bishop of Durham, 1406–37.* 6 vols. Surtees Society 164, 166, 169, 170, 177, 182 (1956–70).

Templeman, Geoffrey, ed. *The Records of the Guild of the Holy Trinity, St. Mary, St. John the Baptist, and St. Katherine of Coventry.* Vol. II. Dugdale Society, 1944.

Thompson, A. Hamilton, "Documents Relating to the Visitations of the Diocese and Province of York." *Miscellanea II*, Surtees Society 127 (1916): 152–210.

———, ed. *Visitations of Religious Houses in the Diocese of Lincoln.* Canterbury and York Society 24 and 29; repr., London, 1968.

Thompson, A. Hamilton and Charles Clay, eds. *Fasti Parochiales 1 and 2.* Yorkshire Archaeological Society 85, 107 (1933, 1943).

Timmins, T. C. B., ed. *The Register of John Chandler, Dean of Salisbury, 1404–17.* Wiltshire Record Society 39 (1983).

Timson, R. T., ed. *The Cartulary of Blyth Priory.* Thoroton Society, Record Series 27–28 (1973).

Towneley, Christopher and Roger Didsworth, transcr., ed. William Langton. *Abstracts of Inquisitions Post Mortem.* Vols. 1 and 2. Chetham Society o.s. 95 and 99 (1875–76).

Train, K. S. S., ed. *Abstracts of the Inquisitions Post Mortem Relating to Nottinghamshire, 1350–1436.* Thoroton Society Record Series 12 (1952).

Way, Albert, ed. *Promptorium Parvulorum.* Camden Society o.s. 25 (1863–65).

Weaver, F. W., ed. *Somerset Medieval Wills* Somerset Record Society 16, 19, 21 (1901–05).

Weaver, J. R. H. and Alice Beardwood, eds. *Some Oxfordshire Wills, 1393–1510.* Oxfordshire Record Society 39 (1958).

Windeatt, B. A., trans. *The Book of Margery Kempe.* Harmondsworth: Penguin, 1985.

Woodruff, C. Eveleigh, ed. *Kent Sede Vacante Wills.* Kent Archaeological Society Record Branch 3 (1914).

Wright, Thomas, ed. *The Book of the Knight of La Tour Landry.* EETS 33 (1868).

Zerbi, Gabriele. *Gerontocomia: On the Care of the Aged*, trans. C. R. Lind. Memoirs of the American Philosophical Society 182, Philadelphia: The Society, 1988.

SECONDARY SOURCES

Achenbaum, Andrew W. *Old Age in the New Land: The American Experience Since 1790.* Baltimore and London: Johns Hopkins University Press, 1978.

Archer, Rowena E. "Rich Old Ladies: The Problem of Late Medieval Dowagers." In *Property and Politics: Essays in Late Medieval English History*, ed., Anthony J. Pollard. Gloucester: Alan Sutton, 1984. 15–35.

Arens, William. *The Man-Eating Myth: Anthropology and Anthropophagy.* New York: Oxford University Press, 1979.

Ariès, Philippe. *Centuries of Childhood: A Social History of Family Life*, trans. Robert Baldick. New York: Knopf, 1962.

Arnold, Morris S., Sally Scully, and Stephen S. White, eds. *On the Laws and Customs of England: Essays in Honor of Samuel E. Thorne*. Chapel Hill: University of North Carolina Press, 1981.

Aston, T. H. "Oxford's Medieval Alumni." *Past and Present* 74 (1977): 3–40.

Aston, T. H., G. D. Duncan, and T. A. R. Evans. "The Medieval Alumni of the University of Cambridge." *Past and Present* 86 (1980): 9–86.

Axon, Ernest, "The Family of Bothe (Booth) and the Church in the 15th and 16th Centuries." *Transactions of the Lancashire and Cheshire Antiquarian Society* 53 (1938): 32–82.

Bailey, Mark, "Blowing Up Bubbles: Some New Demographic Evidence for the Fifteenth Century?" *Journal of Medieval History* 15 (1989): 347–58.

Baring-Gould, Sabine. *Legends of Old Testament Characters*. London, 1871.

Barron, Caroline M. "The Parish Fraternities of Medieval London." In Barron and Harper-Bill, *The Church in Pre-Reformation Society*, 13–37.

Barron, Caroline M. and Christopher Harper-Bill, eds. *The Church in Pre-Reformation Society: Essays in Honour of F. R. H. DuBoulay*. Woodbridge: Boydell Press, 1985.

Beauvoir, Simone de. *The Coming of Age*, trans. Patrick O'Brian. New York: Putnam, 1972.

Bengston, Vern L., Ned E. Cutler, David E. Mangen, and Victor W. Marshall. "Generation, Cohorts, and Relations Between the Generations." In Binstock and Shanas, *Handbook of Aging*, 304–38.

Bennett, Henry Stanley. *Six Medieval Men and Women*. Cambridge: Cambridge University Press, 1955.

———. *Life on the English Manor*. Rev. ed. Cambridge: Cambridge University Press, 1956.

———. *Chaucer and the Fifteenth Century*. New York and Oxford: Oxford University Press, 1974.

Bennett, Judith M. *Women in the Medieval English Countryside: Gender and Household in Brigstock Before the Plague*. New York: Oxford University Press, 1987.

Bennett, Michael J. *Community, Class, and Careerism: Cheshire and Lancashire Society in the Age of "Sir Gawain and the Green Knight"*. Cambridge: Cambridge University Press, 1983.

———. *The Battle of Bosworth*. New York; St. Martin's Press, 1985.

Berkner, Lutz K. "The Stem Family and the Developmental Cycle of the Peasant Household: An Austrian Example." *American Historical Review* 77 (1972): 398–418.

Bideau, A. "A Demographic and Social Analysis of Widowhood and Remarriage: The Example of the Castellany of Thoissey-en-Dombes, 1670–1840," *Journal of Family History* 5 (1980): 28–43.

Binstock, Robert H. and Ethel Shanas, eds. *Handbook of Aging and the Social Sciences*. 2nd ed. New York: Van Nostrand Reinhold, 1985.

Birren, James E., Yonina Talman, and Earl F. Cheit. "Aging." In *International Encyclopedia of the Social Sciences*. New York, Macmillan, 1968. I: 176–202.

Bishop, T. A. M. Review of *Inquisition Post Mortem, XII (39–43 Edward III)*. *English Historical Review* 55 (1940): 328.

Bloch, Marc, "Mémoire collective, tradition, et coûtume." *Revue de Synthèse Historique* 40 (1925): 73–83.

———. *The Historian's Craft*, trans. Peter Putman, intro. J. R. Strayer. Manchester: Manchester University Press, 1954.

Blomefield, Francis. *An Essay Toward a Topographical History of the County of Norfolk.* 11 vols. 2nd ed. London and Norwich, 1806–10.

Boas, Marie. *The Scientific Renaissance, 1450–1630.* London: Collins, 1962.

Bolton, James L. *The Medieval English Economy, 1150–1500.* London: J. M. Dent, 1980.

Bonfield, Lloyd, Richard M. Smith, and Keith Wrightson, eds. *The World We Have Gained: Histories of Population and Social Structure.* Oxford: Blackwell, 1986.

Bowers, R. H., "A Medieval Analogue to *As You Like It*, II, vii, 137–66." *Shakespeare Quarterly* 3 (1952): 109–12.

Brockwell, Charles W., Jr. *Bishop Reginald Pecock and the Lancastrian Church.* Lewiston, NY: Edwin Mellen Press, 1985.

Brown, R. Steward, "The Scrope and Grosvenor Controversy, 1385–1391." *Transactions of the Historic Society of Lancashire and Cheshire* 89 (1938): 1–22.

Brundage, James. *Law, Sex, and Christian Society in Medieval Europe.* Chicago: University of Chicago Press, 1987.

Burgess, Clive, "Late Medieval Wills and Pious Convention: Testamentary Evidence Reconsidered." In Hicks, *Profit, Piety and the Professions*, 14–33.

Burren, James and K. Warner Schare, eds. *Handbook of the Psychology of Aging.* 2nd ed. New York: Van Nostrand Reinhold, 1985.

Burrow, John Anthony. *Medieval Writers and Their Work: Middle English Literature and Its Background, 1100–1500.* Oxford: Oxford University Press, 1982.

———. "Chaucer's *Knight's Tale* and The Three Ages of Man." In his *Essays on Medieval Literature.* Oxford: Clarendon Press, 1984: 27–44.

———. *The Ages of Man: A Study in Medieval Writing and Thought.* Oxford: Clarendon Press, 1986.

———. *Thomas Hoccleve.* Authors of the Middle Ages 4. London: Variorum, 1994.

Burson, Malcolm, "Emden's *Registers* and the Prosopography of Medieval English Universities." *Medieval Prosopography* 3, 2 (1982): 35–51.

Butler, Basil Christopher. *Number Symbolism.* New York: Barnes and Noble, 1970.

Carp, Frances M., ed. *Retirement.* New York: Behavioral Sciences Publications, 1972.

Carruthers, Mary J. *The Book of Memory: A Study of Memory in Medieval Culture.* Cambridge: Cambridge University Press, 1990.

Chandler, Albert R. "Cicero's Ideal Old Men." *Journal of Gerontology* 3 (1948): 285–89.

Chew, Samuel. *The Pilgrimage of Life.* New Haven, CT: Yale University Press, 1962.

Chrimes, S. B. *Henry VII.* Berkeley and Los Angeles: University of California Press, 1972.

Clanchy, Michael T. *From Memory to Written Record: England, 1066–1307.* 2nd ed. Oxford: B. Blackwell, 1993.

Clark, Elaine. "Some Aspects of Social Security in Medieval England." *Journal of Family History* 7 (1982): 307–20.

————. "The Quest for Security in Medieval England." In Sheehan, *Aging and the Aged in Medieval Europe*, 189–200.

Clark, Linda. "The Benefits and Burdens of Office." Archbishop Bourgchier (1408–83), Viscount Bourgchier and Earl of Essex, and the Treasurership of the Exchequer." In Hicks, *Profit, Piety, and the Professions*, 119–36.

Clark, Margaret, "An Anthropological View of Retirement." In Clark, *Retirement*, 117–55.

Clay, Rotha M. *The Mediaeval Hospitals of England*. London, 1909; repr. New York: Barnes and Noble, 1966.

Clough, C. H., ed. *Profession, Vocation and Culture in Later Medieval England*. Liverpool: Liverpool University Press, 1982.

Cochelin, Isabelle. "*In Senectute bona*: pour une typologie de la vieillesse dans l'hagiographie monastique des xiie et xiiie siècles." In *Les Âges de la vie au Moyen Âge*, ed. Henri Dubois and Michel Zink. Paris: Presses de l'Université de Paris-Sorbonne, 1992.

Coffman, George R. "Old Age from Horace to Chaucer: Some Literary Affinities and Adventures of an Idea." *Speculum* 9 (1934): 144–77.

Cole, Thomas R. "Comments on Roland S. Guyot's 'A New Theory About the Ages of Man'." *IJA & HD* 36, 2 (1992–93): 98–101.

Connerton, Paul. *How Societies Remember*. Cambridge: Cambridge University Press, 1989.

Coulton, George G. *Chaucer and His England*. 8th ed. London: Methuen, 1952, 1957.

Courtenay, William J. "The Effect of the Black Death on English Higher Education." *Speculum* 55 (1980): 696–714.

Courtney, Bradley, Leonard W. Poon, Leonard Martin, Gloria M. Clayton, and Mary Ann Johnson. "Religiosity and Adaptation in the Oldest-Old (Centenarians)." *IJA & HD* 34 (1992): 47–56.

Covey, Herbert C. "The Definitions of the Beginning of Old Age in History." *IJA & HD* 34 (1992): 325–37.

————. "A Return to Infancy: Old Age and the Second Childhood in History." *IJA & HD* 36, 2 (1992–93): 81–90.

Creighton, Gilbert. "When Did Man in the Renaissance Grow Old?" *Studies in the Renaissance* 14 (1967): 7–32.

Cullum, P. H. *Cremetts and Corrodies: Care of the Poor and Sick at St. Leonard's Hospital, York, in the Middle Ages*. Borthwick Papers 79. York: University of York, 1991.

Davies, Richard G. "The Attendance of the Episcopate in English Parliaments, 1376–1461." *Proceedings of the American Philosophical Society* 129, 1 (March, 1985): 30–81.

————. "The Episcopate." In Clough, *Profession, Vocation and Culture in Later Medieval England*, 51–89.

Davis, Natalie Zeman. *Fiction in the Archives: Pardon Tales and Their Tellers in Sixteenth Century France*. Stanford, CA: Stanford University Press, 1987.

Demaitre, Luke. "The Care and Extension of Old Age in Medieval Medicine." In Sheehan, *Aging and the Aged in Medieval Europe*, 3–22.

Demos, John. *A Little Commonwealth: Family Life in Plymouth Colony*. New York: Oxford University Press, 1970.

Dennis, Wayne, "Creative Productivity Between the Age of 20 and 80 Years." *Journal of Gerontology* 21 (1966): 1–8.

DeWindt, Edwin B. *Land and People in Hollywell-cum-Needingworth*. Toronto: Pontifical Institute of Mediaeval Studies, 1972.

Dillard, Heath. *Daughters of the Reconquest: Women in Castillian Town Society, 1100–1300*. Cambridge: Cambridge University Press, 1984.

Dobson, R. Barrie, "Richard Bell, Prior of Durham (1464–78) and Bishop of Carlisle (1478–95)." *Cumberland and Westmorland Archaeological Society* n.s. 65 (1965): 182–221.

———, ed. *The Church, Politics, and Patronage in the Fifteenth Century*. Gloucester: Alan Sutton, 1984.

Donahue, Charles, Jr. "Proof by Witnesses in the Church Courts of Medieval England: An Imperfect Reception of Learned Law." In Arnold et al., *On the Laws and Customs of England*, 127-58.

Dove, Mary. *The Perfect Age of Man's Life*. Cambridge: Cambridge University Press, 1980.

Draper, John W. "Shakespeare's Attitude Towards Old Age." *Journal of Gerontology* 1 (1946): 118–25.

Dublin, Louis I., Alfred J. Lotka, and Mortimer Spiegelman. *Length of Life: A Study of the Life Table*. Rev. ed. New York: Ronald Press, 1949.

Duby, Georges. "In Northwestern France: The 'Youth' in Twelfth-Century Aristocratic Society." In *Lordship and Community in Medieval Europe*, ed. Fredric L. Cheyette. New York: Holt, Rinehart, and Winston, 1968: 198–209.

Dunstan, G. R. "Some Aspects of the Register of Edmund Lacy, Bishop of Exeter, 1420–55." *Journal of Ecclesiastical History* 6 (1955): 37–47.

Durkan, J. "Care of the Poor in Pre-Reformation Hospitals." In *Essays in the Scottish Reformation, 1513–1625*, ed. David McRoberts. Glasgow: Burns, 1962: 116–28.

Dutton, Paul E. "Beyond the Topos of Senescence: The Political Problems of Aged Carolingian Rulers." In Sheehan, *Aging and the Aged in Medieval Europe*, 75–94.

Edwards, John Goronwy. "The Emergence of Majority Rule in English Parliamentary Elections." *Transactions of the Royal Historical Society* 5th ser. 14 (1964): 175–96.

Egerton, Frank N. "The Longevity of the Patriarchs: A Topic in the History of Demography." *Journal of the History of Ideas* 27 (1966): 575–84.

Elton, Geoffrey R. *England Under the Tudors*. London: Methuen, 1954.

Emden, A. B. *A Biographical Register of the University of Oxford to A. D. 1500*. 3 vols. Oxford: Clarendon Press, 1957–59.

———. *A Biographical Register of the University of Cambridge to A.D. 1500*. Cambridge: Cambridge University Press, 1963.

Emerson, O. F. "Chaucer's Testimony as to His Age." *Modern Philology* 11 (1913–14): 117–25.

Esler, Anthony. *The Aspiring Mind of the Elizabethan Younger Generation*. Durham, NC: Duke University Press, 1966.

Evans-Pritchard, E. E. *A History of Anthropological Thought*, ed. Andre Singer. New York: Basic Books, 1981.

Fentress, James and Chris Wickham. *Social Memory*. Oxford: Blackwell, 1992.

Ferris, Sumner. "Chaucer, Richard II, Henry IV, and 13 October." In *Chaucer and Middle English Studies, in Honour of Rossell Hope Robbins*, ed. Beryl Rowland. Kent, OH: Kent State University Press, 1974: 210–17.

Fischer, David Hackett. *Growing Old in America*. Oxford and New York: Oxford University Press, 1978.

Fisher, John H. *John Gower, Moral Philosopher and Friend of Chaucer*. New York: New York University Press, 1964.

Foltz, James D. "Senescence and Renascence: Petrarch's Thoughts on Growing Old." *Journal of Medieval and Renaissance Studies* 10 (1980): 207–37.

Forehand, Brook. "Old Age and Chaucer's Reeve." *PMLA* 69 (1954): 984–89.

Fowler, David C., "John Trevisa, Scholar and Translator." *Transactions of the Bristol and Gloucestershire Archaeological Society* 89 (1970): 99–108.

Freeman, Joseph A. "The History of Geriatrics." *Annals of Medical History* n.s. 10 (1938): 324–35.

Freeman, Joseph T., "Francois Ranchin: Contributions to an Early Chapter in Geriatrics." *Journal of the History of Medicine* 5 (1950): 422–31.

———. *Aging: Its History and Literature*. New York: Human Sciences Press, 1979.

Fryde, E. B., D. E. Greenway, S. Porter and I. Roy, eds. *Handbook of British Chronology*. 3rd ed. London: Royal Historical Society, 1986.

Fryer, Alfred C., "Monumental Effigies in Somerset, part ix." *Somerset Archealogical and Natural History* 69 (1923): 14–16.

Fuller, Thomas. *The Worthies of England*, ed. P. Austin Nuttall. 3 vols. London, 1840; repr. New York: AMS Press, 1965.

Gibbs, Vicary, ed. *The Complete Peerage*. 12 vols. in 13, London: St. Catherine Press, 1910–59.

Ginzburg, Carlo. *The Cheese and the Worms: The Cosmos of a Sixteenth Century Miller*, trans. John Tedeschi and Anne Tedeschi. Baltimore: Johns Hopkins University Press, 1980.

———. *Ecstasies: Deciphering the Witches' Sabbath*, trans. Raymond Rosenthal. New York: Pantheon, 1991.

Glascock, Anthony P. "By Any Other Name, It Is Still Killing: A Comparison of the Treatment of the Elderly in America and in Other Societies." In Sokolovsky, *The Cultural Context of Aging*.

Glass, D.V. and D. E. C. Eversley, eds. *Population in History: Essays in Historical Demography*. Chicago: Aldine, 1965.

Goldberg, P. J. P. "Marriage, Migration, and Servanthood: The York Case Paper Evidence." In Goldberg, *Woman Is a Worthy Wight*, 1–15.

———. *Women, Work, and Life Cycle in a Medieval Economy*. Oxford: Clarendon Press, 1992.

———, ed. *Woman Is a Worthy Wight*. Stroud: Alan Sutton, 1992.

Goodich, Michael. *From Birth to Old Age: The Human Life Cycle in Medieval Thought, 1250–1350*. Lanham, MD and London: University Press of America, 1989.

Goodman, Anthony E. "The Piety of John Brunham's Daughter, of Lynn." In *Medieval Women*, ed. Derek Baker. Oxford: Blackwell for the Ecclesiastical History Society, 1978: 347–58.

Gransden, Antonia. "Childhood and Youth in Medieval England." *Nottingham Mediaeval Studies* 16 (1972): 3–19.

Grant, Richard L. "Concepts of Aging: An Historical Review." *Perspectives in Biology and Medicine* 6 (1963): 443–79.

Grauer, Anne L. "Patterns of Life and Death: The Paleodemography of Medieval York." In *Health in Past Societies*, ed. Helen Bush and Merek Zvelebil. British Archaeological Reports International Series 567. Oxford: Tempus Reparatum, 1991, 67–80.

Green, Richard Firth. *Poets and Princepleasers: Literature and the English Court in the Late Middle Ages*. Toronto: University of Toronto Press, 1980.

Green, Vivian H. H. *Bishop Reginald Pecock: A Study in Ecclesiastical History and Thought*. Cambridge: Cambridge University Press, 1945.

Greven, Philip. *Four Generations*. Ithaca, NY: Cornell University Press, 1970.

Griffiths, Ralph A. *The Reign of Henry VI*. Berkeley: University of California Press, 1981.

Grmek, Mirko D. *On Ageing and Old Age: Basic Problems and Historic Aspects of Gerontology and Geriatrics*. The Hague: W. Junk, 1958.

Gruman, Gerald J., ed. *Roots of Modern Gerontology and Geriatrics: Frederic D. Zeman's Medical History of Old Age and Selected Studies by Other Writers*. New York: Arno Press, 1979.

Guyot, Roland S. "A New Theory About the Ages of Man." *IJA & HD* 36, 2 (1992–93): 91–98.

Haber, Carole. *Beyond Sixty-Five: The Dilemma of Old Age in America's Past*. New York: Cambridge University Press, 1983.

Hadas, Moses. *A History of Latin Literature*. New York: Columbia University Press, 1952.

Hajnal, John. "European Marriage Patterns in Perspective." In Glass and Eversley, *Population in History*, 110–43.

Hanawalt, Barbara A. *The Ties That Bound: Peasant Families in Medieval England*. New York: Oxford University Press, 1986.

———. *Growing Up in Medieval London: The Experience of Childhood in History*. New York and Oxford: Oxford University Press, 1993.

Hanna, Ralph III. "Sir Thomas Berkeley and His Patronage." *Speculum* 64 (1989): 878–916.

Haraven, Tamara K. "The Life Course and Aging in Historical Perspective." In *Aging and Life Course Transitions: An Interdisciplinary Perspective*, ed. Tamara Hareven and Kathleen J. Adams. New York: Guilford Press, 1982: 1–26.

Harriss, Gerald L. *Cardinal Beaufort: A Study of Lancastrian Ascendancy and Decline*. Oxford: Clarendon Press, 1988.

Harvey, Barbara. *Living and Dying in England, 1100–1540: The Monastic Experience*. Oxford: Clarendon Press, 1993.

Hatcher, John. *Plague, Population and the English Economy, 1348–1530*. London: Macmillan, 1977.

Heath, Peter. *The English Parish Clergy on the Eve of the Reformation*. London: Routledge and Kegan Paul, 1969.

Herlihy, David. "The Generation in Medieval History." *Viator* 5 (1974): 347–66.

Hexter, J. H. "The Myth of the Middle Class in Tudor England," and "Storm over the Gentry." In his *Reappraisals in History*. Evanston, Ill.: Northwestern University Press, 1961: 71–162.

———. "Lawrence Stone and the English Aristocracy." In his *On Historians*. Cambridge, MA: Harvard University Press, 1979: 149–226.

Hicks, Michael, ed. *Profit, Piety, and the Professions in Later Medieval England*. Gloucester: Alan Sutton, 1990.

Higgins, Anne, "Medieval Notions of the Structure of Time." *Journal of Medieval and Renaissance Studies* 19, 2 (1989): 227–56.

Hilton, Rodney. *The English Peasantry in the Later Middle Ages*. Oxford, Clarendon Press, 1975.

Hollingsworth, T. H. "A Demographicic Study of the British Ducal Families." In Glass and Eversley, *Population in History*, 354–74.

———. *Historical Demography*. Ithaca, NY: Cornell University Press, 1969.

———. *The Demography of the British Peerage*. Supplement, *Population Studies* 18, 2 (1964).

———. "A Note on the Mediaeval Longevity of the Secular Peerage, 1350–1500." *Population Studies* 29 (1975): 155–59.

Homans, George C. *English Villagers of the Thirteenth Century*. New York: Russell and Russell, 1960.

Hopper, Vincent F. *Medieval Number Symbolism*. Columbia University Studies in English 132. Repr., Philadelphia: R. West, 1978.

Howell, Cicely. *Land, Family and Inheritance in Transition: Kibworth Harcourt, 1280–1700*. Cambridge: Cambridge University Press, 1983.

Hughes, A. C. *Walter Hilton's Directory to Contemplation*. Rome, 1962.

Hunnisett, R. F. "The Reliability of Inquisitions as Historical Evidence." In *The Study of Medieval Records*, ed. D. A. Bullough and R. L. Storey. Oxford: Clarendon Press, 1971: 206–35.

Jacob, Ernest F. *Archbishop Henry Chichele*. London: Nelson, 1967.

———. "Reynold Pecock, Bishop of Chichester." In his *Essays in Later Medieval History*. Manchester: Manchester University Press, 1968: 1–34.

James, Mervyn. *Society, Politics, and Culture: Studies in Early Modern England*. Cambridge: Cambridge University Press, 1986.

Jamison, Catherine. *The History of the Royal Hospital of St. Katherine by the Tower of London*. London: Privately Printed, 1952.

Jenkins, Claude. "Cardinal Morton's Register." In *Tudor Studies Presented to Albert Frederic Pollard*, ed. R. W. Seton-Watson. London: University of London, 1924: 26–74.

Jewell, Helen. "English Bishops as Educational Benefactors in the Later Fifteenth Century." In Dobson, *The Church, Politics and Patronage in the Fifteenth Century*, 46–67.

Jones, E. D. "Going Round in Circles: Some New Evidence for Population in the Later Middle Ages." *Journal of Medieval History* 15 (1989): 329–45.

Jones, J. W. "Observations on the Origin of the Division of Man's Life into Stages."
    Archaeologia 35 (1853): 167–89.
Jones, Michael K. and Malcolm G. Underwood. *The Queen's Mother: Lady Margaret
    Beaufort, Countess of Richmond and Derby*. Cambridge: Cambridge University
    Press, 1992.
Judd, Arnold. *The Life of Thomas Bekynton*. Chichester: Moore and Tillyer, 1961.
Kane, George. *The Autobiographical Fallacy in Chaucer and Langland Studies*. The
    Chambers Memorial Lecture. London: Published for University College by
    K. K. Lewis, 1965.
Kastenbaum, Robert. "The Age of Saints and the Saintliness of Age." *IJA & HD* 30
    (1990): 95–118.
Keen, Maurice. *English Society in the Later Middle Ages, 1348–1500*. London: Pen-
    guin, 1990.
Keil, Ian. "Corrodies of Glastonbury Abbey in the Later Middle Ages." *Somerset
    Archaeological and Natural History* 108 (1963–64): 111–31.
Kent, Joan R. *The English Village Constable, 1580–1642*. Oxford: Clarendon Press,
    1986.
Kermode, Jennifer I. "The Merchants of Three Northern English Towns." In
    Clough, *Profession, Vocation, and Culture in Late Medieval England*, 7–48.
———. "Urban Decline: The Flight from Office in Late Medieval York." *Economic
    History Review* 2nd ser. 35 (1982): 179–98.
Kirk, Henning. "Geriatric Medicine and the Categorisation of Old Age: The His-
    torical Linkage." *Ageing and Society* 12 (1992): 483–98.
Krause, Louis A. "Old Age in the Bible and Poetry." *Annals of Internal Medicine* 36
    (1952): 152–56.
Ladurie, Emmanuel le roy. *Montaillou: The Promised Land of Error*, trans. Barbara
    Bray. New York: Braziller, 1978.
Laslett, Peter. *The World We Have Lost*. 2nd ed. New York: Scribner, 1971.
———. "The History of Aging and the Aged." In *Family Life and Illicit Love in
    Earlier Generations: Essays in Historical Sociology*, ed. Peter Laslett. Cambridge:
    Cambridge University Press, 1977: 174–213.
Lehman, Harvey. *Age and Achievement*. Princeton, NJ: Princeton University Press
    for the American Philosophical Society, 1953.
———. "The Production of Masterworks Prior to Age 30." *Gerontologist* 5, 2 (1965):
    24–29.
Levinson, Daniel J. et al. *The Seasons of a Man's Life*. New York: Knopf, 1978.
Lovatt, Roger. "John Blacman, Biographer of Henry VI." In *The Writing of History
    in the Middle Ages: Essays Presented to Richard William Southern*, ed. R. H. C.
    Davis and J. M. Wallace-Hadrill. Oxford: Clarendon Press, 1981: 415–44.
Lowes, J. Livingston. "The Prologue to *The Legend of Good Women*, Considered in
    Its Chronological Relations." *PMLA* 20 (1905): 783–84.
Maddern, Philippa C. *Violence and Social Order: East Anglia, 1422–1442*. Oxford:
    Clarendon Press, 1992.
Makowski, Elizabeth. "The Conjugal Debt and Medieval Canon Law." *Journal of
    Medieval History* 3 (1977): 99–114.

Maxfield, David K. "A Fifteenth Century Lawsuit: The Case of St. Anthony's Hospital." *Journal of Ecclesiastical History* 44 (1993): 199–223.

McFarlane, K. B. *The Nobility of Later Medieval England*. Oxford: Clarendon Press, 1973.

McIntosh, Marjorie K. "Local Change and Community Control in England, 1465–1500." *Huntington Library Quarterly* 49 (1986): 219–42.

———. "Local Responses to the Poor in Late Medieval and Tudor England." *Continuity and Change* 3 (1988): 209–45.

McKisack, May. *The Fourteenth Century: 1307–1399*. Oxford: Clarendon Press, 1959.

Mertes, Kate. *The English Noble Household, 1250–1600: Good Governance and Politic Rule*. Oxford: Blackwell, 1988.

Minois, Georges. *History of Old Age from Antiquity to the Renaissance*, trans. Sarah H. Tenison. Chicago: University of Chicago Press, 1989.

Mitchell, Jerome. "The Autobiographical Element in Hoccleve." *Modern Language Quarterly* 28 (1967): 269–84.

———. *Thomas Hoccleve, c. 1368–c. 1430*. Urbana: University of Illinois Press, 1968.

Mitterauer, Michael and Reinhard Sieder. *The European Family: Patriarchy to Partnership from the Middle Ages to the Present Day*. Trans. Karla Oosterveen and Manfred Horzinger. Oxford: Blackwell, 1982.

Moberg, David O. "Religiosity in Old Age." *Gerontologist* 5, 2 (1962): 78–87, 111–12.

Molinari, Paulo. *Julian of Norwich: The Teaching of a Fourteenth Century English Mystic*. London and New York: Longmans Green, 1958.

Moore, Samuel. "Patrons of Letters in Norfolk and Suffolk, ca. 1450." *PMLA* 27 (1912): 188–207; 28 (1913): 79–105.

Mullins, E. L. C. *Texts and Calendars*. London: Royal Historical Society, 1958.

Nichols, J. G. "The Scrope-Grosvenor Controversy." *Herald and Genealogist* (1863): 385–400.

Nitecki, Alicia. "Figures of Old Age in Fourteenth-Century English Literature." In Sheehan, *Aging and the Aged in Medieval Europe*, 107–16.

Orme, Nicholas, "Sufferings of the Clergy: Illness and Old Age in Exeter Diocese, 1300–1540." In Pelling and Smith, *Life, Death, and the Elderly*, 62–73.

Ormrod, W. R. *The Reign of Edward III*. New Haven, CT: Yale University Press, 1990.

Page, Frances M. "The Customary Poor Laws of Three Cambridge Manors." *Cambridge Historical Journal* 3 (1930): 125–33.

Parkin, E. W. "The Medieval Origins of Wye College." *Archaeologia Cantiana* 102 (1985): 213–17.

Payling, Simon J. *Political Society in Lancastrian England: The Greater Gentry of Nottinghamshire*. Oxford: Clarendon Press, 1991.

Pearsall, Derek. *The Life of Geoffrey Chaucer*. Oxford: Blackwell, 1992.

Peller, Sigismund. "Births and Deaths Among Europe's Ruling Families Since 1500." In Glass and Eversley, *Population in History*, 87–100.

Pelling, Margaret and Richard M. Smith, eds. *Life, Death, and the Elderly: Historical Perspectives*. London and New York: Routledge, 1991.

Perry, George G. "Bishop Beckington and King Henry VI." *English Historical Review* 9 (1894): 261–74.

Phythian-Adams, Charles. *Desolation of a City: Coventry and the Urban Crisis of the Late Middle Ages*. Cambridge: Cambridge University Press, 1979.

Pollard, Anthony J. *John Talbot and the War in France, 1427–1453*. London: Royal Historical Society, 1983.

Pollock, Frederick and Frederic William Maitland. *The History of English Law Before the Time of Edward I*, intro. S. F. C. Milsom. 2nd rev. ed. 2 vols., Cambridge: Cambridge University Press, 1968.

Poos, Lawrence R. "Population Turnover in Medieval Essex: The Evidence of Some Early Fourteenth Century Tithing Lists." In Bonfield et al., *The World We Have Gained*, 1–22.

———. "Life Expectancy and 'Age of First Appearance' in Medieval Manorial Court Records." *Local Population Studies* 37 (Autumn, 1986): 45–52.

———. *A Rural Society After the Black Death: Essex, 1350–1525*. Cambridge: Cambridge University Press, 1991.

Poos, Lawrence R. and Richard M. Smith, "Legal Windows onto Historical Populations: Recent Research on Demography and the Manor Court in Medieval England." *Law and History Review* 2 (1984): 128–52.

Post, Stephen G. "Infanticide and Geronticide." *Ageing and Society* 10 (1990): 317–28.

Powell, J. Enoch and Keith Wallis. *The House of Lords in the Middle Ages*. London: Weidenfeld and Nicolson. 1968.

Prestwich, Michael. *Edward I*. Berkeley and Los Angeles: University of California Press, 1988.

Quadagno, Jill S. *Aging in Early Industrial Society: Work, Family, and Social Policy in Nineteenth-Century England*. New York: Academic Press, 1982.

Ramsay, James H. *The Genesis of Lancaster*. 2 vols. Oxford: Clarendon Press, 1913.

Rawcliffe, Carole. *The Staffords, Earls of Stafford and Dukes of Buckingham, 1394–1521*. Cambridge: Cambridge University Press, 1978.

Reeves, A. Compton. "Thomas Hoccleve, Bureaucrat." *Medievalia et Humanistica* n.s. 5 (1974): 201–14.

———. *Lancastrian Englishmen*. Washington, DC: University Press of America, 1981.

Richardson, Bessie Ellen. *Old Age Among the Ancient Greeks*. Baltimore: Johns Hopkins University Press, 1933; reprint, New York: Greenwood Press, 1969.

Richardson, H. G. "John of Gaunt and the Parliamentary Representation of Lancashire." *Bulletin of the John Rylands Library* 20 (1938): 175–222.

Richardson, Malcolm. "Hoccleve in His Social Context." *Chaucer Review* 20 (1986): 313–22.

Richmond, Colin F. "Religion and the Fifteenth Century English Gentleman." In Dobson, *Church, Politics, and Patronage in the Fifteenth Century*, 193–208.

———. *The Paston Family in the Fifteenth Century: The First Phase*. Cambridge: Cambridge University Press, 1990.

Ritson, Joseph. *Bibliographica Poetica*. London: Printed by C. Roworth for G. and W. Nicol, 1802.

Rosenthal, Joel T. *The Training of an Elite Group: English Bishops in the Fifteenth Century*. Transactions of the American Philosophical Society 60, part 5. Philadelphia: American Philosophical Society, 1970.

———. "Mediaeval Longevity and the Secular Peerage, 1350–1500." *Population Studies* 27 (1973): 287–93.

———. "The Fifteenth Century Episcopate: Careers and Bequests." *Sanctity and Secularity: The Church and The World*, ed. Derek Baker. Studies in Church History 10. Oxford: Blackwell, 1973: 117–27.

———. "Old Men's Lives: Elderly English Peers, 1350–1500." *Mediaevalia* 8 (1982): 211–37.

———. "Sir Richard Choke (d. 1483) of Long Ashton." *Somerset Archaeological and Natural History* 127 (1984, for 1983): 105–21.

———. "Aristocratic Widows in Fifteenth Century England." In *Women and the Structure of Society*, ed. Barbara J. Harris and Jo Ann K. McNamara. Durham, NC: Duke University Press, 1984: 36–47, 259–60.

———. "Lancastrian Bishops and Educational Benefaction." In Barron and Harper-Bill, *Church in Pre-Reformation Society*, 199–211.

———. "Lancastrian Episcopal Wills: Directing and Distributing." *Medieval Prosopography* 11, 1 (1990): 35–85.

———. *Patriarchy and Families of Privilege in Fifteenth-Century England*. Philadelphia: University of Pennsylvania Press, 1991.

Roskell, John S. "The Problem of the Attendance of the Lords in Medieval Parliaments." *Bulletin of the Institute of Historical Research* 29 (1956): 153–204.

———. "John, Lord Wenlock of Someries." *Bedfordshire Historical Record Society* 38 (1958): 12–48.

Roskell, John S., Carol Rawcliffe, and Linda Clark, eds. *History of Parliament: The House of Commons, 1386–1422*. 4 vols. Stroud: Alan Sutton, 1992.

Ross, Bruce M. *Remembering the Personal Past: Descriptions of Autobiographical Memory*. New York: Oxford University Press, 1991.

Ross, Charles, ed. *John Rous: The Rous Roll*. Gloucester: Alan Sutton, 1980.

Rouse, E. Clive and Audley Baker. "The Wall-Painting at Longthorpe Tower near Peterborough, Northants." *Archaeologia* 96 (1955): 1–57.

Rowland, Beryl, "The Three Ages of *The Parlement of the Three Ages*." *Chaucer Review* 9 (1974–75): 342–52.

Rubin, Miri. *Charity and Community in Medieval Cambridge*. Cambridge: Cambridge University Press, 1987.

———. *Corpus Christi: The Eucharist in Late Medieval Culture*. Cambridge: Cambridge University Press, 1991.

Russell, Josiah Cox. *Dictionary of Writers of Thirteenth Century England*. Special supplement, *Bulletin of the Institute of Historical Research* 3 (1936).

———. "The Clerical Population of Medieval England." *Traditio* 2 (1944): 177–212.

———. *British Medieval Population*. Albuquerque: University of New Mexico Press, 1948.

———. "How Many of the Population Were Aged?" In Sheehan, *Aging and the Aged in Medieval Europe*, 119–27.

Sandford, F. *Genealogical History of the Kings and Queens of England*. London, 1707.

Saul, Nigel. *Knights and Esquires: The Gloucestershire Gentry in the Fourteenth Century*. Oxford: Clarendon Press, 1981.

———. *Scenes from Provincial Life: Knightly Families in Sussex, 1280–1460*. Oxford: Clarendon Press, 1986.

Scarisbrick, J. J. *Henry VIII*. Berkeley: University of California Press, 1968.

Scattergood, V. J. "Old Age and Friendship in Chaucer's 'Envoy to Scogan'." *Nottingham Medieval Studies* 35 (1991): 92–101.

Scattergood, V.J. and J. W. Sherborne, eds. *English Court Culture in the Later Middle Ages*. New York: St. Martin's Press, 1983.

Schochet, Gordon. *Patriarchalism in Political Thought: The Authoritarian Family and Political Speculation*. Oxford: Blackwell, 1975.

Scrope, G. Poulett. *A History of Castle Combe, Wiltshire*. London: Privately printed, 1852.

Sears, Elizabeth. *The Ages of Man: Medieval Interpretations of the Life Cycle*. Princeton, NJ: Princeton University Press, 1986.

Seaton, Ethel. *Sir Richard Roos, c. 1410–1482: Lancastrian Poet*. London: Rupert Hart-Davis, 1961.

Shahar, Shulamith. *Childhood in the Middle Ages*, trans. Chaya Galai. London: Routledge, 1990.

Shakespeare, William. *As You Like It*, ed. Horace H. Furness. Variorum edition, 12th impression: Philadelphia: Lippincott, 1918.

———. *As You Like It*, ed. Richard Knowles and Evelyn J. Mattern. Variorum ed. New York: Modern Language Association, 1977.

Sheehan, Michael M., ed. *Aging and the Aged in Medieval Europe*. Papers in Medieval Studies 11. Toronto: Pontifical Institute of Mediaeval Studies, 1990.

Simmons, Leo W. *The Role of the Aged in Primitive Society*. New Haven, CT: Yale University Press, 1945; repr. New York: Archon Books, 1970.

———. "Aging in Pre-Industrial Societies." In *Handbook of Social Gerontology*, ed. Clark Tibbits. Chicago: University of Chicago Press, 1970: 62–76.

Small, Samuel A. "The *Iuventus* Stage of Life." In *Philologica: The Malone Anniversary Studies*, ed. Thomas A. Kirby and Henry B. Woolf. Baltimore: Johns Hopkins University Press, 1949: 235–39.

Smith, Daniel B. "Mortality and Family in Colonial Chesapeake." *Journal of Interdisciplinary History* 8 (1978): 403–27.

Smith, Richard M. "The Manorial Court and the Elderly Tenant in Late Medieval England." In Pelling and Smith, *Life, Death, and the Elderly*, 39–61.

———. "Geographical Diversity in the Resort to Marriage in Late Medieval Europe: Work, Reputation, and Unmarried Females in the Household Formation Systems of Northern and Southern Europe." In Goldberg, *Woman Is a Worthy Wight*, 16–59.

Smyth, John, of Nibley. *The Lives of the Berkeleys*, ed. J. Maclean. 3 vols. Bristol and Gloucestershire Archaeological Society, 1883.

Sokolovsky, Jay, ed. *Aging and the Aged in the Third World*. 2 vols. Studies in Third World Society 22–23. Williamsburg, VA: Department of Anthropology, College of William and Mary, 1982.

————, ed. *The Cultural Context of Aging: Worldwide Perspectives.* New York: Bergin and Garvey, 1990.

Spence, Jonathan D. *The Memory Palace of Matteo Ricci.* New York: Viking Penguin, 1983.

Stanier, R. S. *Magdalen School: A History of Magdalen College School, Oxford.* Oxford Historical Society n.s. 3 (1940).

Steadman, John M. "Old Age and 'Contemptus Mundi' in the 'Pardoner's Tale'." *Medium Aevum* 33, 2 (1964): 121–30.

Stearns, Peter N. *Old Age in European Society: The Case of France.* London: Croom Helm, 1977.

————. "Old Women: Some Historical Observations." *Journal of Family History* 5 (1980): 44–57.

————, ed. *Old Age in Pre-Industrial Society.* New York and London: Holmes and Meier, 1982.

Stevenson, E. R. "The Escheator." In *The English Government at Work, 1327–1336, Vol. II: Fiscal Administration*, ed. W. A. Morris and J. R. Strayer. Cambridge, MA: Medieval Academy, 1947: 109–67.

Stevenson, Hazel A., "A Possible Relation Between Chaucer's Long Lease and the Date of His Birth." *Modern Language Notes* 50 (1935): 318–22.

Storey, R. L., "Marmaduke Lumley, Bishop of Carlisle, 1430–1450." *Transactions of the Cumberland and Westmorland Antiquarian and Archaeological Society* n.s. 55 (1955): 112–31.

Stone, Lawrence. *The Crisis of the Aristocracy, 1558–1641.* Oxford: Clarendon Press, 1965.

Strohm, Paul, "Chaucer's Audience." *Literature and History* 5 (1979): 26–41.

————. "Chaucer's Fifteenth Century Audience and The Narrowing of the Chaucer Tradition." *Studies in the Age of Chaucer* 4 (1982): 3–32.

————. "Chaucer's Audience(s): Fictional, Implied, Intended, Actual." *Chaucer Review* 18 (1983–84): 137–45.

Sussman, Marvin. "An Analytical Model for the Study of Retirement." In Carp, *Retirement*, 29–73.

Sutherland, Donald W. "Legal Reasoning in the Fourteenth Century: The Invention of 'Color' in Pleading." In Arnold et al., *Laws and Customs of England*, 182–94.

Swanson, Robert N. *Church and Society in Late Medieval England.* Oxford: Blackwell, 1990.

Talbot, Hugh. *The English Achilles: Life and Campaigns of John Talbot, Ist Earl of Shrewsbury.* London: Chatton and Windus, 1981.

Tawney, R. H. "The Rise of the Gentry, 1558–1640" and "A Postscript." In *Essays in Economic History*, ed. E. M. Carus-Wilson. Vol. I, 173–214. London: Arnold, 1954.

Thomas, David. "The Elizabethan Crown Lands: Their Purposes and Problems." In *The Estates of the English Crown, 1558–1640*, ed. R. W. Hoyle. Cambridge: Cambridge University Press, 1992: 58–87.

Thomas, Keith. "Age and Authority in Early Modern England." *Proceedings of the British Academy* 62 (1976): 205–48.

Thompson, A. Hamilton. *The English Clergy and Their Organization in the Later Middle Ages*. Oxford: Clarendon Press, 1947.

Thrupp, Sylvia L. *The Merchant Class of Medieval London, 1300–1500*. Chicago: University of Chicago Press, 1948.

——. "The Problem of Replacement Rates in Late Medieval England." *Economic History Review* 2nd ser. 18 (1965): 101–19.

Tierney, Brian. "The Decretist and the 'Deserving Poor'." *Comparative Studies in Society and History* 1 (1958–59): 360–73.

Trinkhaus, Charles E. *Adversity's Noblemen: The Italian Humanists on Happiness*. New York, 1940; repr. New York: Octagon Books, 1965.

Tristram, Philippa. *Figures of Life and Death in Medieval English Literature*. New York: New York University Press, 1976.

Troyansky, David G. *Old Age in the Old Regime: Image and Expression in Eighteenth Century France*. Ithaca, NY: Cornell University Press, 1989.

Turville-Petre, Thorlac. "The Three Ages of Man in *The Parlement of the Three Ages*." *Medium Aevum* 46 (1977): 66–76.

Ulrich, Laurel Thatcher. *A Midwife's Tale: The Life of Martha Ballard, Based on Her Diary, 1785–1812*. New York: Knopf, 1990.

Vansina, Jan. *Oral Tradition: A Study in Historical Methodology*. Chicago: Aldine, 1961.

——. *Oral Tradition as History*. Madison: University of Wisconsin Press, 1985.

Virgoe, Roger. "Three Suffolk Parliamentary Elections in the Mid- Fifteenth Century." *Bulletin of the Institute of Historical Research* 39 (1966): 185–96.

——. "The Crown, Magnates and Local Government in Fifteenth Century East Anglia." In *The Crown and Local Communities in England and France in the Fifteenth Century*, ed. J. R. L. Highfield and Robin Jeffs. Gloucester: Alan Sutton, 1981: 72–87.

——. "Aspects of the County Community in the Fifteenth Century." In Hicks, *Profit, Piety, and the Professions*, 1–13.

——. "The Earlier Knyvetts: The Rise of a Norfolk Gentry Family." *Norfolk Archaeology*, Part I, 41, 1 (1990): 1–15; Part II, 41, 3 (1992): 249–78.

Wagner, Anthony R. *English Genealogy*. 2nd ed. enl. Oxford: Clarendon Press, 1972.

Walker, Sue Sheridan, "Proof of Age of Feudal Heirs in Medieval England." *Mediaeval Studies* 35 (1973): 306–23.

Wall, Richard, "Work, Welfare, and the Family: An Illustration of the Adoptive Family Economy." In Bonfield et al., *The World We Have Gained*, 261–94.

Ward, Jennifer C. "Wealth and Family in Early Sixteenth Century Colchester." *Essex Archaeology and History* 21 (1990): 110–17.

——. *English Noblewomen in the Later Middle Ages*. London and New York: Longman, 1992.

Warren, W. L. *Henry II*. Berkeley: University of California Press, 1973.

Weiss, Roberto. *Humanism in England During the Fifteenth Century*. 2nd ed. Oxford: Blackwell, 1957.

Werner, Dennis, "Gerontocracy Among the Mekromoti of Central Brazil." *Anthropological Quarterly* 54 (1981): 15–27.

Westlake, H. J. *The Parish Gilds of Medieval England*. London: Society for Promoting Christian Knowledge, 1919.

Willis, Browne. *An History of the Mitred Parliamentary Abbots*. 2 vols. London, 1719.

Wrigley, E. A. and R. S. Schofield. *The Population History of England, 1541–1871: A Reconstruction*. Cambridge, MA: Harvard University Press, 1981.

Wylie, James H. *History of England Under Henry the Fourth*. London: Oxford University Press, 1896; repr. New York: AMS Press, 1969.

Yates, Frances A. *The Art of Memory*. Chicago: University of Chicago Press, 1966.

Index